TRAVELS BY GOTHIC ARTISTS

NO AT... ...ADE TO
SHOW ... TAKEN

A RET... ...INDICATED BY ➝

DATES OF JOURNEYS :–

——————— TWELFTH CENTURY
— — — — — THIRTEENTH CENTURY
– – – – – – FOURTEENTH CENTURY
‑ ‑ ‑ ‑ ‑ ‑ FIFTEENTH CENTURY

SOME DATES ARE APPROXIMATE

£6.00

J.H.H. 1950.

THE GOTHIC WORLD

THE BRITISH ART
AND BUILDING SERIES

GOTHIC ENGLAND
By JOHN HARVEY

BRITISH ARCHITECTS AND CRAFTSMEN
By SACHEVERELL SITWELL

THE REGENCY STYLE
By DONALD PILCHER

THE ENGLISH INTERIOR
By RALPH DUTTON

THE OLD CHURCHES OF LONDON
By GERALD COBB and GEOFFREY WEBB

THE AGE OF ADAM
By JAMES LEES-MILNE

STUART AND GEORGIAN CHURCHES
By MARCUS WHIFFEN

ENGLISH CHURCH MONUMENTS, 1510–1840
By KATHARINE A. ESDAILE

NINETEENTH CENTURY ARCHITECTURE
IN BRITAIN
By REGINALD TURNOR

IN PREPARATION

THE TUDOR RENAISSANCE
By JAMES LEES-MILNE

THE AGE OF WREN
By RALPH DUTTON

BATSFORD BOOKS

1 ST. BARBARA, by *Jan van Eyck*, 1437. Note masons' lodge on right, and great wheel of crane seen through tower windows. *Original in Antwerp Museum.*

THE
GOTHIC WORLD
1100 - 1600

A Survey of
Architecture and Art

By

John Harvey

B. T. BATSFORD LTD.
LONDON · NEW YORK · TORONTO · SYDNEY

OTHER BOOKS BY JOHN HARVEY

GOTHIC ENGLAND
A Survey of National Culture, 1300–1550

HENRY YEVELE
The Life of an English Architect, c. 1320–1400

THE PLANTAGENETS
1154–1485

DUBLIN
A Study in Environment

WITH HERBERT FELTON
THE ENGLISH CATHEDRALS

First published, 1950

MADE AND PRINTED IN GREAT BRITAIN
BY JARROLD AND SONS LTD., NORWICH FOR THE PUBLISHERS B. T. BATSFORD LTD.,
LONDON: 15 NORTH AUDLEY STREET, W.1 AND MALVERN WELLS, WORCESTERSHIRE
NEW YORK: 122 EAST 55TH STREET   TORONTO: 103 ST. CLAIR AVENUE WEST
SYDNEY: 156 CASTLEREAGH STREET

CONTENTS

PREFACE

IN the last few years there has been a great revival of interest in the Gothic age—the twelfth to the sixteenth centuries A.D. in Western Europe. The beatific vision of the Victorians: a world steadily progressing, yet to all intents and purposes already perfect, has faded, and left in its place a disillusionment that we hardly care to contemplate. Established values have become discounted, and men's eyes are turning towards a time when Europe was in fact as in theory a living entity, united in a culture, a religion, and a learned language. Our culture may have little in common with that of John of Salisbury, or Thomas Aquinas or Reginald Peacock; we may not share their religion, and it is more than likely that our Latin has become rusty. Yet we may still find apt lessons for our time in an age which was closing five centuries ago.

Again, enormous strides have been made in historical knowledge of the Middle Ages during the last twenty-five years. Much has been done by continental scholars, by Americans (especially by the Mediaeval Academy of America, with its organ *Speculum*), and a respectable amount by Englishmen. English research has been strong in literature and science; American, among others, in music; continental workers have pressed far into the rediscovery of architecture and the plastic arts. There are no national monopolies and it is gratifying to find that there is nothing jingo, and very little sectarian, but a growing and catholic enjoyment of a great epoch. The progress made by scholars is beginning to reach a wider public; twenty years ago, for instance, the late Dr. Tancred Borenius and Professor E. W. Tristram showed the importance of *English Medieval Painting*, and it is now possible for Mr. Cyril Bunt in an admirable survey to relate the English work to its continental and cultural background. The large share taken by fifteenth-century Englishmen under the leadership of John Dunstable in the creation of harmonic music is just becoming recognized, thanks to scholars such as Dom Anselm Hughes and Dr. Manfred Bukofzer. Sculpture, both English and French, is gaining recognition on the shoulders of Mr. Arthur Gardner.

The interest aroused reaches beyond professed enthusiasts of the mediaeval: even so noted an authority on Renaissance architecture as Mr. John Summerson has produced an "interpretation of Gothic" which wittily converts it from the sublime to the aediculous. Such straws prove that a strong wind is blowing, even though the aedicular hypothesis of Gothic may seem to share in the diaphany of the Emperor's new clothes. But Mr. Summerson has done mediaeval studies a service by his insistence that the leading feature of Gothic architecture is not a system of material construction, but the symbolic pointed arch. The verdict of the nineteenth-century preachers of evolution has been greatly modified.

Architecture is of first importance because it was indeed the Mistress Art during the whole Gothic period. After the Renaissance of Roman style and detail, architects were only too glad to acquire their designs second-hand from foreign pattern-books or even from engravers' fancies—title-pages and the like. But from the twelfth to the fifteenth century exactly the reverse had been the case; it was the architect who led the way with his buildings, and all the other artists who gathered round to adorn them, or to adapt his details to their own uses. For four hundred years we have seen the architect led by the nose: by Vitruvius, by foreign interpreters and imitators of Vitruvius, by fashion-plate draughtsmen, by travellers, by dilettanti, by history-books, and lastly by the engineer; in the Gothic age the architect led the way with a flourish of trumpets, while the rest brought up the rear.

Architecture in the Middle Ages took first place among the arts, but like the rest it drew its imaginative qualities from a particular inspiration of the human brain; from what we might call the Gothic Mind. The origin of art in the mind stands in the way of the purely evolutionary explanation of Gothic architecture; indeed, of any single human art or craft. We are asked to believe that the truly distinctive feature of Gothic building is the ribbed vault rather than the pointed arch, which in fact may not appear at all in certain buildings of the Gothic period. But then neither may the ribbed vault. The fallacy is exposed the moment we consider just what the ribbed vault has to do with Gothic painting or sculpture, or with music or poetry. A ribbed vault must be understood in a literal sense, or not at all; but this does not hold true of the pointed arch, which is symbolic before it is structural.

What did the pointed arch symbolize? And the answer must be that it stood for the whole of the re-awakened, quickened life of the twelfth century; for the principle of research, the eager acceptance of new ideas, largely brought from the Near Eastern and Mediterranean region by returning Crusaders and other travellers, and for the establishment of a new conception of humanity, a new ideal. The old insistence on the features of evolutionary development from Romanesque to Gothic structure and forms has cloaked a fundamental diversity. There is indeed a close relation between the plan and structure of a Norman cathedral and those of its Gothic counterpart or successor; but they are only such fossilized relations as exist between the compartment of a railway carriage, and the knee-squeezing stage-coach that preceded it. The railway belongs to an utterly different society from that which travelled by coach; and similarly the social and philosophic backgrounds of Gothic and Romanesque periods are absolutely distinct from one another.

The Dark Ages, in which the Romanesque style existed, were relatively a static period; their art depends on inert masses; even in the case of music this is borne out by the static parallelism of intervals: the introduction of a dynamic element, the changing harmonic intervals of counterpoint, is a sympton of the radically new, Gothic outlook. Of equal significance is the adoption of rhyme in poetry. The massive solidity of Romanesque is altered to an aspiring, unsatisfied outline, ever seeking new heights, new worlds to conquer. Romanesque is blunt and flowing, Gothic leaping and sharp; the pointed arch and the pattern-making lines of Gothic give it a clear-cut definition totally lacking in the earlier style. This quality of definition in aim won the day for Gothic as surely as a comparable improvement of definition secured victory for the rifle over the smooth-bore.

But there is another great quality of Gothic which has been astonishingly overlooked: the fact that it is in all its aspects "classic" art in the highest degree. This may seem a contradiction in terms, but in the most valuable sense, classic art is that in which the mastery of form reigns supreme over the theme of the individual work. In this sense there can be no doubt of the purely classical aspect of Gothic: through and through it is an art permeated by art-forms analogous to the sonata with its repetition and variation; bay follows bay, window succeeds window, yet leading to some climax. Gothic poetry and music are equally founded upon this principle; so are the sequences of illuminations in manuscripts, the wall-paintings of scenes from the lives of the Saints, the reredoses with their pageant of carved imagery. The merely freakish, the exaggeration of the misunderstood "genius", the attitudinizing individuality of the untrained dilettante, are foreign to Gothic art; with rare exceptions, Gothic effects are not calculated to electrify the beholder with astonishment, or to startle him into admiration.

Gothic buildings were no less the product of individual human imagination; one could as well employ the strict use of form at the expense of meretricious content as an argument for the non-existence of John Sebastian Bach. The methods of Bach, or of Mozart, and most of their raw material, were but the commonplace of their times; but by their innate genius and superb, fully trained craftsmanship they gave to their works the stamp of immortality. To find a similar, fully developed tradition in architecture and the plastic arts, we must go back to the Middle Ages. The social revolutions of the sixteenth century, added to religious uncertainty and a violent change of surface fashion, threw overboard old methods of production without finding any satisfactory substitute. Whereas Bach or Mozart could build upon the sure foundation of a living tradition, even the genius of a Wren could not altogether surmount the handicap of working in an artificial style which was not an integral part of structure.

At a later stage it will be important to reach a more precise notion of just how Gothic art was produced: to review the evidence which shows how far religion, philosophy, mysticism on the one hand; and structural necessity, human inventiveness, and environmental factors, combined and interlocked to form a visible and manifest whole—the body of living art which we now see mutilated and more or less abandoned upon the face of Europe. First, I will set out the questions to which this book attempts to find answers. The only excuse for another volume on the art of the Middle Ages is that I have not been able to discover any single work in the English language which deals with Gothic art alone, and which covers the whole of the geographical field. Lethaby's *Mediaeval Art* is by far the finest English work which touches upon this subject, but it is restricted in scope to the period before 1350 and devotes half its space to the forerunners of Gothic. Neither Lethaby nor Graham Jackson dealt with the Spanish and German Gothic schools, which in the later Middle Ages become more important than those of Italy and France. The only detailed account of Gothic in English which is both comprehensive and adequate is that of A. L. Frothingham, filling a volume and a half of the *History of Architecture* begun by Russell Sturgis. What is here attempted is to compress within a moderate compass the answers to the basic questions: What, How, Where and When was Gothic Art?

This book is no more than a modest, interim compilation as a stepping-stone to the better understanding of Gothic, the truer valuation of an extraordinary period of history. To cover the whole area it has been necessary to go beyond the range of personal observation; but this is perhaps more excusable since so much of our knowledge even of the major English buildings in an unrestored state is secondhand. Much of the material for the earlier chapters on Gothic art and artists has been drawn from original English sources; but I have not tried to trace English development in detail, to leave space for treatment of the border regions of Gothic. Similarly, a high proportion of the illustrations is devoted to areas comparatively little known; views of the greater monuments of France and England have been kept to a minimum.

Where possible, I have avoided controversy. My main purpose is to set out a series of significant facts concerning the art of a great period, not to support a particular thesis. But to the reader who requires a thesis, I offer this: I believe the Gothic age to have had an essentially greater significance in human development than the centuries of apparently greater material achievement which have succeeded it. The quality of its output gives the lie to that theory which seeks a quantitative measure of progress in the growth of population. Besides, the appearance of modern material advance is largely illusory. Upon reflection, it is not clear that mechanical inventions from the printing press to the atomic bomb have increased the human perception of beauty, the greatest good of the greatest number, or happiness and health. A cathedral is quite as material as a car, and generally lasts a good deal longer.

But a cathedral was not simply an adequate structure; not merely the material outcome of sound building, but the aesthetic and spiritual child of inspired design. We must distinguish between the functions of designer and builder, even when confounded in one person. It is here the intentions of the designer that concern us; and the aims of the designers of the Gothic cathedrals moved largely on a spiritual plane. They were expressing something beyond physical existence and material convenience. Even where the technical designer took an intention at second-hand from his patron, this spiritual content persisted, and regardless of specific purpose. The same masons might build a castle as well as a cathedral, and the same ship might serve Kings or cut-throats.

Between the Gothic world of A.D. 1100 to 1600, and the modern world built on its ruins, is a far-reaching difference. Gothic men had just climbed from the chaos of a dark age and their dream was of unity. They saw the universe, and its microcosm in western Europe, as an ordered whole. Even in dogmatic religion the thirteenth and fourteenth centuries were able to find much common ground between Christian, Moslem and Pagan. In the field of art the assimilation between motives and traditions of diverse origin was closer still. Thus Gothic art in all its forms was the expression of a spiritual unity; and because of this our attitude towards it should not be one of condescension, but of reverent admiration for our masters.

I offer thanks to the staffs of the British Museum, the Public Record Office, the Guildhall Library, the Victoria & Albert Museum; the libraries of the Society of Antiquaries, the Royal Institute of British Architects, the Society of Genealogists; the London Library; and the Bibliothèque Nationale, Paris. I must also record my gratitude to the City of Westminster Public Libraries; to the authorities of several English Cathedrals; and to the Warden and Fellows of Winchester College.

For the gift or loan of books and other assistance I have to thank Mr. Bernard J. Ashwell, the Rev. Christopher Chitty, Mr. Maurice J. Craig, Miss E. M. Dance, Mr. Ralph H. C. Davis, my father Mr. William Harvey, Mr. F. R. Hiorns, Mr. E. Martyn Jope, Dr. Erik Lundberg, Mr. Walter Oakeshott, Mr. Arthur Oswald, Dr. Xavier de Salas, Dr. W. Douglas Simpson, and Mynheer A. H. Wegerif; and the last of these also for the benefit of his own wide researches in a similar field. Among those who have helped me, some have passed beyond reach of my gratitude: the late Mr. T. D. Atkinson, Mr. George Blackwell, Mr. W. P. Blore, Mr. G. E. Bryant, Mr. Herbert Chitty, Dr. Douglas Knoop, Professor István Möller and his son Dr. Károly Möller. To the following I tender hearty thanks:—

Mr. Kenneth R. Athey, Miss M. J. Becker, Mr. David Black, Mr. Harry A. G. Blackwell, Sir Alfred Clapham, Mrs. M. E. Clegg, Mr. Fred H. Crossley, Mr. D. F. Findlay, Mrs. Dorothy Gardiner, Dr. Rose Graham, Miss M. B. Honeybourne, Mr. R. P. Howgrave-Graham, Dr. G. P. Jones, Mr. E. A. Greening Lamborn, Mr. J. G. Noppen, Mr. Lemuel Powell, the Rev. Angelo Raine, Mr. L. F. Salzman, Mr. L. E. Tanner, Professor A. Hamilton Thompson, Colonel N. H. Waller, and Mr. Francis Wormald. Special thanks are due to Mr. G. H. Cook for the drawing from which Fig. 15 was made; to Dr. Alan M. Easton for assistance in two visits to France; to Mr. Harold G. Leask for much help including the loan of his bicycle; and to Mrs. Mary McEvoy, whose loan of another bicycle to a total stranger enabled me to visit Trim, noblest relic of the English Pale. Finally, I am deeply obliged to Dr. Joan Evans, who has read a set of proofs and given me most valuable advice and help.

To my wife I am indebted for ideas and much hard work, and to my publishers for their patience over details, and particularly for the loan of many valuable books and the immense pains taken to discover wanted illustrations.

John H. Harvey

Half Moon Cottage,
Little Bookham, Surrey.

THE ILLUSTRATIONS

THE illustrations have been chosen to cover the whole field of Gothic architecture, with some emphasis on regions relatively little known, and on the later period of national styles. No attempt has been made to indicate recent destruction or damage to monuments.

The maps and endpapers show all places of importance mentioned in the text. The plans are on a uniform scale of 1 : 2000 (20 metres to 1 cm.; 500 feet to 3 inches); plans of all the English cathedrals to this scale will be found in Sir Banister Fletcher's *History of Architecture*. The sections are on a uniform scale of 1 : 800 (8 metres to 1 cm.; 200 feet to 3 inches). The endpapers show known travels by Gothic artists and especially by architects. Only long and significant journeys have been included.

The frontispiece is unique as a detailed portrayal of the technical processes of building by one of the greatest Gothic artists.

Fig. 9 shows the political and administrative divisions of central Europe in the fifteenth century, as they affected regional schools of Gothic. The north German plain was dominated by the Hansa cities, as was the domain of the Teutonic Order. Silesia, with its capital Breslau, was artistically linked to Bohemia and Poland.

Figs. 10 and 11 are the earliest known Gothic working drawings, but they show the technique of draughtsmanship already highly developed. In both cases the drawings were used as a basis for improvements in design, as other versions of the same or slightly later date exist.

Fig. 12 shows the roofs east of the north transept and south of the chevet, respectively, of Limoges Cathedral; from *Annales Archéologiques*, VI, 1847, at p. 139.

Fig. 14 is from the original in the Archives Départementales du Puy-de-Dôme, Arm. 18, sac B, cote 29. The size of the drawing is 1.40 m. × 0.68 m., and the scale is about 1/30 of the actual building.

Fig. 33 shows only the movements of a few outstanding architects of the period 1350–1420. Another important link was that between the royal craftsmen of Westminster and those in Chester and North Wales.

Figs. 54–57 show the structural solution of the northern cathedrals; compare Fig. 119 for the Catalan solution, and Fig. 232 for the hall-church.

Fig. 99 is from Matthew Paris: *Lives of the Offas*, British Museum Cotton M.S. Nero D.1, f.23 v. Note especially the distinction in dress between the master, speaking with the King, and holding square and compasses, and the working hewers, setters and labourers.

Fig. 105 is from George Godwin: *Churches of London*, 1839.

Fig. 119 shows the Catalan type of section with low clerestory and high aisle, buttressed by an outer range of cellular chapels. This forms a compromise between the northern scheme shown in Figs. 54–57, and the hall-church of Fig. 232.

Fig. 146 shows the quite exceptional character of the plan of Batalha. The nave is of equal overall dimensions to that of Canterbury Cathedral, begun ten years earlier; the open space of the eastern octagon equals that of Ely; the linking vestibule to the octagon reflects the English retrochoirs; the octagon within a square of the south-western Founder's Chapel is based on the plan of the Chapter-House and Cloister of Old St. Paul's in London.

Fig. 180 is a typical example of the two-aisled plan of friary church with a central range of columns, derived from ultimately secular originals.

Figs. 183 and 184 show, in their treatment of the same subject, the initial and final stages of Gothic realism.

Fig. 200 omits several places in Poland and the Baltic area, which appear on the endpaper map.

Fig. 232 shows the structural system of the hall-church. Compare the northern system of Figs. 54–57, and the Catalan solution of Fig. 119.

Fig. 240 is from a drawing by Professor Ramsay Traquair in *R.I.B.A. Journal*, 3rd series, XXXI, p. 46, Fig. 19.

ACKNOWLEDGMENTS

THE Author and Publishers here express their indebtedness to the following persons and institutions for the illustrations mentioned:

Mr. Robert M. Adam, for fig. 134; Fratelli Alinari, Florence, for figs. 101, 102, 104, 234–236, 289 and 290; Herr Arthur Bach, Alba Iulia, for figs. 195 and 196; Messrs. Black Star Pub. Co. Ltd., for figs. 218, 274, 282, 283 and 286; The Trustees of the British Museum, for fig. 99; Rev. C. Chitty, for fig. 83; Messrs. Compagnie des Arts Photomécaniques, Paris, for fig. 62; Mr. G. H. Cook, for fig. 15; Courtauld Institute of Art, for figs. 50, 64, 94, 113, 115, 161, 175, 177, 178, 210, 245, 246, 248 and 254; Mr. F. H. Crossley, F.S.A., for fig. 111; Czechoslovak Embassy, for figs. 22, 27, 183, 185, 187, 190, 258 and 261; Danish National Museum, Copenhagen, for fig. 184; La Dirección de Monumentos Coloniales, Mexico, for figs. 154–157; The Dominican Legation, for fig. 153; Messrs. Dorien Leigh, for figs. 148, 158 and 270; The Estonian Legation, for figs. 217 and 278; Messrs. Exclusive News Agency Ltd., for figs. 17, 21, 29, 32, 36, 39, 48, 51, 52, 59, 61, 96, 97, 103, 109, 121, 139, 142, 149, 159, 174, 176, 189, 201–206, 208, 209, 213–215, 219, 220, 229, 230, 243, 244, 252, 255, 257, 268, 273, 276, 277, 279–281, 288 and 294; Mr. Herbert Felton, F.R.P.S., for figs. 78, 79 and 81; Finland National Museum, for figs. 28, 224 and 285; Messrs. Fotofilm, Cluj, for fig. 192; Mr. R. P. Howgrave-Graham, F.S.A., for fig. 87; National Library of Ireland, for fig. 128; The Irish Tourist Association, for figs. 131 and 132; Mr. Fred Jenkins, Southwold, for fig. 82; Mr. A. F. Kersting, F.R.P.S., for figs. 80, 106 and 140; Lichtbeelden-Instituut, Amsterdam, for figs. 3, 168, 212, 250, 251 and 256; Messrs. Foto Marburg, for figs. 122, 123, 186, 188, 191, 194, 247, 263, 265, 266 and 267; Mr. T. H. Mason, Dublin, for figs. 89, 93, 129 and 130; Messrs. McLeish and Macaulay, for fig. 90; The Norwegian Embassy, for fig. 88; Messrs. Paul Popper Ltd., for figs. 2, 6, 7, 13, 30, 37, 38, 43, 49, 53, 112, 138, 147, 166, 167, 216, 238, 241, 253 and 295; Mr. C. Raad, Jerusalem, for fig. 34; Rijksdienst v.d. Monumentenzorg 's-Gravenhage, for fig. 264; M. Jean Roubier, Paris, for figs. 4, 5, 20, 24, 35, 40–42, 124 and 242; Société français du Microfilm, for fig. 14; Spanish State Tourist Department, for figs. 66–69, 71, 114, 150, 237 and 239; Swedish Institute for Cultural Relations, for figs. 16, 19, 63, 211, 226, 275, 284 and 287; Swiss National Tourist Office, for figs. 260, 269, 271 and 272; The late Will F. Taylor, for figs. 133 and 135; Messrs. J. Valentine & Son Ltd., for figs. 95 and 228; Sr. Winocio, León, for fig. 70; Mr. Reece Winstone, A.R.P.S., for figs. 108 and 249; Sir Robert Witt, for fig. 1. Figs. 31, 65, 141 and 259 are in the Author's collection.

The Editor of *The Builder*, for figs. 91 and 92; Messrs. Raymond Dupriez, for figs. 23, 25 and 26 (from Comte J. de B. d'Altena: *Œuvres de nos Imagiers Romans et Gothiques*, 1944); Messrs. R. Piper, Munich, for fig. 10 (from G. Dehio: *Das Strassburger Münster*, 1922); Messrs. Salvat Editores, Barcelona, for figs. 151 and 152 (from D. Angulo Iñiguez: *Historia del Arte hispano-americano*, 1945); Messrs. A. Schroll & Co., Vienna, for fig. 110 (from K. M. Swoboda: *Peter Parler*, 1943, pl. 19), and for figs. 291–293 (from *Denkmäler der Kunst in Dalmatien*); Société Nationale des Antiquaires de France, for fig. 60 (from *Bulletin Monumental*, LXXXI); Professor Ramsay Traquair and The Royal Institute of British Architects, for fig. 240. Figs. 8 and 160 are from J. Ainaud, J. Gudiol and F. P. Verrié: *Catálogo Monumental . . . de Barcelona*, 1947); figs. 45–47, 55–58, 72–75, 100, 107, 116–119, 145, 163–165, 172, 173, 198, 199, 207, 221, 232 and 233 are from G. Dehio and G. v. Bezold: *Die kirchliche Baukunst des Abendlandes*, Stuttgart, 1901; figs. 11 and 12 are from Didron: *Annales Archéologiques*, vols. V, VI, 1846 and 1847; figs. 77, 137 and 143 are from R. de Lasteyrie: *L'Architecture religieuse en France à l'époque gothique*, 1926; figs. 76, 120, 180 and 181 are from D. Líbal: *Goticka Architektur a vČechách a na Moravĕ*; fig. 98 is from J. J. van Ysendyck: *Documents Classés de l'Art dans les Pays-Bas*. The remainder are from the Publishers' collection.

The endpapers and figs. 9, 18, 33, 44, 85, 86 (after a photograph by E. Lefèvre-Pontalis in *Congrès Archéologique*, 1902–3), 125, 126, 127 (after a plan in the 82nd Report of the Commissioners of Public Works in Ireland 1913–14), 136, 144, 162, 179, 182, 197 (after a plan by the late Professor I. Möller in *Magyarország Műemlékei*), 200, 222 (after a plan by Dr. Erik Lundberg in *Byggnadskonsten i Sverige 1400–1650*), 223 (after a plan in P. A. Munch: *The Cathedral of Throndheim*) are from line-drawings by the Author.

Introduction

BEFORE the concept of Gothic art can have much meaning to us, we must have some notion of what we mean by Art itself; and it is necessary to make a careful definition of terms. Such terms, to be used throughout this book, are: artist, craftsman, architect; and some more general, such as: utility, beauty. But first to enunciate one or two main propositions which I shall throughout take for granted: that there are both universal and particular human values; that the universal values remain constant; and that the particular values change with circumstances. Local cases will modify universal requirements. What is more, this applies to other things than the material elements of existence; human morality, custom, and religion, while sharing certain fundamental propositions, are on a sliding scale, varying from time to time and place to place. From this it follows that praise or blame allotted to individual works of man must not be taken as final awards or condemnations, valid under all circumstances alike. Material circumstances and mental and spiritual habits alter cases, so that an English village church would be as out of place in tropical Africa, as a communal hut from Papua would be as the new House of Commons.

There are then groups of local circumstances within which grows up a single, essentially suitable and natural style, and all cultural activities conform to its standards. Until the Italian Renaissance, every building ever built had been erected in *the only conceivable way*. Of course this does not mean that there was no room for individual treatment in the ages before 1500 A.D.—we know that there were in fact great differences between the works of the Greek, Roman, Byzantine, Romanesque and Gothic masters. But in any one cultural area at any one period there was, broadly speaking, room for only one artistic method at a time. The exceptions, as in Spain and Palestine, occur where two historically and geographically distinct cultures meet or overlap. Absorptive as Gothic was, it never assimilated the true dome, and even had difficulty in using the centralized plan itself. It is clear that such limitations had little or nothing to do with structure, for the ingenuity and skill of the greatest Gothic architects was unlimited. Here was rather an inhibition of the Gothic spirit.

By investigating the limitations of Gothic, we find its mental frontiers and ultimately come nearer to discovery of what it was. Among fundamental forms, Gothic accepted the rectangular, rejected the central plan; accepted the arch, as far as might be rejected the lintel; accepted the vault, rejected the dome. Catholic in its choice of materials, it preferred homogeneity, and did not normally employ mosaic or marble panelling. But the Ruskinian notion of Gothic "Honesty" is completely false: not only iron tie-rods, but concealed iron reinforcement (as in Salisbury steeple), brick core inside coursed ashlar (as at Bell Harry tower, Canterbury), and rubble infilling, were widely employed. It is nevertheless true that many local and guild regulations of the Gothic age were directed towards adequate materials and workmanship, and the fixing of the "just price".

Gothic art was the outcome of a way of thought, the product of a special kind of imagination. It is pure fantasy to attempt to derive the whole towering achievement of the artists of the twelfth to sixteenth centuries from the half-accidental structural evolution of the ribbed vault. Yet this is what we are asked to believe by the materialist historians, and even by so enlightened and erudite an antiquary as M. Marcel Aubert, who tells us that architecture dominates mediaeval art, and that the basic element of this architecture is the ribbed vault and its necessary complement, the flying buttress.

More to the point than methods of construction are the leading ideas behind design; we have to remember with Dr. Pevsner, that architecture is concerned with space. By itself this does not take us very far, but we may go further and consider the characteristics of Gothic space. The first and outstanding characteristic of Gothic is its vertical expansion, its tendency to upwardness. Consider the section of a Greek temple and a thirteenth-century cathedral; the elevations of the Monument of Lysicrates and of one of the Eleanor Crosses. Kindred as are the ultimate, universal values of Gothic and Greek, it is the aspiring tendency of Gothic which singles it out from the remainder of man's works, and more especially from those which, like the Greek, renounce the arch and emphasize the beam. But the vertical space of Gothic is not merely high; it is also jagged, leaping, like a flame. Here it is in marked contrast with the works of Byzantium and of the Roman Renaissance. Santa Sophia, before the Turkish minarets were added to it, St. Mark's at Venice, St. Peter's at Rome, have none of this soaring quality, though they lift great volumes of man-shaped space high into the air. Only the northern architects, Wren at St. Paul's, and superabundantly in the spires of the City churches, Soufflot in the Panthéon, could infuse into their essays in Roman style some of this ardour, this implacable determination to scale the skies.

Gothic style expresses a certain temperament; its impulse is essentially ethnic. Uniting the pointed arch of the East with the linear pattern of Atlantic cultures and the human proportions and realism of Greece, the synthesis is conditioned by its home. With its fiery, upward leap, Gothic is a northern art. Its steep roofs, ritual in origin, threw off northern snow; its piercing outlines tell in an atmosphere where mass and colour are obscured; its pillared construction reflects the branching deciduous forests where the timber builders worked. As Lethaby wrote: "Northern Art had the mystery of the great forests behind it." Gothic cathedrals are not direct imitations of the branching glades of a forest; but they are the outward expression of minds formed among the trees, living for generations in the knowledge of their growth, their strength, their beauty.

It is time to return to those basic definitions to which I earlier referred, and without which all discussion is futile. We are considering the works of man, the products of man's skill as distinct from surrounding nature. Used in the most general sense, we already express the sum total of man's productivity as "art"; but so manifold are these works that they have become subdivided, classified into "fine" and "applied" arts, and we tend to segregate the fruits of modern mechanical invention, the railway engine, the aeroplane, the wireless set, as not works of art at all. Mechanism must be considered later; but for my purpose all the works of man rank equally as art, though only in this general sense. It follows that every human being who makes anything at all, is to that extent an artist. Various as are the degrees which lead from the shaping of a hedge-plant into a rude stick, to the design of a cathedral or the composition of a symphony, all are one art, the common heritage of mankind.

Having recognized this, we may still find it possible to define more closely certain species of art, of human work. The most fundamental distinction is that between the work which is simply imitative, the copy of a model or of a known manual process; and that which initiates. We know that there exist in the world communities entirely ruled by tradition and by imposed unchanging sanctions; in such a community all art *copies the model*, is purely imitative; all is in a state of fossilization. But outside such bodies of men, change is the rule: it is the many single alterations making this total of change which flow from the initiative, creative impulse in man. To such men as *initiate*, however much they may be rooted in tradition, in the common form of their time and place, I shall give the term "artist". Secondly, to such as carry out imitative work, which nevertheless demands a special degree of trained skill, I assign the word "craftsman". In the third place, those who do but carry out instructions, bearing burdens and waiting upon the men of craft, are "workmen". There is no suggestion of mutual exclusiveness or watertight compartments in this definition; but the words are necessary to define quite separate *functions*, even though those functions may in certain cases be carried out by the same person.

Artists are of many kinds, but one species had peculiar importance in the Middle Ages, especially in the Gothic period: the architect. I have already said that it was distinctive of Gothic art that architecture led the way: all other arts and crafts tended to be subordinated to its fashions, its methods. We need, of course, a definition of architecture as well as of architect. Some would have us believe that the term "architecture" is purely artificial, that it denotes no more than *building*; others, Dr. Pevsner among them, would have us believe that "the term architecture applies only to buildings designed with a view to aesthetic appeal". Besides noting the introduction of a new term, "design", we should consider how far this definition covers the greater buildings of the Gothic age. Just how far can we go in attributing to the building masters of the twelfth century a conscious intention to build, not merely in a way fitting to purpose, functional, but also to appeal to the senses? On the answer to this question will depend very largely our estimate of the Gothic artists and their output.

The question can only be answered by reference to the historical facts; but I suggest that it is irrelevant to the definition of architecture. The architect, in a literal sense, is the chief of those who make, particularly of those who make buildings. Remembering our former definitions of workman, craftsman, and artist, we must apply the word in its best sense, and consider the architect as the chief artist concerned in building. The architect is then *in function* he who lays down the particular scheme according to which a certain building is made; by hypothesis, this scheme contains elements that are new, or put together in a new way, for as an artist even the most traditional of architects does more than perpetuate the fossil of a pre-existing art. I stress the distinction of function for two reasons: it might happen in the case of a small building that its form was decided, its parts determined, its members hewn, its materials carried and placed in position, entirely by one man, who would combine in himself the separate functions of architect, craftsman, and workman or labourer. The fact that he performed the lesser tasks would in no way decrease his responsibility for the major performance of laying down the form that the work was to take—its design. The second reason why we should carefully distinguish function from individual performance, is that in the Gothic period, as we shall find, it was common for one man at different stages of his career, and even at one and the same time, to perform different functions.

We must now define the new term which has entered the discussion— "design". The design of a building (or of any other work) is the predetermined form which it is to take, existing in the mind of the architect or other creative artist; design is a work of the imagination before it can become the work of the hands. We speak of an architect's design, or more commonly in the plural of his "designs", meaning loosely the material series of lines, geometrically disposed on paper, which translate the imaginative design into a practical form which can be made of solid stone or brick or wood. But these drawings on paper or some other material are only the reflection of the original design, which is immaterial, existing in the imagination. Much of the controversy which has raged around mediaeval art has sprung from a failure to distinguish clearly between the design, which is essential, and the material interpretations of it—the "designs"—which might at one time be elaborately drawn out on sheets of paper, at another be set out upon the ground or directly on the solid materials themselves.

Having gone so far, we may turn back to the problem of the aesthetic appeal, which I have rejected as inessential. The architect is the maker of the design, he whose imagination is fired by a creative spark; he is not in function necessarily also the builder, and in fact his design may never find expression. The necessary requirement of the design is that it shall adequately fulfil a purpose: primarily material, as in the case of a house or a bridge; primarily spiritual, as with a temple or a church; or usually some mixture of the two. If the building adequately fulfils its purpose, and is durable (a vital qualification), its designer is a good architect. We must not import into the problem the question of appearance, of aesthetics, for this introduces the variable and fallible senses of the observer. All the same, separate from the two great categories of the material and the spiritual, there has grown up a great class of artefacts, including some buildings, whose primary purpose is to minister to the senses. The extent of this category in Gothic times was already considerable.

Architecture is then building which has been designed and built for a specific purpose; and the architectural content resides in the specific design. Even the simplest of buildings, if the outcome of fresh creative thought, is a work of architecture, and the only buildings to which the term architecture must be denied are firstly mere copies, and secondly the products of a rigid tradition which permits no departure from precedent. Architecture (and all other art) which durably fulfils its purpose, has *utility*, irrespective of the nature of the purpose. We have cleared the ground, and have now to reach some understanding of the final problem, the residue which has been excluded from the previous definitions, namely aesthetic appeal, or "beauty". This book is not a treatise on aesthetics, but to appreciate Gothic art it is essential to reach some conclusion as to the intentions of the artists.

At the outset we are faced by the difficulty that men of the Gothic period did not discuss the problems of aesthetic criticism, or if they did, their views have not been preserved. On the other hand, their philosophers had a great deal to say of art and beauty in the abstract, and many features of Gothic architecture and art can only be explained as the outcome of a purposeful search for the beautiful and the appeal to the senses. But there is another difficulty in assessing the aesthetic views of the Gothic age: we cannot be certain to what extent the same views were current throughout four centuries, nor how far the views of philosophers and writers represent those of the artists themselves. It is indeed probable that there was, then as now, a considerable gulf between theoretical precept and actual practice. Even in other more talkative periods, great artists have seldom been at the same time aesthetic critics; the creative urge and the anxiety to dissect and analyse the creations of others are seldom united. For this reason, and contrary to what might at first sight be supposed, the deductions which can be made from the buildings and works of art are a more trustworthy guide than the most explicit written statements.

All the same, since many of the mediaeval philosophers held high position in church and state, and so ranked as patrons of art, it is reasonable to suppose that their views to some extent expressed the results of their own observation of artists and craftsmen, and conversely that their theories found some concrete expression in works carried out at their bidding. What then were the views of the Gothic writers? At the very opening of the period there were two sharply opposed schools of thought; both were to find their exponents through the whole age. On the one hand were the ascetics led by St. Bernard (1090–1153), and comprising such men as Abbot Aelred of Rievaulx (1109–1166), who sternly opposed all appeals to the senses: to them, physical beauty of all kinds was a delusive snare, a hindrance to the fuller spiritual life at which they aimed. Leader of the more human school opposing asceticism and seeking, even in the monasteries, a rational middle way, was Abbot Suger of St.-Denis (1081–1151), a great states-man and historian as well as monk. Dr. Panofsky has recently retold the con-troversy between Suger and Bernard: how the Abbot of St.-Denis justified with quotations from Scripture his condemnation of Cistercian asceticism, his own belief in "super-resplendent architecture".

Both views were to have results of the highest importance in the history of mediaeval art. Both Suger and Bernard had reached manhood before there was the slightest breath of Gothic art—yet at their deaths, only a generation later, not merely were the elements of Gothic architecture in existence, but its first great monuments were complete, and western Europe was becoming a new world. Bernard's Cistercian Order became one of the chief vehicles by which the pointed arch, and later the fully developed Gothic style, were disseminated, though without the enrichments and decoration elsewhere customary. This was perhaps due to the enormous power and influence of the order, and to its institution of lay-brothers, attached to the houses of the order and doing its work. These lay-brothers were certainly in some cases artists and craftsmen who had trained as laymen, and only entered the order later in life. Some of them must have been among the pioneers of Gothic construction, and were able to adapt the new ideas in building to the special requirements of their order. On the other hand, the older orders were already housed in great Romanesque buildings, and in most cases were not ready to undertake the vast expense of rebuilding in a new fashion-able style. But it so happened that at St.-Denis, the chief royal abbey of France, the church was a much earlier, Carolingian structure, in need of repair. Thus Suger, bringing together in his enthusiasm the best artists from all parts, was able to give Gothic a flying start by his completion of a new west front between 1132 and 1140, and the building of a chevet in 1140–44.

At the same time, 1140–49, a French master was erecting a new church two thousand miles away from St.-Denis, the Church of the Priory of the Holy Sepulchre in Jerusalem. It is astonishing how closely details of the two churches resemble each other: just as at St.-Denis, so at Jerusalem do Corinthianesque capitals with debased acanthus jostle naturalistic leaves, vines and budding bracken-fronds. Though the Church of the Holy Sepulchre has groined vaults in the aisles and ambulatory, the high vaults are ribbed, and with ribs of a great torus mould-ing as at St.-Denis. The two great churches, at opposite ends of the western world, typify a new outlook, new methods, and new canons of beauty. Within a genera-tion these first tentative outpourings will have coalesced into a coherent style, including not only new types of enrichment, but also the gaunt austerity of Cis-tercian art. As always, actual practice, the creation of new forms, precedes the production of a rationalization, a theory of art. Neither St. Bernard on the one hand nor Suger on the other, standing at the roots, strangely assorted god-parents of Gothic, had a coherent theory of aesthetics. That was to come a century later, when the lava-flow had cooled and crystallized.

The new life and the new art of the twelfth century had taken Europe by sur-prise; it was not until the middle of the following century that the schoolmen, led by the intellects of the new Dominican Order of preaching friars, were able to codify the experience of the past hundred years, and provide a workable theory. Into this theory, scholastic philosophy, were fitted by the immense ingenuity and stupendous labour of St. Thomas Aquinas, no less than the whole of the life of the universe as then conceived, and all knowledge, both human and divine—the latter being revealed in the Scriptures. In this enormous task St. Thomas (c. 1227–74) was greatly helped by the reintroduction to western Europe of a large proportion of the works of Aristotle, previously unknown. The twelfth-century renaissance which gave birth to Gothic art had been founded in physical and mental exploration, on the principle of free inquiry—but the rediscovery of Aristotle by the scholastic philosophers, and especially by the Dominicans with their obsession by dogma, was to lead to a blind reverence for authority and an almost complete suspension of first-hand investigations. This was to have serious effects upon mediaeval society, less serious effects upon art.

In so far as any currently accepted theory reveals the mind of an age, the scholastic theology and philosophy of St. Thomas Aquinas give an authoritative picture of the views of the foremost intellectuals of the thirteenth century—precisely the time which saw the production of the greatest spiritual works of the Gothic period in art: the majority of the cathedrals, abbeys and greater collegiate churches of France, England, and western Germany. Just what this theory was in its relation to art has been most ably expressed by M. Jacques Maritain in a book covering all the ramifications of the subject.* By ample quotation from the scholastic philosophers themselves, M. Maritain shows the complete falsity of many modern notions concerning mediaeval thought. In particular it was laid down that *Art imitates Nature by operating in Nature's way* (and not by mere copying of natural forms), and that *The operation of Art is based on the operation of Nature, and that upon the Creation.* Such a doctrine emphasized the ultimate responsibility of God, and not of the individual artist, for the work; but at the same time it was insisted on that there must be a perfect discrimination between the end to be served by the workman (which might be the earning of his wages, or any other human intention), and the end to be served by the work, which must be made for its own perfection alone.

Further, and utterly contrary to the ideas that would have us believe that mediaeval art sprang purely from the blind exercise of technique, of manual skill, "the Schoolmen . . . did not consider that the virtue of the *artifex* lay in strength of muscle or in nimbleness of fingers . . . nor was it merely empirical dexterity . . . art cannot dispense with such a talent, but it remains extrinsic to art". Art is essentially of the mind, and it was held that manual skill, so far from being of the essence of art, merely removed a physical obstacle to its practice. This, though expressed with precision by John of St. Thomas at the close of the Gothic age, simply restated the sense of the scholastic dissertations of the thirteenth century.

As to "beauty" in the abstract, it was defined by St. Thomas Aquinas as "what gives pleasure on sight" (*id quod visum placet*), and he or his master Albertus Magnus (d. 1280) developed the idea in the *Opusculum de Pulchro et Bono*: "Beauty consists in its nature of several things, namely the brilliance of essential or accidental form shining upon the proportioned and settled parts of matter." (*Pulchrum in ratione sua plura concludit; scilicet splendorem formae substantialis vel accidentalis supra partes materiae proportionatas ac determinatas.*)

Scholasticism was to give rise to a period of "classic" equipoise at the end of the thirteenth century, when men were deliberately to seek harmony and unity. But itself stood on the shoulders of an earlier period of unification, of reduction to order: the period ruled over by the great kings of emergent Europe, Frederick I Barbarossa, Henry II of England and Anjou, and Philip II Augustus of France. This earlier unification of the twelfth century was in fact the founding of the Gothic age, and it had been marked by an impressive transfer of power from monastic to secular and lay hands. The great period of Romanesque art, ending in the middle of the twelfth century, had rested largely, though not entirely, upon the knowledge and skill of monks of the Benedictine Order, and of its reformed, Cluniac offshoot. Reading, writing, science, history, had been almost monastic preserves, and during the Dark Ages of constant invasions and turmoil this was

* Translated into English as *Art and Scholasticism*, 1930.

inevitable. Shelter from the stormy blasts of the world was the preoccupation of thinking men, and a prerequisite of any flourishing art.

The revolution of the twelfth century changed the face of Europe in more senses than one: the growth and establishment of lay power implied the creation of an army of secular clerks and of lay officials. The improvement of political conditions made travel safer and easier; for the first time (save for the short interlude under Charlemagne) since the breakdown of Rome, it was possible for scholars from all parts of Europe to meet together and to exchange ideas. Their eagerness for acquiring knowledge led to the erection of the universities, essentially guilds of masters or scholars founded for the purpose of amassing and handing on methods of thought, just as the craft guilds were engaged in the perpetuation of methods of manufacture. Nothing could be more significant than this close connexion between the idea of education and the idea of technique. In origin, the University was founded upon the practices of lay craftsmen; and if, as time went on, the outlook of the scholars tended to become remote from the empiric knowledge of the crafts, it did not prevent the two bodies from showing their kinship by the use of identical or closely similar organization and titles.

The scholar, the bachelor, and the master of the schools had their close counterpart in the apprentice, the journeyman, and the master of the shops. When Pierre de Montreuil, the great Parisian mason-architect, died in 1266, his epitaph in the abbey-church of St.-Germain-des-Prés called him "doctor latomorum". Three ranks of masons are implied by the terms on which Étienne de Bonneuil was to leave Paris for Uppsala in Sweden in 1287; Bonneuil himself was "master of the church work of Uppsala", and was to take with him "companions and bachelors" of the art of masonry. The schoolman had his cap and gown; so had the master craftsman, who is indeed distinguished by these articles in innumerable extant carvings and drawings, as well as in more specific documentary records.

Of equal or greater importance for the history of Gothic art is the adoption of lay ideas and the empiric methods of laymen. That this was already a commonplace by the end of the twelfth century is proved by the Latin narrative of Richard Cœur-de-Lion's crusade,* where reference is made to a degree of beauty, "the lineaments of which a painter working very hard could not exactly imitate". (*qualem nec pictor plurimum laborans linealiter imitaretur ad unguem.*) It is here accepted as normal that the artist should seek to imitate nature, and implied that he did so by methods of trial and error. Half a century later, the thoroughly practical "building encyclopaedia" of Villard de Honnecourt, a Picard master-mason, with its lion "portrayed from the life", carries the same principles into the whole realm of Gothic artistic practice. The value of experiment in agriculture was recognized in contemporary England by Walter of Henley, who speaks of practical trials of the yield of milk of cows, and of the produce of home-grown and bought seed-corn: "Plough two selions at the same time, and sow the one with seed which is bought and the other with corn which you have grown: in August you will see that I speak truly."

As time went on, the new Aristotelianism of the Scholastic philosophers tended more and more to put life and art into a carefully designed strait-jacket; an ideal scheme was devised for everything. The whole of the decorative aspects of art were for a time subordinated to detailed iconographical arrangements, and the artist's freedom of design could only be exercised within narrowly determined limits. Though much relaxed during the fourteenth century, these standard schemes of iconography can be traced from beginning to end of the Gothic age, first as tentative re-arrangements of notions familiar from the Romanesque period, then crystallized as parts of the unified pattern of scholasticism, gradually

* And again in the metrical life of St. Hugh of Lincoln, *c.* 1225.

disintegrating under pressure from the increasedly lay outer world of affairs. Coulton brought together a series of illuminating documents showing the conflict between empiricism and authority over the portrayal of Christ on the Cross. Thirteenth-century artists, including Villard de Honnecourt, had increased the realism of the Crucifix by showing both feet, crossed one upon the other, pierced by a single nail. This development, the result of "working very hard" in the imitation of nature, had taken place before 1250; within a generation it had provoked a counterblast from Bishop Luke of Tuy in Spain in a treatise against heresy, and as late as 1306 the Bishop of London caused a crucifix of this type, made by Tidemann, a German carver, to be removed from his diocese "either at early dawn or late in the evening, when it can be done most secretly and with least scandal".

I said above that the effects of scholastic authority were less serious in art than in society generally; this was due to the fortunate predominance of architecture. The rigid theories and iconographical schemes intimately affected the details of sculpture and painting, but could have little effect upon the development of building. The requirements of the Church changed from time to time, demanding first the great processional churches of the monastic orders, then the more popular secular cathedrals, later still the open preaching space required by the friars, and the large and brilliant parish churches formed in imitation, at least in Germany and England. The potential scope for the designer was very wide, and steadily becoming wider still: in spite of extensive imitation, and the swift spread of fashion, there is infinite variety in the buildings of the fourteenth and fifteenth centuries. The recognized dominance of architecture was admitted by the end of the thirteenth century in the comparison made between power and art—the schoolmen holding that spiritual power was in relation to secular power, as architecture is to the subordinate arts.

Besides, the art of rearing up great buildings demanded a technique which was generally quite beyond the grasp of the academic thinkers who ruled in iconography. Very few of the great churches were designed by monks, or indeed by "clerics" of any sort, unless it were by Cistercian lay-brothers. The bishops and others responsible for the great wave of Gothic building and rebuilding made no attempt to be their own architects, but called in the professionals of the new art. In 1215, for instance, the Bishop of Auxerre is recorded as having determined that in the place of his old cathedral there should rise a new building made and adorned "by those skilled in the art of masonry", that it might equal any other.

Emulation of others was then as at all times the driving force behind changing fashion. From Suger onwards, each of the great works of building was undertaken in the hope and with the intention of excelling what had gone before, and frequently of casting into the shade some neighbouring work. The building contracts of the period refer again and again to the standard of "as good as the work at ——, or better". The Chapter of Seville in 1401 passed and recorded a resolution to "build so great a church to the glory of God that those who come after us will think us mad even to have attempted it". Henry VI, in his proposals for King's College Chapel, took care that it should exceed in size every comparable building, even while he deprecated extravagant superfluities of ornament. Robert and William Vertue, designing the choir vault for the new Bath Abbey in 1503, assured their patron that "ther shal be noone so goodely neither in England nor in France".

It is essential to remember that the Gothic age throve upon apparent inconsistencies of viewpoint. Too many arguments are based upon modern ideas of compatibility, and it is frequently alleged that mere human rivalry is negatived as a motive by the fact that the Middle Ages built to the greater glory of God. But it was not so; we have seen how, even in theory, a most careful distinction was made between the end or aim of the work, and that of the workman. In practice, even barefaced swindling might be employed by great churchmen for the glory of God, or for their own comfort, as in the case of Abbot Litlyngton's methods of "borrowing" lead from the convent of Westminster for his own new lodging. Motives almost always are mixed, and it would ill become the twentieth century to accuse the fourteenth of hypocrisy.

To many mediaeval, as to most modern patrons, beauty was a relative term depending upon fashion, and upon the safe maxim: "I know what I like." Ideas, and the customs and habits formed by them, tend always to slide downwards in the social scale; the refuge of the modern Philistine was the proud boast of the mediaeval King or prelate. In actual practice, all that may be said of the positive side of Gothic aesthetic concepts, is that they reflect the taste, the personal liking, of Emperors, Kings, Popes, Bishops, and lay and church noblemen. Side by side with this liking there flowed a stream of dislike: the reprehension of the ascetics and puritans, angered by extravagance or grudging others a delight in material beauty which they were not formed to appreciate. But this counter-current was not always purely negative, though in its early manifestations it seemed likely to be so. The Cistercians in 1182 ordered that all coloured glass should be cast out of their churches within two years; they had already, in 1157, decided that neither monks nor lay-brothers might work for secular patrons, but this statute was not universally observed. The lay-brother John of Waverley, probably the designer of Hayles Abbey, also built fish-ponds for Henry III. By *c.* 1180 an Orléans formulary contained a letter suitable for the King to send to an abbot, asking for a craftsman (*artifex, architectus*) competent to build a castle tower.

Cistercian rigour was not everywhere appreciated, even in the stricter monastic circles. The Premonstratensian canons, founded by St. Norbert who was a personal friend of Bernard, at first welcomed Cistercian visitation of their houses, but early in the thirteenth century the visitants condemned paintings in the refectory of the Premonstratensians at Vicognes near Valenciennes; the owners refused to suppress them, and relations were broken off. On the other hand, objections to art did not come only from followers of St. Bernard; Alexander Neckam, who was an Augustinian canon, writing about 1200, was horrified by the numerous and unlawful "inventions" or new ideas in building: "Look at the superfluous and vain inventions in buildings, in clothing, in foodstuffs, in jewellery, in furniture . . . O vanity!" But gradually this attitude of moral condemnation softened into a wise restraint in applied ornament. We have noticed how Henry VI objected to "superfluities of too great curious workes of entaile and busy mouldinge", and a few years earlier the University of Oxford had ordered the mason of the Divinity School, Thomas Elkyn, to avoid overmuch curiosity in the work, consisting of tabernacles, "batements", casements, fillets and other frivolities. As their reason they alleged that the part of the work completed by Elkyn's predecessor, Richard Wynchcombe, had been criticized by several magnates of the realm and other knowing men.

It must be admitted that much English work of the fifteenth century did invite such criticism by its tendency to rely for effect upon a lavish display of repetitive carving and detail, and at all periods there had been some whose appreciation of art lay chiefly in an ability to make a shrewd estimate of its cost. Some high contemporary estimates were due to local patriotism, and we must make some allowance for this in considering the panegyric of the St. Albans annalist on the great reredos of the High Altar made by Abbot Walynforde, which "fills with pleasure the eyes of beholders, and which to all who gaze upon it is the most divine object in the realm". But some travellers had been more objective, and there is even a trace of professional criticism in the descriptions of the buildings seen by Simon Simeon and his artist friend Hugh the Illuminator on their journey from Dublin to the Holy Land in 1323. Lichfield Cathedral, then nearing completion, was said to be "most gracious and of wondrous beauty, with very high stone steeples or belfries, paintings, and carvings, and excellent well enriched and adorned with other church furnishings". In the middle of St. Paul's Cathedral, at London, they saw "that most famous steeple, crowned with incomparable grandeur, and five hundred feet high, so it is said, while at the east end of the church is the majestic chapel of the Blessed Virgin". Francesco Florio, an Italian visitor to Tours, wrote in 1477 that its cathedral was "joyous and faultless and so well proportioned in all its parts that the mere sight of it, from within or without, turns sorrow into happiness and sadness into joy".

Literary descriptions of buildings are seldom informed by much technical knowledge or appreciation, but are either told for the sake of rich effect, as was Lydgate's description of Troy, and Chaucer's *Hous of Fame*, or else, like the Friary in *Peres Ploughman's Crede*, for the reprobation of ecclesiastical hypocrisy and luxury. Lydgate frankly admits that he had not read Euclid, "That the maister and the foundour was Of alle that werkyn by squyre or compas", and was not well up in the terms of the trade. Chaucer eventually had experience of administering building operations as Clerk of the King's Works, and with his shrewd eye for various conditions of men described to the life three separate carpenters of different rank: the wealthy burgess with his snobbish wife; the resident carpenter of Oseney Abbey, in the *Miller's Tale*; and the Reeve, who was a simple village wright.

In all the mediaeval discussions on the legitimacy or otherwise of costly art employed in the service of God, we find no reference to those economic questions of shop-work, mass-production and the use of machinery, so dear to the heart of the modern controversialist. It would be too facile an answer to say that these problems simply did not exist; they did, though not on an enormous scale, and not as major problems of social-aesthetic morality. Shop-work grew inevitably as the demand for artefacts increased, and for two reasons. Of these the first was that the amount of employment available for the craftsmen was inconstant and intermittent. The man dependant on his position as a carver employed on church works might suffer long intermissions when he could only save himself from the alternatives of starvation or charity by exercising some by-occupation. This might in some cases be small farming or the sale of materials, but it could most easily be the manufacture and sale of articles connected with the worker's trade.

The second reason was purely a matter of demand. A higher standard of living consequent on political stability and improved commercial relations led in the later Middle Ages to a great investment of surplus wealth in churches and objects of art and luxury. These could not have been made in sufficient quantity by the old individual methods, and the existing shopmen were driven to increasing their numbers of journeymen and apprentices or learners as far as guild regulations would permit. The efficiency, on the whole, of these regulations, is shown by the extraordinarily high technical quality maintained by most of the surviving shop-made artefacts, not only in England, but in France, Germany and Spain. By the fifteenth century, shop-work in many cases involved actual mass-production: alabaster carvings, statues of St. John the Baptist, and even ready-made parts for chapels and churches, were being turned out on a large scale by workshops which were already factories in miniature.

The application of machinery was still in a rudimentary stage, but columns and capitals, of stone, marble and wood, were turned in the lathe, stencils and stamps were employed for painted and gesso work, and before the Gothic period closed, engraving and printing were well established. Ever since the thirteenth century, flooring tiles with elaborate patterns had been made by a partly mechanical process of stamping, and there was extensive application of mould-casting to such minor objects as pilgrims' signs. The best wrought iron of the fourteenth century was made by water-power hammers. But though the machinery of manufacture was still in its infancy, other machinery, of process, was not. The classical treatises of Vegetius and Vitruvius were studied for engines of war, and through the whole period extensive use was made of many types of hoisting engines and tackles, of water-driven mills and pumps, and special pieces of apparatus such as Honnecourt's device for pushing back to the vertical the framework of a leaning timber house. The master masons and master carpenters were also engineers, and both in peace and in war were full of invention and experiment.

Metallic reinforcement of buildings has been mentioned already; it is merely nonsense to suppose that the mediaeval engineer had the slightest scruples of conscience about using any material which he found suitable to his purpose. Every large window, every steeple, every pinnacle, of the thousands of Gothic churches throughout Europe, with the exception of those entirely framed of timber, made extensive use of wrought iron for cramps, stays, tie-rods and dowels. Frequently, as at Westminster Abbey, the tie-rods were exposed and frankly linked the piers across the springing of the arcades; sometimes, as in the Ste.-Chapelle in Paris in the thirteenth, and the tower of Salisbury Cathedral in the fourteenth century, hidden reinforcement was largely used. Nor was the knowledge of these engineers confined to structural expedients; they had a very considerable practical experience of the properties of materials, prevented their iron from rusting by boiling it in tallow, forestalled stone-decay by the use of resin, pitch, and linseed oil, and by habitual lime-washing.

We shall see as we go on something more of the details of Gothic methods in building and in art; we must remember always that the superb results obtained were informed by the spirit of the age. As in every other age there was jerry-building, slacking, striking, and inefficiency; but as in few other ages in recorded history, there was a hard core of energetic purpose. In spite of their internal differences, their bitter controversies, Gothic men were certain of themselves, knew where they wanted to go and went, well assured that their paths led towards God. In their eagerness to build, and to build magnificently; in their love of exuberant ornament and profusion of every form of art; in their underlying hatred of usury and sharp practice and their belief in the just price; above all in their love of gaiety and bright colour, of song and dance, of ceremonial and humour everywhere, even in church, the men and women of the Gothic age proved themselves truly human, and more than human. The final refutation of the materialist, the rationalist, the sceptic, lies in the tangible, unsurpassable remains of Gothic art.

I

The Production of Gothic Art

WORKS of art do not just grow of themselves; they are the product of human hands as well as of human brains. It follows that for the production of works on a large scale, especially great buildings, a high degree of organization is required. Such an organization presupposes not only a relatively complicated social civilization and system of administration behind it, but also the needful economic means to the desired end. That is to say, the great building projects of the Gothic age implied great schemes of finance, and of the application of the money in an appropriate way. Now we know that the great building employers of the period were precisely the people who had the necessary financial and administrative machinery: the Kings, the Church in its various ramifications, and as time went on, the great municipalities.

In England, where the archives of the Crown have been particularly well preserved, the direct evidence of an existing Pipe Roll proves the high degree of financial organization to have existed before 1130: a time earlier than the first traces of the Gothic style in art. In other words, the material organization was already in existence before the new outpouring of artefacts began. It is as well to emphasize this, for it might otherwise be suggested that the artistic impulse came to fruition in spite of a surrounding chaos of barbarism. This was very far from being the case; the Gothic seed fell upon a fruitful and already well-tilled ground.

The well-known letters and chronicles of 1145, relating to the building of Chartres Cathedral and other churches in northern France and Normandy, and describing the swarms of people of all classes who flocked to help the works, have been considered as evidence tending in a contrary direction. Here, if any-where, is the proof of general co-operative construction, on the building-bee principle. But this is not what the documents record. The most famous, a letter from Abbot Haimon of St.-Pierre-sur-Dives in Normandy to the Prior of his cell at Tutbury, in England, refers to thousands of men and women, including kings, princes and others of noble birth, as binding bridles on their necks and dragging waggons of "wine, corn, oil, lime, stones, timbers, and other things needful for sustaining life or the fabric of churches". These works of piety did not include anything so unlikely as the shaping or setting of masonry or beams, but simply provided an abundance of unskilled labour. Similarly records such as that of 1236 which tells us that the work of Amiens Cathedral was carried out after con-sultation with the clergy and laity of the city (*accedente consensu Ambianensis cleri et populi*) at most imply that a referendum was held (as happened in modern times over the completion of the front of the Duomo at Florence) upon pre-existing designs; not that there was spontaneous "folk-design".

Even so, these manifestations were relatively uncommon, and the normal Gothic building patron or committee could not rely on such adventitious aid. Both before and after these outbursts of devotion, unequivocal records prove the existence of highly skilled craftsmen who were responsible for actual building work. Abbot Suger, who himself records the assistance of laymen in providing transport, mentions his crowd of skilled masons, sculptors and other craftsmen, and describes how he consulted not only his own carpenters, but those of Paris, as to where he might find twelve great beams of a certain size. Getting a negative reply, he took the measurements and his own carpenters with him for a day in the

2   THE GOTHIC SCENE.   Regensburg: the city and Cathedral from the Danube.

3   MUIDEN: Castle, early thirteenth century.

4   CAHORS: Pont Valentré, 1308–80.

FUNCTIONAL GOTHIC

woods, and in spite of the grinning disbelief of the foresters, succeeded in discovering exactly twelve sufficient trees. In taking such a close personal interest in the work, Suger was exceptional—most later patrons were content to abide by the decisions of their technical advisers.

That the normal organization of finance was on the basis of a fabric fund is amply proved by the institutions of confraternities, which, beginning in France in the eleventh century, had by about 1175 reached England. Dr. Rose Graham has recently given a sketch of this system of raising church funds, referring to such institutions at St. Paul's, London, c. 1175; Winchester Cathedral, 1202; Lincoln Cathedral, 1205; and Worcester Cathedral in 1224. In each case contributors were urged to undertake annual subscriptions and to make bequests; in return the clergy of the church and diocese would sing Masses for both the living and the dead members of the confraternity. Similarly, hundreds of papal and episcopal indulgences were granted to those who should aid the building of specific churches, monasteries, or chapels.

During the early part of the Gothic period, the economy of western Europe was to a large extent based on agriculture, and the endowments of the great monasteries and cathedrals, and later of colleges and schools, consisted of land, and to a certain extent of house property. The ability of these institutions to build and to keep their buildings in repair, depended upon the management of their estates. Very often we find that the raising of the money and its outlay upon new building were in the hands of the same man, both able and eager in administration. In the case of monastic buildings, such work gave scope to men of enterprise who were by their vows cut off from personal ambition and private glory. This was not the case with the secular clergy, whose higher ranks were able to amass considerable private fortunes; thus a large proportion of the great building works at the English cathedrals was carried out with money given or bequeathed by wealthy bishops.

However acquired, the funds for the fabric needed careful administration. One or more officials would be entrusted with the care of the money and its outlay on the work. The names and precise functions of these officials differ from place to place in almost infinite variety, and reveal several different methods of organization. At the secular cathedrals, where there were of course no obedientiaries, it was usual to appoint one of the canons as Master or Keeper of the Works or Fabric; all other persons concerned with the fabric and its maintenance: the artists, craftsmen and labourers, the sacrist who had charge of the sacred vessels, and such minor officials as the bell-ringer, were paid by the Master of the Fabric. In most monasteries it was the Sacrist, an obedientiary, who himself took the place of the administrative Master, and to whom the craftsmen and minor officers were responsible. But while the Master at a secular cathedral would probably have charge of all works, including the repairs to house-property and estates of the Chapter, the monastic obedientiaries took charge of the various works within their own spheres of influence. So at Norwich we find that the cloisters, of interest to the whole monastery, were built by the Communar; at Westminster the great rebuilding of the Infirmary in the fourteenth century was managed by the Infirmarer, and the construction of a new range for the Cellarer came under that official's supervision. If a Prior or Abbot built a new lodging for himself, it might be paid for from a separate household account, or by the monastic Treasurer.

So far I have described only the arrangements made for the building and upkeep of the great churches and religious houses, for they provided most of the employment for artists and building craftsmen during the twelfth and thirteenth centuries. But there was in addition a great and growing organization devoted to the production and maintenance of secular buildings. This was the department, a sort of excrescence upon the Royal Household, which dealt with the King's buildings, his castles, fortifications, manor-houses, fish-ponds, harbours, and where the King was responsible for them, roads and bridges. This department, the Royal Works, seems to have attained a much higher degree of organization and independence in England than it did in continental countries during the Middle Ages. The reason for this is probably to be sought in the much higher degree of English national unity than was attained by the European states, and in her rapid concentration of administrative power into the King's hands. Similar household organizations undoubtedly existed at the Courts of France, Spain, Burgundy, and in the German and Scandinavian countries, but so many of these territories were petty feudal states rather than national entities. Later we shall see something of the alternative forms of organization which grew up on the Continent.

In England, the Office of the King's Works did not begin to take definite shape until the middle of the thirteenth century, and it did not become completely organized and permanent until 1336. In its final form it was administered by a Clerk of the Works (sometimes termed the Surveyor, and later to be the Surveyor-General of Works and Buildings), who had financial and administrative charge of all operations, assisted by deputies as occasion might require, and by a staff of clerical assistants whose duties were to enter and engross the rolls and books of accounts; to issue imprests of cash and materials, and to keep check on materials and time spent. Attached to the department was a purveyor, armed with royal writs giving him the power to buy all materials required at the King's price, and to impress craftsmen and labourers. The power of impressment included the right to imprison objectors, and to arrest fugitives from the works; but craftsmen already employed by ecclesiastical bodies were generally exempt. As a safeguard against maladministration and abuses, a separate official kept an independent account of all receipts and expenditure, and was known from this counter-roll as the "controller".

None of the members of the staff so far described, except upon occasion the controller, had charge of the actual conduct of the works themselves, and none of them required technical knowledge of the design and construction of buildings. Technical control was entirely in the hands of a separate series of officers, the master-craftsmen and their assistants. Chief of these were the Master Mason, supreme over planning, design and execution of all works to be carried out in stone; the Master Carpenter, who had similar charge of all woodwork; the Master Plumber; the Master Glazier; the Master Smith; and the Master Joiner. There is some evidence that both masons and carpenters were technically capable of taking charge of each others' work, but this is obscured by mediaeval craft exclusiveness.

The controller was sometimes a craftsman, as for instance William and Hugh Herland, the carpenters, on several important English works in the late fourteenth century, and William Swayn, mason at King's College Chapel, Cambridge, at the opening of the sixteenth century. There are also examples of craftsmen being associated in the administration of the works with the clerical Keeper. Master James of St. George, a mason who designed most of the castles and fortifications of North Wales for Edward I, also held high administrative office, both in connexion with their building and later; several craftsmen are named even earlier, as joint "keepers" of Henry III's works at Westminster Abbey and Windsor Castle; and outside the royal works, Master Roger the Mason (*fl.* 1299–1310) was one of the Keepers of the New Work of Exeter Cathedral. Such appointments indicate a high degree of confidence in the craftsmen concerned, and also point to their literacy, for even though the rolls might be written out for them by a clerk, it is difficult to suppose that they could be held responsible for their accuracy, and for auditing them (as Master Robert of Beverley did in 1282 and 1284), if unable to read.

At the inception of a new work, the first charges usually relate to the acquisition of materials: timber for scaffolds and centering; rubble or chalk for foundations, and possibly piles of alder, elm or oak; and stone for the masons, all had to be procured and their carriage to the site arranged. We have seen Abbot Suger taking an excursion to the forest in search of timber, and the records are full of instances where the master carpenter with his assistants, sometimes accompanied by one of the clerical administrators of the work, spent time in finding and marking suitable trees to be felled. The master mason likewise visited the quarries, either to arrange for consignments of stone, or to hire the whole quarry for a given period. Many of the great religious houses and other constant building employers owned their own quarries. Special materials, such as Purbeck marble for columns, lead for roofing, and glass, had to be ordered from the quarries, mines or glasshouses, and surviving letters and contracts refer to such trade supplies.

After deciding upon the materials, and finding appropriate sources of supply, carriage had to be arranged. Religious houses, many of whose tenants owed labour-services as rent, could make use of the carts and teams of their own dependants; so could the greater lay-landlords. For royal works, the King could make use of his power of impressment, or hire at his own price. There was already an official scale of payments for travel to pressed men in England by 1233, when 16 carpenters impressed at Reading and sent to Painscastle, a distance of 120 statute or 80 "long" miles, were allowed 16d. each, a rate of 4d. for every 20 "long miles". By 1515 this rate had increased to 6d. Upon the means of carriage available depended in many cases the choice between various sources of materials. Land carriage was most expensive, while water-transport was comparatively cheap, if it were practicable. Even in the thirteenth century, foreign materials could be obtained at competitive prices. In addition to Caen stone from Normandy brought over because of its excellent working qualities, timber was bought from the Hansa cities: in 1274 the master carpenter of Norwich Cathedral went to Hamburg to buy timber and boards, and two masons voyaged to Caen to purchase stone. Stone and timber were alike shipped to Great Yarmouth, and thence brought up the Yare to Norwich, thus avoiding all land-carriage except the few hundred yards from wharf to the cathedral. Christ Church, Canterbury, even sent to Ireland for oak timber, and throughout the Middle Ages London and East Anglia found it worth while to ship Magnesian Limestone from the quarries which were accessible by way of the Humber and long sea passage.

While the financial arrangements were in the hands of the Clerk or Master of the Works, an administrative official, it is important to remember that it had necessarily to be a competent technical man who visited quarries or timber-yards to discover suitable material; such visits were among the influences which contributed to the spread of style, and formed links for example between the brick-builders of the Low Countries and North Germany and their imitators in England, or in the contrary direction carried English patterns of stellar vaults to the later Gothic churches of the Baltic region. In many cases, however, materials lay close at hand, and near the greater cities it was already possible in the thirteenth century to rely to some extent upon "builders' merchants", tradesmen who dealt, generally as a by-product of their own craft, in such commodities as hewn ashlar, scantlings of timber and boards, and ironmongery.

An important branch of mediaeval building was concerned with the equivalent of modern "contractor's plant", the ladders, scaffolding, tools, and especially machinery needed on large and high buildings. The early masons and carpenters were also skilled in military engineering and siegecraft, and were the experts of their time upon problems of mechanics. Various forms of cranes and hoisting engines were devised for dealing with heavy loads, and great wheels belonging either to the treadmill or hand-operated types of hoist survive in the towers of several cathedrals, notably Canterbury, Salisbury, and Peterborough (**1**). In these cases the engine was probably preserved for use in raising and lowering the bells after building operations had ceased. Sometimes, as nowadays, the larger engines were hired, for William Orchard the master mason paid the Abbot of Rewley ten shillings for the use of a crane during the building of Magdalen College, Oxford, in the late fifteenth century. At Westminster Abbey in 1413, a wheel and other apparatus for a crane were bought ready-made from Nicholas Walton, a prominent carpenter.

Setting aside the planning and design of the work, which will be dealt with later, the first operation on a clear site was to set out the lines of the main walls and the positions of the piers on the ground. This was done, then as now, with pegs and string: Gerald the Welshman, writing in the 1180s, referred to his dream of the King's son, John, "in a green plain . . . after the fashion of surveyors . . . marking the turf, making lines on all sides over the surface of the earth, visibly drawing the plan of a building". Cords for setting-out commonly appear in mediaeval accounts, and in 1434 the contractor for Fotheringhay Church undertook "to make all the groundwerk", "to void hit" and to "latlay it" under proper supervision. The late Professor Knoop and Dr. G. P. Jones have shown that "groundwerk" is equivalent to foundations, while "voiding" the site was clearing it before the start of work. The operation of "latlaying" was that of setting or laying the measuring-lath or "latt" upon the ground to mark out the dimensions. Other references occur to the due supervision of building measurements, doubtless with a view to checking quantities and payment, as well as accuracy for its own sake. Right-angles were set out simply by means of the triangle whose sides are in the proportions of 3, 4 and 5, a proposition in practical geometry well known to the Gothic builders. At the end of the period we get more specific descriptions of the preliminary operations in the accounts for Wolsey's works at Whitehall and Oxford between 1515 and 1525. The masons and bricklayers were paid for "mesuring and setting out of ground", and at Oxford the master masons and their assistant went on the site "to se the platte (plan) with the grownde", i.e. to compare their sketch design with the actual boundaries of the property, for it was not until six months later that they were ordered "to set forth the ground" ready for the foundation trenches.

As soon as the plan had been set out, a gang of labourers with picks and shovels were employed to dig the foundation trenches, and the soil was carried away by basket-carriers, hodmen, and bearers of hand-barrows. The last, similar to stretchers, were steadily being replaced by wheelbarrows through the Gothic period. On a wet site, or where a sea- or river-wall had to be built, squared piles, with ends sharpened and shod with an iron point, were driven down into the sub-soil, and levelled off. On the heads of the piles, and sometimes quite elaborately dowelled into them, was laid a continuous flooring of heavy planks in one or more layers, and on this level platform the footings of the stone wall were placed in position. Where solid rock was near the surface, it was cut away to form a similar level plane for the footings; but in the majority of cases all that was done was to dig a trench judged to be roughly adequate to the proposed weight of walls and piers, and to fill it nearly to ground-level with chalk, stone rubble, flints and rubbish rammed hard. But in the case of some important buildings, a better foundation was made with strong concrete of rubble and lime-mortar.

While work on the foundations was in progress, the carpenters had run up timber sheds and shelters for the permanent staff of craftsmen, particularly the "lodges" for the masons who were to work at their bankers on cutting the stones to shape (1). It must be emphasized that there was originally no peculiar or esoteric significance attached to the masons' lodge; other craftsmen with a permanent quota of indoor work to perform, notably glaziers, were provided with lodges, and the term is also found applied to mere storehouses and sheds. But for a number of reasons, chiefly perhaps the fact that for centuries they had no local guilds, the masons came to use their lodges for other purposes than as mere workshops. On important works where there was no shortage of money, a staff of mason-hewers could be kept steadily engaged through the winter in the lodge, preparing stone for the next season. The setters, on the other hand, unless there was indoor work such as vaulting to be done, were laid off when the frosty weather began, and the unfinished walls were protected with a covering of straw-thatch, heather, or fern, gathered for the purpose.

As soon as the walls were a few feet above ground-level, scaffolds became necessary; they were framed with poles* and putlogs resting in holes left in the wall-face, but instead of planks (an expensive luxury obtainable only by pit-sawing) the gangways were formed of hurdles. The purchase of hurdles for scaffolds is a constant item in the building accounts, and that they were for this purpose is specified by some of the accounts for the fourteenth-century work on St. Stephen's Chapel, where also leather thongs are mentioned, for tying the scaffold together. Centering for the larger windows, and later for vaults, was a more highly skilled task, carried out under the personal supervision of the master carpenter, who had to set out his centres geometrically from the working drawings, allowing the necessary clearances. The growing use of detailed drawings, and the improvements in technical knowledge during the thirteenth and fourteenth centuries, enabled the masters of the late Gothic period to attain a far greater degree of accuracy and precision than their predecessors.

The rate of progress of Gothic buildings was governed by the available finance rather than by technical considerations, but precautions were taken where heavy work such as a tower was concerned. The surviving contracts suggest that a height of about ten or twelve feet per year was considered the best for tower-building, and this caution was justified by the survival of "leaning towers" such as that of Pisa, and those of the Temple Church, Bristol, and Pinchbeck, Lincs., in England. In these cases the piecemeal method of work made it possible to correct the inclination progressively as the tower went up. Caution was also necessary in arranging the order of operations in a building provided with vaults and flying buttresses, for the flyers and vaults had both to be allowed to set firmly before the centerings could be struck. The pinnacles, so characteristic a feature of the Gothic aesthetic system, were structural necessities as counterweights to control the vault-thrusts.

Where stone vaults were to be covered by a timber roof, as was generally the case in northern Europe, the roof was erected on completion of the walls, and the construction of the vaults undertaken at leisure, beneath its shelter. Once the roofs were up, the building could be consecrated and used, in spite of work proceeding upon the vaults. This was the method adopted at St.-Denis, the first great Gothic building with high vaults, where services were actually in progress during the great gale which threatened the vault-ribs after the roof had been put up, but before the webs of the vault had been filled in between the ribs. It may have been with such risks in mind that Count Raymond VI gave orders that the immense vault of the cathedral nave of Toulouse should be completed in 1211, although the "crusaders" of Simon de Montfort had already laid siege to the

---

* These were sometimes omitted; the putlogs running through the wall, and having platforms on both sides, acted as balanced cantilevers. I am indebted to Mr. H. A. G. Blackwell for telling me of this practice, which is confirmed by mediaeval drawings and illuminations.

city. The vault in fact bears the count's badge upon its keystone, and was evidently complete before Raymond's defeat and exile in 1213.

There was no fixed rule as to carving, whether it was to be carried out before or after the stone was set in position. In general, moulded stones and tracery were completed at the banker and carefully stacked until wanted; and at least some carving was done in the same way. But carving *in situ* clearly diminished the risk of damage, though in the event of the stone being spoilt it could not be replaced, except perhaps with great difficulty. The evidence of unfinished work proves that, at any rate in the earlier part of the period, a certain amount of carving was done in position, but in some cases it seems more probable that partly finished stones were used up after they had remained some time in store during temporary cessation of work. This may account for the well-known instance of the east window of Carlisle Cathedral, and the blocked-out but only part finished tower parapet of Walberswick Church, Suffolk (**82**). Towards the end of the period, moulded and carved details could not only be cut on the site at the banker, but even purchased ready-made from a quarryman-contractor. The east window supplied to the Infirmarer of Westminster Abbey for Battersea Church by Henry Yevele in 1379 was made ready for insertion, presumably at Yevele's shop in St. Paul's Churchyard.

Window-bars of wrought iron were inserted as the work went up, and spires and pinnacles were held together with iron cramps, dowels, and rods. These were purpose-made by the smith as occasion required, and so were the more ambitious reinforcements used by the very daring masters. In the mid-thirteenth century a chain was imbedded in the walls of the Sainte-Chapelle at Paris, and the vaulting ribs were strengthened with iron bars; while in the great steeple of Salisbury, a century later, a whole system of wrought-iron reinforcement was laid within the masonry, and remained unknown until discovered by Mr. W. A. Forsyth in his recent work of conservation. Colonel N. H. Waller has found similar bars in the work of *c.* 1330–50 at Gloucester. Contrary to commonly received opinion, vast quantities of iron nails were made and used in the Middle Ages, all hand-forged, and wonderfully rust-resisting. It is said that this "stainless" quality of mediaeval ironwork was obtained by tempering in boiling tallow, and it is certain that the Gothic builders were aware of a number of special methods and receipts which found a useful application in the course of their work. There is, for example, documentary evidence of the use of linseed oil, pitch and resin in mortar, the oil being expressly used to preserve stone of poor weathering quality.

Lead was used not only for covering flat roofs and those of low pitch, but also on higher roofs and even on spires. For this reason it was the plumbers who were the mediaeval steeplejacks, as Lydgate mentions: "plummers on stieplis and towris clymming aloft", while John Stow tells how, after one Robert Godwin had fallen to his death while trying to re-fix the weathercock on Paul's steeple, it was successfully set up by "Burchwood the King's plumber", i.e. John Byrchold. Many of the great churches kept a plumber in constant employment on repairs, while some also retained a glazier. But the glazing of real importance, with painted glass, was done by specialists working in a few centres, enumerated by Dr. Christopher Woodforde, of which the most important in England were Canterbury, Coventry, Exeter, Ipswich, London, Lynn, Norwich, Oxford, and York. The work of the glaziers, who designed and painted windows, fired them, assembled them in lead cames, and finally attached the complete panels to the iron bars in the windows, has carefully to be distinguished from that of glass-makers, who produced the raw material, the pot-metal and flashed sheets of glass of various colours, on which the glaziers worked. Some glass was imported from the Continent, including a large proportion of the coloured glass used, but from the fourteenth century pot-metal, flashed and composite glass in many colours was being made at Chiddingfold in Surrey, at first by a family called Alemayne, presumably from Lower Germany, and after 1368 by the Shurterres, whose name has been supposed to be a corruption of Chartres.

The glazing of the windows would normally have been the last work carried out before taking down the scaffolds, to minimize the risk of breakage to the glass. But after the walls, roof and vaults had been completed, much else remained to be done. The floor was paved, often with patterned tiles brought from some famous pottery; in England the most important centre of such work was at Chertsey. Painters set to work upon the walls and vaults, joiners fitted screens and stalls, and the prepared stones of altar-screens, pulpitum and sedilia were erected. All this, and the many minor fittings, embroideries, tapestries, carpets, plate, provided work for an army of artists and craftsmen, some working in and around the building, others in their own houses and shops, close by or at some more or less distant centre.

Except for the absence of machinery (apart from a limited use of wind- and water-power), all this work was carried on by means closely similar to those of the present day. The actual processes of hewing and carving stone and timber are still the same, except where power-driven saws or planes can be used; the making of scaffolds and centering are still closely akin to what they were in the twelfth and thirteenth centuries; for the most part there has been no radical change in the technique of the other crafts or of the minor arts. But some distinction must be drawn between the mediaeval building trade and the contemporary crafts. Building was almost the only occupation of the Gothic age which involved large numbers of men, and a considerable variety of skill. In general, mediaeval industry was conducted on a small scale, and within corporate towns, where the members of each craft could easily band themselves together for mutual protection and benefit. These craft guilds, which combined social, economic, practical and religious functions, were organized on an intensely local basis. They resisted all tendencies towards the practice of the craft by non-members of the guild, whether they were fellow-townsmen, fellow-countrymen from outside the municipality, or aliens from a foreign country.

It followed that non-members of the appropriate guild could only practice their craft outside the limits of the municipalities, and this meant in fact that they must either obtain work from an employer in the country, e.g. a monastic house; or else live and work in a liberty or exempt jurisdiction, outside the control of the neighbouring municipality. These exempt liberties were so numerous in the Middle Ages that they must almost have cancelled the protection afforded by the guilds to their own members. Painters, glaziers and other artists swarmed in the liberties of London and Southwark, in the "Soke" of Winchester, and in the many "peculiar" precincts adjoining other cities and towns throughout the country. In London, especially towards the end of the period, it seems to have been almost the exception, rather than the rule, for the really distinguished masters to be members of their London Company. Some were aliens, but many were Englishmen who by impressment or chance had been drawn into the royal service and thus found adequate employment free from municipal control, or who were protected and at least partly employed by some religious house. In Germany and central Europe these non-local masters belonged to the system of Lodges, which operated independently of the local Guilds.

There was no rigid pattern of guild organization; in any case the craft guilds did not exist at the opening of the Gothic period, though the guild idea was symptomatic of Gothic, and grew with Gothic art. Craft guilds sprang from the advantages to be derived from collective bargaining and mutual protection, as the trade union movement was later to do. But the guilds included both employers and journeymen, all of them fully skilled in their particular craft. The earliest craft guilds were mostly formed to protect groups of small men from the greed of the town oligarchs who formed the exclusive Guild Merchant. By the end of the fifteenth century, the craft guilds themselves, in England and all over Europe, had become oligarchical, and tended to promote mainly the interest of a few wealthy families who were entrenched in them. This was noticeably so, as Mr. John A. Knowles has shown, with the glaziers of York. In France the *Compagnonnages* developed, to protect the journeymen's interests.

But in their hey-day the guilds at least aimed at an idyllic state of affairs. In the guild there were no class-distinctions, no member was irrevocably a wage-slave. Membership was open only to the man who had attained full mastery of the technique of the craft. The two normal methods of obtaining membership were by patrimony, when the father presented his son, whom he had trained personally; and by apprenticeship, where the master presented his apprentice. There were limitations on the number of apprentices that a master might train simultaneously, and the standards demanded were high. In accordance with the underlying theory of group-responsibility which inspired mediaeval policing and criminal law, the guild was held responsible for the faulty work of its members, and therefore its officers had powers of search, which included the right to destroy without compensation to the defaulting worker any work found to be below standard.

Such methods were rigorous, and to be maintained even for two to three centuries, as they were, with a considerable degree of success, they had to be inspired by a fundamental belief in the value of good work and honest dealing between man and man. Like mediaeval legislation on markets, the guild system in its prime insisted upon the just price, whereby the buyer paid what the article was worth, and the seller was enabled to live in reasonable comfort from the proceeds. Critics of the Middle Ages point with glee to the denunciations of mediaeval moralists as proof that the system never worked at all; but the excellence of the material works produced, and the certain knowledge that those extant are but a small fraction of the original total, speak eloquently to the contrary. In spite of its imperfections, the mediaeval system based on the two great commandments of duty towards God and one's neighbour, did represent the most notable approach to a perfect condition that the western world has seen for two thousand years.

In the earlier Middle Ages, the majority of guildsmen were small capitalists, each with his own little shop, and master of perhaps two apprentices and a servant, who might be a young man out of his apprenticeship or training, saving up and seeking an opening for a shop of his own. There was a good chance in this system for most employees to become in time employers on their own account, and everything conspired to encourage good work. Notwithstanding this, there are numerous recorded cases of poor and inadequate work, and even fraud, but considering that extant records are largely legal, and that the extant work itself is good, we must not lay undue stress upon mediaeval shortcomings, amusing as some of them are.

The building crafts, like the rest, formed guilds, but more slowly in many cases, for their work was not equally concentrated in the towns. The masons in particular, whose work led them all over the country, developed their local organization late, and in London apparently not until somewhere about 1360. For this reason it will be convenient to return to the masons a little later, and first to consider the other crafts connected with building and the arts. I have mentioned mediaeval trade-exclusiveness; this was founded upon a theory roughly expressed by the saying: "Jack of all trades is master of none." It was moreover fostered by the growth of similar trades from diverse origins. Each individual had his own specific place to fill, in theory, and it was only with considerable difficulty that a craftsman could transfer from one trade to another. In actual practice there was

5 ROUEN: Palais de Justice, 1499-1526, by *Roger Ango*
and *Roulland le Roux*.

6 AVIGNON: Palace of the Popes, main front, 1344-52. Designer *Jean de Loubières*.

PALATIAL GOTHIC

7   AVIGNON: Palace of the Popes, Audience Chamber, 1344–50, by *Jean de Loubières*.

8   BARCELONA: Royal Palace, the Tinell, 1359–70. Designer *Guillem Carbonell*.

GOTHIC SPACE

very extensive subdivision of labour, though perhaps to a less extent than theory would suggest. The main effect of such regulations was to provide work for as many hands as possible, and in relation to building, to delay the advent of the general contractor.

The municipalities themselves appointed searchers of the various crafts, and so far as building was concerned, those chosen to view the work of masons and carpenters had powers similar to those of the District Surveyors of modern times. In London, for example, there were elaborate building by-laws from the twelfth century, and the sworn searchers administered these in addition to the good work provisions of their respective guilds. Similar arrangements were in force in York, Norwich and other great cities of England, and in Paris and elsewhere on the Continent. The guilds, for their part, took fees for licences which would now be granted by the District Surveyor; the records of the Carpenters Company of London, for example, show that in 1514 Humphrey Coke the famous carpenter paid for licence to raise a frame (i.e. set up a timber-framed house) in Fleet Street, and there are many other instances.

A large proportion of artistic work must always have been done in the shops of the "little masters", and was none the worse for that, but it is at first sight surprising to find as early as 1272 that worked masonry was being supplied to order. Even in Norman times we know that Tournai produced a special kind of black marble font, which was widely exported, but the thirteenth-century document shows two stone-cutters of Tournai agreeing to provide and send to the Abbot of Cambron in Bruges an extensive collection of masonry at piece-work prices. The items include columns, quoin-stones, cornices, windows according to the design sent (*selon les molles ki en sont livré*), voussoirs, sills, and cornices by the foot-run. Gothic art must have been infinitely less parochial than our notions of mediaeval transport make us believe.

It is indeed in connexion with the masons of the Middle Ages that this fact is forcibly brought home. Disregarding the exploded legend of the "Comacine" Masters who secretly travelled the roads of Europe and built all the great cathedrals, one after another, the truth is very nearly as startling. As we shall see, documentary records of very wide travel by named masters are frequent, and it is possible to trace across the map of Europe the personal links in the development of Gothic style. But besides this there was indeed organization of a remarkably widespread kind, or rather several organizations different in form, but presenting definite analogies.

The clearest evidence of such organization comes from Germany, where both written records and masters' drawings have been, or were until recently, preserved in unusually large quantity. The principal documents are the Lodge Ordinances which were promulgated by periodical chapters of master masons, held in various cities of the Empire at frequent intervals from 1459 until relatively modern times. It is certain that the meeting of 1459 was not the first of its kind, but no specific data relating to earlier meetings are forthcoming. The very detailed regulations laid down, and altered and amended from time to time, are described as and clearly are ancient usage (*altes Herkommen*). Equally interesting is the territorial representation, covering all parts of Germany except the North-East, and also the Swiss Confederation and Hungary. The meeting of 1459 was at Regensburg, and consisted of nineteen masters and twenty-six *Gesellen*, journeymen. It was laid down that the Master of the Lodge at Strassburg should always have pre-eminence, while separate spheres of influence were under the charge of the Masters at Vienna (for Austria, Hungary and the Danube lands), Berne (for Switzerland), and Cologne (**9**). Of special importance among the regulations are those which enjoin that no non-mason shall be instructed in the secrets of design, and that no one shall be taught for money. It should be noted that this German organization applied only to the Lodge-Masons who worked for the greater churches; it was entirely distinct from the guilds of local masons in the towns and cities who worked for lay patrons.

The German evidence of a continuous tradition can be carried back by means of the drawings which survived until modern times. These show that scale drawings were made as early as the thirteenth century, and that careful copies of them were made and passed on by the masters, altered and amended in the process, and gave rise to new developments of style and design. On the other hand, the existence of a definite body of technical and aesthetic knowledge, as distinct from craft or lodge organization, is proved by the statements made in the printed and manuscript treatises of the close of the period. Three of these are of great importance: that of Hans Schmuttermayer of *c.* 1484 refers to the rules of composition and design as "not discovered by myself, but from many other great renowned masters, as the 'Junckheren' of Prague, Master Ruger, Nicholas of Strassburg and many others who brought the 'new art' to light". Matthaeus Roritzer, in his booklet printed in 1486, speaks of "the older (masters of) the art and particularly the 'Iungkher' of Prague", while Lorenz Lacher in 1516 mentions "the old usage". The "Junkers" of Prague were the members of the famous Parler family, who diffused the new Sondergotik through the Germanic area at the end of the fourteenth century. It is clear that Schmuttermayer's "new art" refers to the developments which were perfected, even if not originated, during Peter Parler's work at Prague Cathedral. A Spanish treatise was written by Rodrigo Gil de Hontañon.

Just as in 1459 the Master of Strassburg was to have jurisdiction over the German Lodge-Masons, and one of their governing regulations was the injunction to secrecy, so in Paris in 1268 the *Livre des Métiers* of Étienne Boileau laid down that whereas the King had given the mastery of the Masons to Master Guillaume de Saint Patu, he and his successors as masters of the craft should have the lesser justice and the fines of the masons etc., and it was further ordered that masters should not impart to outsiders the points of the mistery. For England the evidence is less adequate, and it is at least a tenable hypothesis that this may be partly due to an even more conscientious adherence to the rule of secrecy than was the case abroad, where the late German text-books, and the thirteenth-century album of Villard d'Honnecourt throw light upon the secrets of the craft. What we do know is that before the end of the fourteenth century the English masons had formulated a legendary history of their craft, and a series of ordinances closely related to those of Paris and Regensburg. The two early versions of the "Articles and Points of Masonry" are quite specific as to the existence of assemblies or congregations to which the masons were bidden, and which they must attend; and there are independent references in Statutes of 1360 and 1425 to the existence of congregations and general chapters of the English masons. It has been suggested that these latter congregations were entirely unconnected with those of the "Articles and Points", but this is very improbable. It seems evident from the wording of the Statute of 1425 that it was the recent illegal action of the chapters (in attempting to raise wages above the statutory limits) that was objected to, rather than the existence of masons' congregations for legitimate purposes.

In England, as in France and Germany, there was then a professional body representative of masons, or at any rate of those masons who were not included in the municipal craft guilds; periodical assemblies were held, and regulations laid down for the governance of the members. Obviously, as in the continental cases, the assembly must have had some legal basis of jurisdiction, and though its records are lost, the existence of an analogous jurisdiction as early as 1305 can be proved. At that date Master Walter of Hereford, King's Mason and master of the works of Caernarvon Castle, petitioned that he might be allowed to have his "free Court of his workers of the said Castle" as he had had in the past, and his prayer was granted, the answer specifying that he was to hold his Court and to have "the

BOUNDARY OF THE EMPIRE
///// BURGUNDIAN LANDS
\\\ LANDS OF TEUTONIC ORDER
● PLACES REPRESENTED AT
REGENSBURG CONGRESS 1459
+ PLACES REPRESENTED AT
SAXON CONGRESS 1462
⊚ R REGENSBURG
*The Master of the Strassburg
Lodge had his own region, and
also general Jurisdiction over
the regions controlled from
Bern, Cologne and Vienna.*

9   Central Europe, showing the organization of the Building Lodges in the
fifteenth century.   For France see **44**; for Flanders see **162**; for Bohemia see **179**;
for Germany see also **18**, **200**; for Hungary see **182**.

amends of transgressions of conventions and contracts made between the same workers". From such glimpses as this, and the evidence of the numerous masons' marks, which must have been assigned upon some principle, and have been shown to be subject to hereditary differences, we must reconstruct in imagination a highly developed organism of technical men. Securing the preservation and transmission of the rules and secrets of their craft, these great societies of the building masters played a decisive part in the production of Gothic art.

10 Strassburg Cathedral: drawing "A", *c.* 1250–60, showing the design of Master Rudolf for the western porches and rose-window.

II

The Design of Gothic Art

BEFORE any work of human skill can be produced it must first be imagined. In essence, it is this human power of imagining something which did not exist before, that we term "design". The word has of course acquired more specific meanings, including that of the actual picture or model made, firstly as a means to the proper making of the article itself, and secondly to show to the artist or to his client the form of the proposed work. Preparatory drawing or marking-out of materials is an essential preliminary of almost all technical processes. Paintings of elaborate composition, figure sculpture, and large buildings are all examples of art which cannot be accomplished without previous sketching, modelling, or setting out.

Not only is this forethought and preliminary deliberation inevitable, but it was realized as such by the men of the Gothic age. Writing at the end of the twelfth century on the parallel development of the "new poetry", Geoffrey of Vinsauf declared that the writing of poetry required as much care as the building of a house: "He who would found a house sets no rash hand to work, but metes it out first with the measuring-line of his heart." The Latin original was paraphrased by Chaucer in his *Troilus* two centuries later, and there is no doubt that the idea had a wide circulation. Vinsauf continues to elaborate the theme, and states that "the inner compasses of the mind must encircle the whole quantity of material" (before the work begins). The juxtaposition of ideas: measuring-line and compasses, and the Platonic archetype, whose production by the imagination is the subject of Vinsauf's reflections, is most significant. Mediaeval iconography pictured the Almighty as Creator, holding a pair of large compasses in His hand, and therewith measuring out the universe. Geometry was considered fundamental both in religion and in mundane affairs, even though practical knowledge of its operations was limited.

"As above, so below": the activities of the Creator were reflected and echoed in the works of human artists, and those works depended for their utility, durability, and beauty upon properly composed geometrical relations. The relations of buildings to human scale, and of their parts and those of other works of art to one another, were a practical expression of geometrical truths. This fact, and its particular connexion with the practice of architecture, had been detailed by the Roman architect Vitruvius, writing some twelve centuries before the Gothic age began. It is commonly implied that the work of Vitruvius was lost to the world in the Dark Ages, to re-appear only in the fifteenth century in Italy. This is a misconception, for numerous copies of his work, and of epitomes and abstracts of it, are known to have been made throughout the Middle Ages. In England alone there is evidence that there were copies in the monastic libraries of Bury, Ely, and St. Augustine's at Canterbury, and in that of the Austin Friars at York, while a further copy was made at St. Augustine's in the year 1316, and is now at St. John's College, Oxford.

At Monte Cassino in Italy one of the monks had made a compendium of Vitruvius in 1100, and it cannot be a coincidence that "ordinatio" and "dispositio", the two primary components of Architecture described by the Roman writer, were used throughout the Middle Ages to describe the work done by the chief building masters who had charge of works of architecture. It is moreover a stupidity to deny to these masters the title of "architect", for by derivation it has the precise meaning required by the facts: the chief or master builder. Eliminating the details of the classic orders, almost the whole of Vitruvius was applicable to Gothic architecture, engineering, mechanics, and art generally; hardly any of the technical aspect of the work but can be paralleled in mediaeval practice. It is not suggested that mediaeval architects had a rare and costly manuscript of Vitruvius lying on a shelf of their chamber; but the presence of copies in libraries, and the close adherence to Vitruvian technique shown by the works themselves, is good evidence of the strong if not absolutely direct influence of the book.

As examples of technical devices contained in Vitruvius, and put into practice by the Gothic builders, may be instanced: the use of bond-timbers, and of bond-stones (*parpeyns* in mediaeval parlance) running from face to face of a wall; the use of alder-wood or oak for piles; the relationship of the human body and of numbers to the proportions of buildings; acoustic vases (in Classic theatres, and Gothic choirs); the structural theory of piers and arches, requiring end abutment; methods of levelling. Even Vitruvius's remarks on the moral probity of architects, brought up in honest ways as well as in skill by their parents, so that they might safely be entrusted with large sums, find an echo in the positions of trust held during the Middle Ages by master craftsmen.

We have seen that towards the end of the fifteenth century German masters were beginning to issue for private circulation the geometrical secrets of planning and design, consisting in the practical application of square and compasses to the production of parts proportioned to the whole. A century earlier, there is abundant evidence of the discussions as to methods of proportion to be used in the design of Milan Cathedral, when Heinrich Parler was called in from Germany in 1391. Rival systems of proportion, favoured by German, French and Italian masters, were invoked in justification of various heights proposed for the vault. A hundred and fifty years earlier still, Honnecourt's album shows that he and his friend Pierre de Corbie produced an ideal plan for a church by discussion, "*inter se disputando*". Honnecourt also sketched down towers, windows and other details on his travels, because they pleased him; and since his whole book is of the nature of a practical exemplar or builder's cyclopaedia, the purpose that lay behind these sketches was clearly the intention of using them for reference in fresh designs.

Indeed, the Gothic masters took as great pains over improvements upon the work of their forerunners as Renaissance architects ever did over their variations upon the theme of the classic orders. The extensive study of the surviving German drawings by Herr Otto Kletzl has demonstrated that Gothic style was largely diffused by means of the drawing-board: a plan at Strassburg plays upon the choir-plans of the cathedrals of Paris and Orléans; a version of the plan of Rodez was elaborated for use at Prague by the French master Mathias of Arras, and remains at Vienna; in 1414 King Sigismund of Hungary sent to Siena for plans of the Ospedale della Scala, to serve as models for a hospital in Buda. Many drawings based on the great tower at Freiburg-im-Breisgau exist.

The scope for individuality in tower-design was very considerable, and steeples and vaults in all European countries within the Gothic region prove that mediaeval architecture was not solely functional, not the child of blind adherence to tradition, but allowed full scope to originality. Various refinements, introduced as time went on, tell the same story. In the late thirteenth-century choir of Exeter Cathedral, many additional ribs were introduced into the vault; by itself, this innovation might be purely structural. But when the nave came to be vaulted, a generation or so later, the curve of the diagonal ribs was kept back, stilted, not to interfere with the suave and flowing lines of the sheaves of ribs. A few years later still, about 1375, the same thing was done in the vaulting of the south aisle of Westminster Abbey, as Mr. Howgrave-Graham has pointed out. Before the end of the century this process was carried even further in the splendidly modulated vaults of the nave of Canterbury Cathedral.

Many works of art are made by their designer with his own hands, but this is not possible with large buildings. Hence the division which now exists between architect and builder, each function being represented by a separate person or group. Mediaeval architects had usually been trained as building craftsmen, but on becoming primarily designers, that function was a first charge upon their time and energy. The documentary records are perfectly clear on this point, and it is difficult to understand the emphasis which is so often placed upon the mistaken idea that the mediaeval master was simply *primus inter pares*, craftsman on the same level as his fellows. There is no positive evidence of any kind in favour of this view, and it contradicts common sense.

On the contrary, the evidence is all in favour of the architect-masons of the class that planned and designed cathedrals, from the twelfth to the sixteenth century, having left the lodge (in the sense of the working mason's banker and tools) and entered the tracing-house, where they took to the drawing-board or tracing-floor, square, compasses, and measuring-rod. The crucial passages of *c.* 1261 from sermons of the Dominican Nicolas de Biard show that at that date it was already customary for the chief masters on large jobs to do no manual work themselves. The passages, literally translated, run as follows: "Masters of masons, holding a (measuring-)rod and gloves in their hands, say to others: *Cut it for me this way*, and do no labour; and yet they receive a higher fee, as do many modern prelates." And the other: "Some work by word alone. Note: that in these great buildings, there is wont to be one chief master who only ordains by word, and rarely or never sets hand (to the work); and yet he takes higher pay than the rest. Many such are in the Church, etc."

Nothing could be much more explicit than these contemporary statements of thirteenth-century practice in France; and from about the same date comes the English evidence of a drawing, perhaps by Matthew Paris, showing a number of building craftsmen at work, while King and Master Mason, in long robe, wearing gloves, and holding square and large compasses, stand by in conversation (**99**). In 1225 the Countess Joan of Hainault sent to Valenciennes architects (*architectores*) and carpenters, to devise (*ut disponant*) the building of a convent for the Friars Minor. The transaction is described in greater detail as the sending "from the Isles" of a master of works with certain architects (*architectoribus*) to consider and view the place where the church and other buildings might be set. The masters raised various objections of a technical nature, and it is evident that they were exercising precisely the functions which would be carried out in such a case by architects at the present day.

The contrast between the persons, as well as the functions, of architects and builders is again brought out in the accounts of S. Maria del Fiore at Florence in 1366, when six barrels of wine were purchased to celebrate important stages in the work, to be consumed by the masters and the handworkers (*pro magistris et manualibus*). Further, this division of function is implicit in the arrangement whereby large works were carried on under the supervision of a master who did not reside on the spot, but visited from time to time. That this already occurred in the thirteenth century, if not earlier, is evidenced by the precautions taken by employers in engaging masters: the Abbey of St.-Ouen at Rouen insisted upon their master undertaking not to work for other patrons; and in 1278 the Abbey of Winchcombe in England made a similar stipulation in regard to their master, Walter of Hereford, but excepted from the condition the King's works. And we know from abundant records that Master Walter was in fact one of the busiest architects under Edward I, and have seen him holding his "free Court" at Caernarvon Castle. Earlier in the century there is a high probability that the Master Alexander who was mason of

Worcester Cathedral *c.*1220–40, and the Alexander, mason and master of the work of Lincoln Cathedral about the same time, were one and the same man. By the early fourteenth century the procedure had become common form.

At Ely Cathedral in 1323 "a certain man from London" was paid for "ordaining" the new work of the octagon, said by the chronicler to have been "imagined with wonderful ability of mind"; within the next few years Master William de Ramsey and his brother John were being paid by Norwich Cathedral for journeys to and from London in connexion with the building of the cloister, and the same William de Ramsey, who had become the King's Chief Mason in 1336, was in 1337 engaged by the Dean and Chapter of Lichfield to pay visits from London "to supervise the fabric of the church and to give his discreet counsel as to the repair of defects and his ordinance and instruction to the other masons". In 1334 the Chapter of Salisbury Cathedral engaged the services of Master Richard of Farleigh, he undertaking to give them a due proportion of his attention in spite of his prior commitments at Bath and Reading. When a new cloister was to be built at Exeter Cathedral in 1377, Master Robert Lesyngham was sent for from Gloucestershire to "supervise and ordain" the work, and he spent seventeen weeks at first, and paid shorter visits in successive years, while at the beginning a sheet of parchment was bought "to show the form of the work". Nearly seventy years before, in 1311, the Exeter accounts record a payment of 25*s.* to Master William de Schoverwille, a mason from Salisbury who came to "visit" the new work.

Later references to part-time supervision are extremely numerous, and we shall refer to some of them in dealing in greater detail with the masters themselves. But from the middle of the fourteenth century the direct evidence as to design becomes so overwhelming that it is quite unnecessary to introduce the collateral proofs. Henry Yevele, who became King's Master Mason in 1360, is almost immediately afterwards described as "devizer of masonry of the works"; in 1381 he was supplying designs (again the word is "*devyse*") for work to be carried out by a contracting mason, while in 1395 work was to be done according to a "form and mould" made by Yevele's advice. His colleague, William Wynford, often associated with him on the royal works, was also master mason for William of Wykeham's works, and in Wykeham's will was appointed to have the "disposition and ordinance" (the words of Vitruvius again) of the rebuilding of the nave of Winchester Cathedral.

Similar records relate to continental masters: Raymond du Temple, master mason to Charles V of France (1364–80), was described by the poetess Christine de Pisan as "a learned artist, who very well understood geometry, which is the art of measure and square, compass and line, and who showed his knowledge in the designing (*en devisant*) of his buildings". Ulrich von Ensingen, the master at Strassburg Cathedral, was in 1414 paid to supply a design for the north tower of Basel Cathedral, and in 1499 Burkhard Engelberger, a master mason of Augsburg, supplied a drawing showing his design for the church tower of Bolzano in the South Tyrol, which was exhibited for several weeks in the church on a pillar close to the offertory chest. A Parisian master concerned in a lawsuit laid emphasis on the fact that he was a "great geometrician and carpenter, which is superior to a mason", and in 1425 the master of the cathedral works at Bordeaux, Colin Tranchant, was described as "*maître en geometrie*". More than two centuries earlier, at the close of the twelfth century, one Master Simon, in charge of the fortifications of Ardres near St.-Omer, was described as "so learned in geometrical work", and as "proceeding in magistral manner with his rod, and here and there setting out (*geometricantem*) the work already conceived in his mind, not so much by his measuring-rod as by the yard-stick (*pertica*) of his eyes."

John Lydgate, writing his *Falls of Princes* in the 1430s, referred to Nembroth "makyng his masouns For to compasse and castyn there devises, Gemetriens in ther dyvysiouns". About the same time, actual building contracts mention windows in the church tower of Dunster, Somerset, as to be made "acordyng to the patron y made by the avyce of Richard Pope fremason" in 1442, and three years later the Angel Inn at Andover, Hants, was to be made "cordyng to the portatur". Parallel evidence comes from other arts: in the 1350s the painter Master Hugh of St. Albans was drawing the figures on the walls of St. Stephen's Chapel in Westminster Palace, for other subordinate painters to fill in, and "ordaining" the painting of several images. At the same time Master John of Chester, glazier, and five other masters were drawing the images for the glass windows of the Chapel, and in 1405 John Thornton of Coventry, in contracting to make the east window of York Minster, undertook to draw (*portroiabit*) the window and the subjects, figures and any other things to be painted on it, but he was to engage workmen (*operarios*) to do the painting, only himself painting it in so far as might be needful. The designs of embroideries were not produced by the broderers themselves, for the King's Broderers from Robert Ashcombe in 1396 onwards were given writs to impress not only broderers and workers in that craft, but painters as well.

It is inescapable that the masters, at any rate those able to design and supervise the greater works, had already abandoned the banker and the habitual use of hammer and chisel by the middle of the thirteenth century, if not much earlier, and that they never relapsed into a condition of mere building foremen. In so far as they did themselves do manual work, it was as specialist carvers and figure sculptors, not as mere hewers of stone, once they had passed out of their training or apprenticeship. Even masons who were not masters might spend a part of their time in the drawing office, as William Netylton did at Louth Church, Lincs., in 1500, "trassyng and makyn molds" for the spire. "Tracing" is used in the sense of drawing and marking out, as cognate words in Latin and French had been for some two centuries before. By the fourteenth century masons such as Yevele and painters like Gilbert Prynce, who died in 1396, had many servants in their houses and shops. Prynce in his will mentions four servants and two apprentices by name, and refers to other "serving workmen" (*famulos meos operarios*).

Even where a master spent his whole time upon one job, he would not necessarily do much, if any, of the cutting of stone. In the case of a great cathedral, and still more where a monastery required extensive buildings as well as a large church, the amount of time necessary for reflection and active design, sketching and drawing, whether upon paper or parchment, or on boards or a gypsum tracing floor, and marking out shaped stones to be hewn by the craftsmen, could well take up the whole energy of one man, together with the exercise of general supervision of the work in progress. That this specialized function not only deserved but obtained higher pay, we know from the sermons, and from the abundant accounts and other financial records. This aspect of the matter will be dealt with later, but it will be well to consider here the actual processes of mediaeval design.

The earliest surviving drawings which are strictly architectural are those in the album of Villard de Honnecourt, which certainly belongs to the first half of the thirteenth century. Their exquisite quality, precision and finished technique show that the capacity to produce both freehand and scale drawings could have been no new thing at that period. From only a little later, *c.*1250, comes the first considerable collection of designs drawn to scale, those of the Reims palimpsest, which had already been erased and written over at a date between 1263 and 1272. They comprise three elevations of façades, another elevation, a ground-plan, and details of a choir-stall, besides fragments (**11**). Also dating from *c.* 1250 is the earliest of the drawings for Strassburg Minster (called "A") (**10**), possibly drawn by Master Rudolf the Elder, who at a later date, *c.* 1274, may have made the elaboration of the same design known as "A 1".

Such large and elaborate drawings upon sheets of parchment could only have been made upon drawing-boards, or trestle tables of the kind used by the Gothic glaziers for drawing their cartoons. What may well be a reference to such boards occurs in the account for works at the Tower of London in 1274, when Salamon the Joiner (*le Iongnur*) provided two fir "tables" with trestles and other harness (*Gernes'*) for the King's work (or use; *ad opus domini Regis*) and at the same time "forms" for timber for Master Robert of Beverley, the master. Early in the fourteenth century an illumination in Queen Mary's Psalter shows an artist at work upon such a trestle board, and thenceforward references to "tracing", to tracing-houses and to tracing-boards become fairly numerous. In 1332 Master Thomas of Canterbury was working at St. Stephen's Chapel, Westminster, in ways described as "*tractanti super trasuram*" (probably drawing upon the tracing-board or tracing-floor); and "*in trasura super moldas operanti*" (working upon the moulds, either "in

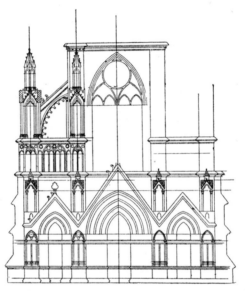

11   Reims: *c.* 1250, elevation for a church,
possibly by Hugues Libergier.

drawing", or "in the tracing-house"). In 1350 repairs were carried out at Windsor Castle on the "*trasour*", which is again mentioned in 1397; at Exeter in 1375 nearly £10 was spent by the Cathedral Fabric upon the building of a new "trasyng hous"; in 1381 Master Henry Yevele was paying rent to St. Paul's Cathedral for his shops and little garden in St. Paul's Churchyard "next the tracing-house of the Dean and Chapter" (*iuxta trasuram*). A "trassour" at Ely Cathedral appears in 1387 when its paving was being laid; in 1400 two tracing boards were part of the equipment of the masons' lodge at York Minster; from 1436 to 1474 references occur in the Norwich Cathedral accounts to a solar above the tracing-house (*supra le Trasour iuxta le Cloccher*); in 1451 and 1456 "traseris" were among the rooms belonging to the office of the King's works in Westminster Palace; and in 1462 a door was made for the "Trasynghous" of Westminster Abbey. When Nicholas Ellis was granted the office of King's Master Mason in 1547, he was to have charge of all the lodges, "traceries", etc. in the Tower of London and other royal castles and buildings.

The alternative to drawing-boards was a "tracing-floor" consisting of a large wooden platform or slab of plaster-of-Paris. Such a slab already existed at Strassburg in 1490, and survived until 1759, when it was accidentally burnt. For full-size setting-out on jobs where there was no permanent organization, a space of ground in the open might be cleared for the purpose. The trusses of Westminster Hall were set out on the ground in 1395 at a place called "the Frame" near Farnham in Surrey, and in 1501 at Louth two labourers were paid for "leffeyng (levelling) the ground for to sett the broch (spire) upon and remewyng stone be 3 dais". A large inscribed plan on the stone floor of the chapter-house at Wells Cathedral is supposed to be the setting-out for the "St. Andrew's Arches" inserted under the crossing *c*.1340, and it is said that a piece of wood found in the roof of the choir of Glasgow Cathedral bore upon it the lines of the crypt vaulting, which dates from the thirteenth century. At Christchurch Priory, Hants, there are architectural drawings upon the wall-plaster.

Foreign references to drawing-boards include that used in 1386 at Dijon by Drouet de Dampartin when drawing the plans for the Charterhouse of Champmol, and the making of a large board by the joiner of the lodge at Strassburg in 1418, on which Master Ulrich von Ensingen might prepare the main drawing for the top of the tower. A century ago Didron published examples of setting-out on

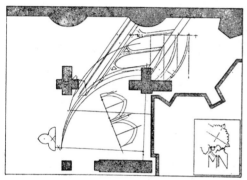 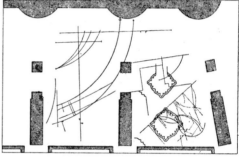

12 Limoges Cathedral: geometrical setting-out on granite slabs of aisle roofs, probably by Master Jean des Champs or his son Pierre, *c*. 1300.

level roof-slabs (**12**). From study of the German drawings and records, Herr Otto Kletzl has been able to reach definite conclusions as to the instruments used in mediaeval drawing. Lead-pencil is found only occasionally, and red chalk not until the late Gothic period. Axes and construction-lines were made with a round-pointed metal stylus, and something of the sort would seem to have been used by the painter or illuminator of St. Augustine's Abbey, Canterbury, who about 1300 designed geometrical panels surrounded by ogee tracery on the flyleaves of what is now Christ's College, Cambridge, MS. Dd.1.1.

Parchment was smoothed with pumice, and bone-meal was rubbed into the surface; the finished drawing was made in ink, the freehand lines with a quill or reed pen, but both straight lines and circular arcs with some form of ruling-pen. No example of such a pen dating from mediaeval times seems to be known, but examination of actual drawings leaves no doubt whatever that such must have been used, as the lines are often extremely thin and perfectly regular. They are, moreover, of varying thickness on the same drawing, so that the pens were provided with some form of regulating screw. For work on wood or stone there were drawing-needles, pieces of strong wire, pointed, and bent to form a hand-grip. A few pairs of compasses and calipers have survived, a fine pair of large wrought-iron compasses, probably of the fifteenth century, being kept in the chapter-house at York Minster. During the work on the Norwich cloisters in 1345 a compass was bought for 1*s*., and in the next year 4*d*. was spent on a small compass, and in

1346 a cord for measuring was purchased for 4*d.* In 1436 the Sacrist's inventory taken at Norwich showed that the glazier's house contained "1 peir of gret compas of iron", while at Westminster Abbey in 1471 and 1483 small cords and "lyne and Whipcord" were bought for the masons. In 1485 at York Minster "metroddes" (measuring rods) were obtained for the carpenters. What is presumably a reference to ruling-pens occurs in the Westminster accounts of 1531, when 8*s.* was paid for "two payre skrewis for tracerye roddis provided for the maister mason to drawe with in his tracery house".

Gothic technical drawings are not provided with a figured scale, and setting-out could for the most part be accomplished proportionally by means of a standard unit, such as the rod, pole or perch, of (in England) 16½ feet, or some similar dimension. At Ely Cathedral a fir-pole of 24 feet was bought *c.* 1387 for the master to measure his work. Herr Kletzl refers to a contract of 1407 for the shrine of St.-Germain at Paris, which was to be made according to a *portraiture et patron*, only one dimension being given. Various national and local units can be traced in different parts of Europe, and also the introduction into one country by foreign craftsmen of another system of measurement. Thus it is said that old English units have been found in those parts of Linköping Cathedral in Sweden which were built under English influence or by English masons. Proportional compasses or dividers seem to be shown on the tomb-slab of Hugues Libergiers at Reims, 1263, and a century later as a badge upon the shield of Master Mathias of Arras beneath his bust in Prague Cathedral. More elaborate instruments may be implied by Abbot Suger's description of the setting-out of the alignment of his new work about 1140, "with geometrical and arithmetical instruments".

Documentary references to smaller units of measurement, such as feet and inches, and to such measurements being carried out by or in the presence of building masters, prove that they must also have used divided measuring rods, cords and scales. Leonardo of Pisa, writing *c.* 1220, states that "Fields and the dimensions of houses are measured with poles and linear feet and inches", and there is no reason to suppose that this did not apply all over Europe. On the other hand, it seems to have been characteristic of northern Gothic that no complete designs for a whole building were made, but only a plan, and elevations and sections of parts, as each came to be built. And the drawings which were made were often reduced to their simplest terms, only one half or one repeat of several being shown in detail, and the rest merely indicated. Similarly, while models of parts were made, the earliest models of complete buildings made to the North of Italy seem to belong to the fifteenth or possibly even the sixteenth century; the claim that a model of the Church of St.-Maclou in Rouen is as early as 1414 is strongly disputed.

In his detailed investigation of the drawings extant before the recent war, Herr Kletzl was able to show that they could all be assigned to one of six different groups, according to their purpose. These groups are: (1) pupils' drawings, for purely educational reasons; (2) designs and sketches; (3) copies made by masters for their use and study; (4) copies made for lodge use; (5) elaborations of pre-existing designs; (6) show drawings, intended for the information of patrons and clients, and therefore pruned of technicalities such as the superimposition of one plan upon another, and more decoratively produced. In England, the only strictly architectural drawings earlier than the fifteenth century seem to be the fragments which occur on leaves of the Pepysian MS. sketchbook at Magdalene College, Cambridge. These include a scale drawing of a window with cusped intersecting tracery, apparently an original design, for more than one radius has been attempted; three large-scale sections of mouldings; and the remains of the setting-out of an ogee-headed window or arch. All, according to Sir Alfred Clapham, can be securely dated to the half-century 1350–1400.

13 METZ CATHEDRAL: interior looking east. Nave arcades, 1239–60, completed
1326–48; choir rebuilt 1503–20.

THE GOTHIC FLAME

14 CLERMONT-FERRAND CATHEDRAL. Design for west front, *c.* 1496: *Le patron et Pourtraict des portaulx Et de ce quil reste a parachever a leglise de Clermont.* (About $\frac{1}{7}$ actual size.)

From about the middle of the fifteenth century comes the great drawing of the projected tower of Henry VI's King's College, Cambridge. This is clearly a show drawing, not intended for practical use, and is in incorrect perspective. But in 1450 in Italy, large-scale working details were being made for Orvieto Cathedral. Of early sixteenth-century date is the north perspective-elevation of the whole of King's College Chapel, as actually built. This, too, is clearly a show drawing, but whether made before or after the building was completed cannot be determined with certainty. A somewhat earlier scale drawing is preserved at Canterbury Cathedral, consisting of the rejected design for the pinnacles of the central tower. This is to a scale of half an inch to one foot, though not so figured, and can, fortunately, be connected with a letter of *c.* 1493 from Prior Sellinge to Cardinal Morton, referring to a visit from John Wastell, the cardinal's master mason, who had drawn out "ij patrons of . . . the pynacles of your new towre here". This further agrees with the accounts for the year running from August 1493, which contain the item of 20*s.* reward given to "a certain master mason sent by the lord Cardinal".

Gifts and bequests of "patrons" and "portraitures", as well as of "moulds" or templates, by master masons and other craftsmen occur with some frequency, and they were certainly regarded as possessions of value until the full flood of the Renaissance in the sixteenth century put an end to their usefulness, when almost all were destroyed. Fortunately, a sufficient number was intentionally or accidentally preserved on the Continent to prove the existence of technical drawings of admirable execution at any rate as far back as the thirteenth century, when their style and assurance suggest a much longer pedigree. Without counting Italian examples, there are, or were recently, important collections at Reims, Strassburg, Cologne, Regensburg, Ulm, and Vienna; an early fifteenth-century design for the west front of Barcelona Cathedral; and one of great splendour for the west front of Clermont-Ferrand Cathedral, to be dated about 1496 (**14**). In 1506 Jean Gilde was paid for a drawing of the cathedral towers at Troyes, and in 1510 Roulland Leroux provided drawings and supervision for the tomb of Georges d'Amboise at Rouen.

Germany again provides the best series of documentary references to architectural drawings. In 1407 a drawing formed the basis of the contract by which Hans Krumenauer undertook to vault a church; in 1416 Michael Savoy, invited by the Abbey of St.-Gall to become master of their works, sent his son to them, bearing a design for a tower; and when Master Simon the stonemason of Vienna died in 1419 he left to his brother-in-law his "art upon paper or parchment" (*mein kunst in dem papir oder pyrmeid*). Article 10 of the Ordinances of 1459 laid down that when a Master had shown the client a design (*Visierung*), he was bound to adhere to it in carrying out the work, and provided that candidates for the Mastership should have two extra years of learning in which to study drawing especially. Master Hans Niesenberger, working on the Convent of Weingarten in 1462, was asked to provide drawings for the Pyx of Ulm Minster, and Ulm decreed in 1470 that all drawings prepared by a master during his term of office should become the property of the Lodge, and in engaging Moritz Ensinger insisted that "at his retirement he shall hand over . . . not only all the designs which his father Master Matheus Säliger made for the Minster and Tower, but also those he made at Berne and here, and those also which Master Moritz himself has made or shall make in future". At Berne in 1483 Erhard Küng was bound to provide a substitute master at his own costs if he should be sick, and to give up to his employers the drawings and patterns (*die visierung und muster*). In 1486, when Salzburg decided to build their chief parish church, the town sent as far as Nuremberg for designs, and in 1503 the Council of Frankfort ordered Master Niclas Queck to return one of the great drawings of the tower of their cathedral which he had taken with him from the Lodge when he resigned in 1497 to become master at Mainz. In 1506 Konrad von Tübingen appeared before the supreme Tribunal of the Lodge of Strassburg on the charge of having stolen drawings which were the family property of the Böblinger family, while in the following year Hans Schweiner of Weinsberg was being paid an annual fee of 6 gulden for drawings and supervision (*Riss und Aufsehen*) at St. Kilian in Heilbronn.

Though the English references are seldom quite so explicit, it is at least clear that master masons preserved their designs and working details, though how far these consisted of drawings, and how far of moulds and templates, is uncertain. In 1417 Stephen Lote, the King's Master Mason, left to his friend Thomas Mapilton all his "patterns" (*patronos*), and in 1459 John Clerke bequeathed all his "toles patterns and pertenances" to his erstwhile apprentice Henry Janyns. In 1525 St. John's College, Cambridge, paid the master mason of Ely for "drawing a drawght" for Bishop Fisher's tomb. Henry Smyth, mason at the Savoy Hospital, left in 1517 a legacy of "all my Bokis of purtiturys", which suggests a series of albums comparable to that of Honnecourt, or to a late Gothic pattern-book preserved in the Vienna National Library, and the "book which Master Hans bequeathed" to the lodge of St. Theobald in Thann about 1470. By the end of the period, in 1546, John Molton, master mason to Henry VIII, could leave to his apprentice and two of his former assistants "all my portratures, plaates, books, with all other my tools and instruments".

Regarding the form taken by the English drawings, we have the evidence of the fragments incorporated in the Pepysian sketchbook that some were on parchment in the later fourteenth century, and this is borne out by the sheet of parchment to show the form of the new cloisters at Exeter, bought in 1378. Parchment was bought for making moulds at Norwich in 1335–37, in addition to wooden boards. Patterns were sent abroad or to distant quarries, to enable stones to be worked to shape before transport. These were known as "false moulds" and are mentioned in the accounts for Westminster Palace of 1324, when three yards of canvas were bought to make false moulds to be sent to Caen in Normandy for stones to be shaped there. Patterns were sent from Norwich to Corfe in 1345, and in 1424 the Westminster Abbey accounts refer to the mason Robert Westerley going to the quarry with "Faussemoldis". A later account of 1480 mentions elm planks for making "falsmolds" at the quarry, and throughout the Middle Ages occur mentions of boards, especially "Estrichbords" from the Baltic, to be used for moulds by the masons. Hugh Herland the great carpenter, was granted by Edward III a little house in the Palace of Westminster for keeping his tools (*instrumenta*) and for making his models (*formis, formulas*) and moulds (*moldis*).

Other materials mentioned in connexion with the making of "moulds" by the master masons are glue, sprig nails, "Chalkelyne" or "Tracyng lyne", and in 1323 at Ely iron cramps (*crombis ferreis*), though these may have been drawing-needles. It seems likely that the word "moulds" at least sometimes included what we should term models, rather than mere templates. Even in the later Gothic period, some drawings were made upon wood, as was the case at the building of Roslin Chapel in 1446, when the Earl of Orkney "causd the draughts to be drawn upon Eastland boords and made the carpenters to carve them, according to the draughts thereon, and then gave them for patterns to the masons". It may have been similar wooden templates (*formas*) that were delivered to the stone-hewers in 1175 by William of Sens at Canterbury. Two lead templates, probably fourteenth-century, with holes for hanging up, were found at March. Setting-out also continued to be done on stone slabs, one such containing tracery of *c.* 1475, having been found when the old chapel of St. John's College, Cambridge, was demolished. A fine Geometric window is set out on a crossing-pier of Leighton Buzzard Church (**15**). It may even be that the slab from the side of a high tomb at Callan in Ireland described and illustrated by Mr. Conor O'Brien, and containing three technical drawings in relief, served its turn as a set of working drawings before it was ingeniously turned to account by the mason in his monumental practice. In the Archaeological Museum at Dijon is part of the tomb-slab of Abbot Hugue d'Arc of St.-Bénigne (1269–1300), carved with elevations of the abbey church built during his abbacy; the whole design was preserved by Gaignières.

But even apart from the existing drawings on parchment which take us back to 1250 or earlier, there is abundant evidence of the growing practice of making separate drawings, side by side with the more primitive method of drawing direct

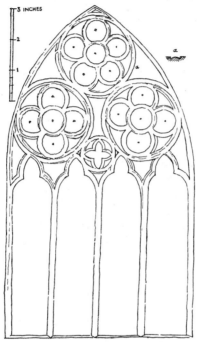

15   Leighton Buzzard Church:
design for a Geometric window,
cut on the south-east pier of the
crossing.
From a drawing by Mr. G. H. Cook.

upon the stone, or upon the boards destined to be cut into templates. The references already given to "portraitures" certainly relate to such technical diagrams, and we find that Capgrave in his *Life of St. Katherine* of *c.* 1440, mentions "Euclidis bokys wyth his portraturys." As early as 1337 the painters at Ely Cathedral were supplied with canvas and parchment for "moulds" which in this instance must have been cartoons, and in 1352 at Westminster the sum of 1*s.* 8*d.* was paid for two quires of royal paper for the painters' "patrons". Just two centuries later "Paper Riall for platts" was bought for the use of John Lubbyns, master mason at Hampton Court; the "Royal" size, about 19 or 20 inches by 24 or 25, was no doubt the largest size commonly obtainable during the Middle Ages. Paper itself was one of the inventions or re-inventions typical of the Gothic age, and which comprised the compass, the rudder, the blast-furnace, gunpowder, and clocks showing hours and divided into minutes and seconds, all of which were known by the early fourteenth century, by which time paper was in common use.

Whether on paper or parchment, easily portable drawings were common in England by the fifteenth century, and probably earlier. About 1421, Henry V's master mason at Calais wrote to his sovereign with an account of the work done on the chapel in Calais Castle, sending with the letter a "patrone" to show the extent of what had been done. In 1448 a drawing (*portratura*) of the proposed chapel of Eton College was submitted to Henry VI, and in 1496, John Brian, one of Henry VII's carpenters, petitioned for £9 in respect of alterations which had resulted in waste of worked timber, after "Your Grace had a sight bi picture of the ruffe of your hall of Wodestoke". In his will Henry VII refers to "a plat signed by our hande" showing the design of his chapel at Westminster, and in 1512 John Wastell and Henry Semerk, masons, undertook to vault King's College Chapel, Cambridge, "accordyng to a platt thereof made and signed with the handes" of Henry VII's executors. At Eton College in 1510, Humphrey Coke, master carpenter, drew out plans for the cloister there (*pro figuratione edificii le platt*), and six years later he and two master masons, William Vertue and Henry Redman, were rewarded for their work "on a paper book containing the form of the new building for the College court thought out by them, (namely) the plan" (*formam novi edificii ad quadrum Collegii per predictos excogitatum le platte*). The reference to the brainwork of design is noteworthy. William Horman, Fellow of Eton College, and Bursar at the time of these works, included a long chapter on building in his English-Latin phrase-book *Vulgaria*, published in 1519. One of the sentences is: "He is nat worthy to be called maister of the crafte, that is nat cunnyng in drawynge and purturynge." (*Non est architecti nomine dignus qui graphidis peritus non est.*) By no means all the drawings were made for important royal works: in 1503 a "wellome skyn for to draw the broch in" was bought for the spire of Louth Church, Lincs., and in 1520 paper was bought to draw the draft of the rood-loft in Banwell Church, Somerset. A contract of 1515, and the drawing referred to in it, survived at Notre-Dame-de-l'Épine.

Thus far we have considered the facts of design in mediaeval art, and the practical methods of designing. What was it that lay behind these surface facts, and provided a motive force; what were the aims of Gothic design? The records, laws, contracts, guild ordinances and the rest will only speak to us of certain aspects of the problem. We learn from them that the Gothic age was preoccupied with a high standard of structure and technical execution, and furthermore with the welfare, spiritual as well as physical and economic, of the artists, craftsmen and labourers. In this the story of the documents is amply corroborated by the works of art themselves. Beyond this, it is plain that function counted for a great deal; churches were planned with a view to the service of God which was to be carried on within; castles were to provide defence, houses shelter, bridges to maintain communication. Yet when we look at Gothic art, it is obvious that its roots go deeper even than the ideal of perfect functionalism and fitness of structure.

An infinitude of detailed researches, and works of patient and loving synthesis such as the studies of M. Emile Mâle, have disentangled the intricacies of mediaeval iconography. The elaborate decorative schemes, the Poor Man's Bible, the sets of symbolic figures, were no haphazard imaginings of the men who portrayed them, but exemplified a theology and a philosophy which from tentative beginnings were brought together to form one vast integrated system. But this was interpenetrated by another system, half-forgotten but of exceeding vitality, the older pagan world of legend, tradition, and popular festivals and observances, which still lived in the hearts and memories of the European peoples, and especially among those of the North. Mediaeval chivalry, knightly custom, hopeless passion and the Courts of Love, the Cycles of the great Romances and the code of

16   MALMÖ: Church of St. Peter, from the south-east, *c.* 1320–80.

NORTHERN GOTHIC

17 BATALHA: Friary church from the north-west, 1387–1415, by *Affonso Domingues*. The Founder's Chapel (on the right), 1415–34, by *Huguet*.

SOUTHERN GOTHIC

behaviour which glows through the pages of Malory and was parodied with wistful affection by Cervantes, were the outcome of this interpenetration of the best of Paganism and the best of Christianity. All these were the essence of the Gothic cultural pattern, but its visible, tangible features were the works of Gothic art.

The driving force of this system was a real belief and faith in God as a personal Creator of the universe and of man, who reflected, however dimly, the image and attributes of the Almighty. A century and a half before the great age of Aquinas and the schoolmen, Honorius of Autun, writing shortly before 1130, had reduced the parts of the church built with hands to a symbolic system imparting higher truths. "The transparent windows, which keep out the weather and bring in the light, are the doctors who withstand the hurricane of heresy and pour in the light of Church doctrine. The window glass, through which the ray of light is thrown, is the mind of the doctors, viewing heavenly things as in a glass darkly." The art-motive of the Creator as the Architect of the Universe, which has already been mentioned, goes back to the end of the Romanesque period, but has a continuous history only from the beginning of the thirteenth century. Closely connected with this idea was that of geometry as the fundamental harmonizer of the universe and of human life. The fourteenth-century English masons or their chaplain who formulated the traditions of the craft insisted that "Geometry is the science that all reasonable men live by" and that "among all the crafts of the world . . . masonry hath the most notability and most part of this science of Geometry". At the same time Heinrich von Mügeln, court poet of Charles IV at Prague, was writing that "the art of Geometry teaches us proportion", and Chaucer in the *Knight's Tale* makes Theseus bring together for the design and building of his theatre every "crafty man That geometrie or ars-metrik can".

The master builders may then be expected to have had a preoccupation with geometry, and this is confirmed by the ingenuity of their designs for tracery, the optical refinements* (such as the modification of vaulting ribs already described) which they introduced, and the capacity of foreseeing spatial effects evidenced by their work. It was very largely from them that the other artists derived their inspiration and their technical equipment. The early master masons, in so far as they worked with their hands, were carvers and sculptors, and like Villard de Honnecourt, freehand draughtsmen. It is now generally admitted that painted images on the flat derived from painted sculptures in the round, and that the minor arts took their cue throughout the Middle Ages from architecture and from illumination, itself largely inspired by architecture. Glaziers took their iconography and much of their method from illuminators and painters, and quite recently Miss C. K. Jenkins has shown reasons for thinking that the early monumental brasses were made by masons accustomed to drawing cartoons for the production of effigies in the round, and possibly in some cases direct from such cartoons. The English evidence that some masons, notably Henry Yevele in the late fourteenth, and William Hyndeley at York in the late fifteenth century, were concerned with latten work and with engraving on plate, certainly favours this view.

On the subject of portraiture, too, the older view is giving way to the admission that actual likenesses were attempted from early Gothic times. Here again we have the evidence of Honnecourt, who noted that his drawing of a lion was done from the life, and later in the thirteenth century the effigies, carved heads, and again the brasses in many cases are clearly intended to show individuality. From the very beginning of the century I have already quoted the narrative of Cœur-de-Lion's crusade which speaks of a painter's assiduous imitation of the lineaments of beauty, and the beginning of this search for exactness in imagery may safely be placed back in the twelfth century, as an original

* I cannot accept the reality of most of the early Gothic "refinements" advanced by Goodyear, and approved by Frothingham; they have been shown to be due to structural distortion under stress.

37

component and symptom of the Gothic spirit. In the fourteenth century there is record of the sending of a painter to make portraits of three princesses at the Courts of Bavaria, Austria and Lorraine, from which Charles VI of France was to choose his queen; in 1444 a portrait of Henry VI was painted to hang in the Guildhall of Reading, Berkshire; and in 1548 the effects of John Hylmer, a London Freemason, included "pictures of a lord and a lady and many other portraits of men and women", which we may suppose were connected with the making of effigies or brasses.

The Gothic artist was, therefore, first and foremost imitating his Creator to the best of his power and ability; and he was secondly striving to imitate Nature. The first aim taught him deliberately to seek harmony and just proportion, while the second implied an inevitable consonance and fitness in his results. As we shall see in considering the designers themselves, these aims did not lead to any suppression of individuality: the never-ending variety of Gothic churches, tracery, ornament, illuminations, and of every other product of human art, not merely equals, but excels that of other periods. The fact that the Gothic artist attained his ends within the limits of an integrated system, and without seeking to cultivate an egocentric "originality", heightens rather than lessens the credit due, as it must the respect in which we hold him. The exquisite balance between imitation of nature and adherence to conventions, that equilibrium where, as Goethe saw, Law alone can give us Liberty, is the true glory of Gothic design.

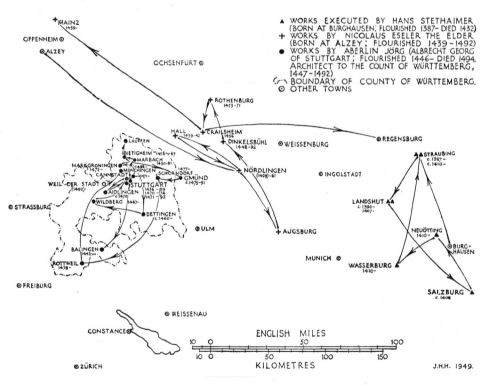

18 Map showing works and journeys by three South German Masters in the fifteenth century.

III

Gothic Designers

FOR some two or three generations controversy has raged over the problem of Gothic "architects" and artists of other kinds. Extreme views are on the one hand that mediaeval culture both artistically and as a whole was anonymous, the product of a group and not of individuals; and on the other that there was no essential difference between the Gothic and later periods, but that "professional" architects and artists existed as members of the literate intelligentsia of the age, namely the clergy. Examined in the light of the ascertainable facts, neither of these views will hold water.

Much of the discussion has been vitiated by lack of adequate definition of terms, and this applies not merely to the modern controversialists, but to the records of the Gothic age themselves, whose usage of words is often ambiguous. Words and phrases divorced from their contexts and preconceived theories have been bandied about as substitutes for impartial research; worse still, professional pride and social snobbery have become involved in the question. It has been common for present-day architects to uphold the view of the importance of their mediaeval predecessors, and for critics of Renaissance and modern architecture to claim that the beauty of Gothic art was due to its production by working men, without the pernicious interposition of an unwanted supernumerary, the "professional man".

It is true that Hugh of St.-Victor, writing about 1130 at the opening of the Gothic period, stated that the mechanic arts, including *architectura* were suitable only for plebeians and sons of the low-born (*plebei et ignobilium filii*), but this sneer is countered by the mediaeval masons' own view (in the early Constitutions) that their craft originated with "grete lordis children". A good deal of the arguments advanced on both sides would be merely ludicrous were it not for the profoundly important issues at stake. The discussion has also become involved with cross-currents emanating from the controversy between the "Catholic" and "Protestant" schools of historians. On the whole, the last twenty years or so have seen a diminution in the fierceness of the dispute, partly owing to a waning interest in the social approach to art which interested Ruskin, Morris and the late Eric Gill, partly to the happy tendency for the swinging pendulum to come to rest at a point of equilibrium. But it remains true that the historic facts concerning Gothic art are less well appreciated in England than they are in most of the continental countries.

It takes a long time for the effect of *ex cathedra* pronouncements to disappear; such was the considered statement by the late Professor Prior that "behind the Renaissance in the history of mediaeval art personality vanishes entirely. We know that individual hands must have carved each figure of Wells front, a certain mind set out the tracery of each Exeter window, but no distinction lies in the personality, just as no record remains of the name of the artist. . . . The conclusion is that the power of designing art in mediaeval times was common property, not merely very usual, but what could be demanded of any workman, and was existent in the masses of the people . . . Artists . . . were just folk generally, and the credit of their art must not be attributed to extraordinary personalities, but to the life history of the race."

The fact that mediaeval masters made their designs and working-drawings piecemeal, as they were required, and commonly built up their great works from many vertical sections or bays horizontally juxtaposed, has given rise to the misleading idea that Gothic drawings were generally made in respect only of minor works or alterations, and that even then they were show- not working-drawings. Examination of the evidence from Germany and France provides a complete refutation of this view.

We have seen that Horman in 1519 equated *architectus* with "maister of the crafte" (i.e. building, *res aedificatoria*), and Sir Thomas Eliot's *Dictionary* of 1538 defined *architector* or *architectus* as "maister of the warkes, deviser of buildyng". A letter of Bishop Fox remarks that "the maistre carpenter (Humphrey Coke) . . . shall advantage you large monee in the buildynge (of werkes of your owne), as well in the devisinge as in the wirkenge of yt". It is plain that to Eliot, a man of the budding Renaissance who must have been well aware of the significance of *architectus* in its Vitruvian sense, "deviser" of building meant designer (as opposed to builder), and this agrees with the various occurrences of *devyse*, *deviser*, and *devisour* which we have already met as far back as the fourteenth century, and with Lydgate's description of King Priam sending for workmen to rebuild Troy, "And for everyche that was good devysour, Mason, hewer, or crafty quareour."

To return to the proposition that the Middle Ages did not think it worth while to record artists' names, the evidence of the records at least casts considerable doubt upon its validity. Neglecting the survival of names in legal records, contracts, accounts and the like, we are left with literary references, inscriptions, signatures, and at least certain types of memorial, which indicate more than the family piety of relations. In the eleventh century, the Chronicle of St. Maxentius of Poitiers records the building of the monastery at the behest of Emma, Queen of Canute, by the hands of one Walter Coorland; later in the century the extensive early Norman work at Canterbury Cathedral is recorded as being carried out by Blitherus, "*praestantissimus artificum magister, templique spectabilis dictator*". The St. Albans Chronicle of the Abbots refers to Robert the mason of the great abbey church at the end of the century, "who excelled all the masons of his time". (*qui prae omnibus caementariis suo tempore pollebat.*) At the opening of the twelfth century the Chronicle of Croyland Abbey relates the rebuilding work done by Arnold "a most learned master of the masons's craft". (*caementariae artis scientissimus magister.*)

Turning to France, Ordericus Vitalis, in the second quarter of the century, records that the Castle of Ivry was built by Lanfred, *architectus*, the praise of whose talents outdid all the craftsmen who were then in Gaul (*cuius ingenii laus super omnes artifices qui tum in Gallia erant transcenderet*). Some doubt exists as to whether Geoffrey de Noiers, mentioned as the builder of the new Lincoln Cathedral in the *Great Life of St. Hugh* (*nobilis fabricae constructor*) was really the designer, or simply an administrative chief, but there is no uncertainty regarding the contemporary master at Durham, Richard of Wolveston, who was described as "a most accomplished man at his work and a clever architect . . . best known by name and craft to all the dwellers of the region". (*vir artificiosus fuisset opere et prudens architectus . . . cunctis regionis hujus incolis arte et nomine notissimus.*) We have already seen the spirited account given of the fortification of the castle of Ardres by Master Simon, about 1200, and shall find that there is compensation for the literary silence of the thirteenth century in records of other types.

Moving on to the fourteenth century, the St. Albans chronicler refers to work done in the first quarter of the century under the master carpenter Geoffrey "an accomplished man by whose industry the work attained the desired effect" (*virum artificiosum . . . per cujus industriam dictum opus effectum sumeret adoptatum*), and by Master Henry Wy, to whom the rebuilding of the fallen bays of the south nave arcade was entrusted in 1323. At Evesham Abbey, record was preserved of the

19 STOCKHOLM: The Great Church, *c.* 1470.

NORTHERN SPACE

20 BOURGES: Hôtel Jacques
Cœur, 1443–51.

21 (*above right*) BOURGES CATHE-
DRAL: kneeling statue of Duc Jean
de Berry, *c.* 1390, by *Jean de
Rupy* of Cambrai.

22 PRAGUE CATHEDRAL: Bust of
Peter Parler, *c.* 1375.

GOTHIC REALISM

rebuilding of the chapter house, dormitory, refectory and abbot's hall by Master Henry the mason (*Latomus*), who died in 1319. As we have seen, Raymond du Temple was later in the century referred to by Christine de Pisan, and Froissart in 1390 devoted a paragraph to the importance of the painter André Beauneveu.

Inscriptions and artists' signatures occur in considerable numbers: on the plinth of the South Portal of Notre-Dame de Paris the beginning of the work in 1258 is recorded, with the name of the master, Jean de Chelles, mason: "*Kallensi lathomo vivente Johanne magistro.*" At Elne the work of Master Bartholomew with his two sons from Perpignan in 1294 is commemorated. At both Amiens and Reims Cathedrals were prominent labyrinths in the paving, with effigies of the master masons who had charge of the works, and commemorative inscriptions; that at Amiens, which included an effigy of Bishop Evrard, the founder, was laid in 1288. At Mont-St.-Michel are named busts of the architects (thirteenth century) with the Archbishop, and similarly at Prague Cathedral in the fourteenth century busts of Master Mathias of Arras and Master Peter Parler appear in the triforium in series with Emperors, royalty, Archbishops and the clerics who administered the works (**22**). In just the same way the glass of the east window of Winchester College Chapel, of 1393, contained named portraits of King and Founder, Clerk of Works, Mason and Carpenter.

To these may be added the account of the building of the new Church of St. Stephen Walbrook in London in 1429–39, copied into the church Inventory a generation later, which gives the names of all those who laid foundation stones, among them being "Maistir Thomas Mapilton the kyngis mason than beyng Maistir mason of the seyd Chirche werke". If diligent search were made of the mediaeval literature and chronicles of Europe, it cannot be doubted that further references would be found.

But another aspect of the problem must be taken into account in estimating the relative amount of interest in the artist's personality in Gothic and post-Gothic times. At all periods the understanding of technical procedure by persons without technical training has been very small. Since printing encouraged men of all types to venture into print, a great deal has been published by writers with a background of technical knowledge; in the Gothic age this was not and could not be so. The typical writers of the Middle Ages were monks or secular clergy, with interests running along well-defined and possibly rather narrow lines. One would search in vain for evidence of a keen preoccupation with art among more recent men of comparable position. In general, literature and history are written by those who have no acquaintance with the plastic arts except that of the dilettante and the amateur. It is not merely that no need *was* recognized in the "anonymous" Middle Ages for recording the name of him who conceived a church building; no such need is generally recognized to-day.

We have seen, in dealing with the production and design of Gothic art, what was actually done, and how the masters arranged that it should be done. The remaining problem is to discover what sort of people these masters of building and of art were, what their family, education, social position, and technical and economic status. That they were not members of a distinct professional class, divorced by birth and education from craftsmen generally, is already certain; but it is all the same fair to conclude that most of them did form a kind of superior caste of craftsmen, springing from families already distinguished in their art, and probably of relative wealth.

Mediaeval society was sharply divided into the two great sections of the free and the unfree: the latter greatly predominating in numbers until the progress of individual and group enfranchisement had thinned their ranks. The unfree were not bond-slaves, though some such also existed, but were in theory bound to the community of which they were members, and unable to claim the protection of the national laws. The state of modified serfdom, which disappeared from England by 1600, lasted much longer in most European countries. It is this background of freeman and villein which distinguishes the typical skilled craftsman of the Gothic age from the mere labourer. In theory at least, only a free man could enter the craft guilds or such organizations as those of the Lodge Masons. The fourteenth century English Articles of Masonry insist that "no master for no profyte take no prentis . . . that is bore of bonde blode", for practical reasons, and also because according to the legendary history the craft had taken its rise "of grete lordis children frely begetyn". Theory is confirmed by actual record. While there is a number of instances of bond craftsmen, who were the property of their lords and could be bought and sold, there is nothing to suggest that these men were in any sense upon a level with masters who were responsible for planning, design and supervision. On the contrary, from the twelfth century onwards, the masters appear as grantors and grantees of free tenements, as witnesses to charters (who were by implication freemen), and freemen's sureties, who had themselves to be free. They were also sent on missions of trust, as William Orchard was on behalf of Oxford University in 1482, or Humphrey Coke, sent by Bishop Fox to Oxford in 1517 with the foundation deed of Corpus Christi College, and other documents and money.

Not only did the masters belong to the significant minority of freemen, but within that division of society they were often men of consequence. At a time when only a very small number of people made wills, for they had so little to leave, masons, carpenters and other artists formed a fair proportion of the total of testators, and bequeathed articles of value as well as extensive landed property. In 1229, after the death of Master Adam Lock, mason of Wells Cathedral, the sub-dean and one of the canons acted as his executors, and other canons including the famous Elias of Derham were witnesses to subsequent grants of his property. Richard of Wolveston, the famous twelfth-century master at Durham, had also been a landowner, and so were important masters at Lichfield, Lincoln, York, and elsewhere. Similar records abound on the Continent, and leave no doubt that master craftsmen who had charge of cathedrals or royal works, and other artists of comparable standing, were more often than not men of relative wealth. Kletzl states that the instruments of a leading master might be of silver, and were bequeathed as treasures to the lodges.

The same conclusion can be reached, with greater precision, from a study of the fees and perquisites obtained by the masters as compared with the standard of wages received by the rank-and-file of the crafts. Fully to appreciate what the monetary values mean, some attempt has to be made to translate them into present-day purchasing-power. This must necessarily be an approximation, but the late Dr. Coulton showed good reason for using the multiplier of 40 to bring mediaeval money to the values understood shortly before the war of 1939–45. During the years of war and post-war inflation, money-values in England have again fallen so that sums have to be multiplied further by about two-and-a-half; that is to say, we must apply the multiplier of 100 to money-values of the Gothic age to give a very rough notion of their real worth. Dr. Coulton's figures were mainly based on a study of prices in England during the fifty years preceding the Black Death; for the century-and-a-half after the Black Death a closer multiplier would be 80; and for the first half of the sixteenth century, with a rapid drop in purchasing power, about 55. Readers are referred to the notes for details of the actual sums concerned; the figures given here have been subjected to multiplication by the appropriate ratio, and those for France are based on the careful estimates given by Mr. Martin S. Briggs in *The Architect in History* (1925 values), multiplied by two only, to allow for the considerable drop in prices between 1925 and Dr. Coulton's estimates of 1934.

To set against the income of the masters, we must first arrive at an approximation to the yearly earnings of a skilled craftsman. Unlike the chief masters, who received overall fees, and were commonly paid for every day in the year, Sundays and feasts included, the craftsmen were paid only for working days, and it is safe to assume that even with full employment no mason, carpenter or other artisan would obtain in the year more than 300 daily wages. He might in addition be able to make some profit or at least subsistence out of farming, mainly conducted by his family, but by-occupations and other opportunities for making extra money apply with equal or greater force to the masters, and are therefore disregarded. The predominant rates found for masons (and applying to most other skilled craftsmen) by the late Professor Knoop and Dr. G. P. Jones, can be broadly stated as $4\frac{1}{2}d.$ per day up to 1350; 6d. per day from 1350 to 1500; and 7d. per day from 1500 to 1550. At these rates, the equivalent yearly income to keep in mind amounts to £562 before 1350, £600 thence to 1500, and £480 to the close of the Gothic age proper.

Taking the English instances in some detail, and dealing first with chief masters of the Royal Works, we find that Ailnoth, Henry II's engineer, received £1,065 yearly, and Maurice, a specialist in castle-building, £1,825 and clothing. Under Henry III, Ralph Burnell and several other carpenters had £744 each when fully employed, and at the beginning of Edward I's reign Master Robert of Beverley, the chief mason, took £913 and a clothing allowance of £75; in 1275 when he was promoted to be surveyor of the King's Works, these terms were doubled, yielding £1,975. The great military engineer, James of St. George, was given £5,475 yearly, and his colleague Richard "Lenginour" of Chester, £1,825 besides opportunities to profit from the farm of mills and fisheries. Successive chief craftsmen were usually paid at this rate of £1,825, and normally with a clothing allowance of £100 in addition.

After 1350, and comparing with the skilled craftsman's basic income of £600, Master John Tichmarsh, concurrently mason of Chester and murager of the city, received £1,216; William Wynford, when in full employment at Windsor Castle, and inclusive of a clothing allowance of £80, took £2,340; Hugh Herland at the end of his official career as master carpenter of the royal works, £3,533. The basic rate for chief masters through the fifteenth century was normally £1,540, including clothing allowance, and a subordinate master such as Henry Janyns at St. George's Chapel in Windsor Castle in 1481, received £1,266. In the sixteenth century, owing to the drop in the value of money, while the rates of fees remained much the same, chief masters obtained only £1,004 and £55 clothing allowance, comparing with the £480 of the skilled craftsmen, while subordinate masters such as the chief carpenter at Chester or Berwick might get one-half or two-thirds as much (£502 or £670). In all these cases, it must be stressed that the chief masters, and such subordinate masters as those in charge of provincial offices of works, were able to take on private commissions in addition to their official pay.

Some commissions were paid for by means of allowances in kind, such as the corrody granted by Winchcombe Abbey to Master Walter of Hereford in 1278, whereby he was to have his food and clothing, candles and firewood, and allowance for two servants and two horses. But in other cases it is possible to attach a monetary value. For instance, Master William Hurley of London, called in by Ely Cathedral to advise as to the roofing of the great octagon in 1334, charged a fee equivalent to £800 a year, which caused the Sacrist to run into debt. William Joy, as master mason at Wells Cathedral, had a retaining fee of £200 yearly, and weekly pay when actually at work equivalent to £750 in a full year of 300 days. In the second half of the fourteenth century, John Lewyn who was also a great mason-contractor, drew £1,120 a year for his fees and clothing as mason to the Bishop of Durham; William Wintringham, chief carpenter of the Duchy of Lancaster under John of Gaunt, had £1,600 as well as clothing. In the fifteenth century William Colchester had at first fees of £460, and later of £860, as consultant to Westminster Abbey, while Master Richard Winchcombe when employed on the Oxford Divinity School was given retaining fees and clothing worth £214, free lodging and hay for his horse when engaged on the works, and weekly pay amounting to £800 in a full year. The master mason of Spalding Priory in 1439 refused 12 marks (£640) a year, insisting upon a pension for life.

In the early sixteenth century retaining fees varied from as little as £18 up to the £1,004 enjoyed by Henry Redman as master mason of Wolsey's works, concurrently with £502 as master mason at Windsor Castle, another £502 as jointholder with William Vertue of the office of King's Master Mason, and clothing worth about another £50. Redman's total income at this period, inclusive of a further £311 as chief mason to Westminster Abbey, amounted to £2,365, or approximately five times that of a skilled mason: under Redman at Westminster Abbey the fortunate men who were kept in full employment received £504 including clothing. This disproportion between the rate for the artisan and that for the master of architectural status remains just as striking, however approximate our translation into modern values. Nor is there any marked change in the ratio as we proceed from the twelfth to the sixteenth century. Specialists such as Master Maurice at Newcastle and Dover Castles under Henry II, or Richard Lenginour under Edward I, could earn more than three times as much as the fully skilled craftsman, and exceptional men like Redman and James of St. George received from five times to nearly ten times as much. Intermediate in time is the case of Henry Yevele, which it is possible to follow in considerable detail.

Yevele, who had taken up the freedom of the City of London in 1353, was able in 1358 to take a contract of 221l. (£17,680) worth of building work for the Black Prince, all of it paid by the end of eighteen months. This in present values equals £11,800 per year; if the clear profit amounted to 5 per cent, the income from this work alone was £590, or about the total wages of a skilled mason. But this was clearly not the whole of Yevele's income, for in 1359 he was also engaged in transporting victuals to Calais under licence, and probably had other mason's work in hand too. In 1360 he was appointed King's Master Mason, an office worth £1,540 a year; in 1365 he added a further £800 as a Warden of London Bridge; about 1372 he became master mason to Westminster Abbey at £460 yearly; for over twenty years his annual income from these regular sources amounted to £2,800. Beyond this he undertook large contracts for St. Paul's Cathedral, the London Charterhouse, and John of Gaunt, carried out private architectural work for John, Lord Cobham, and probably acted as architectural adviser to William of Wykeham from 1380 or earlier. Towards the end of his life he was concerned with the works of Canterbury Cathedral and St. Albans Abbey, and in partnership with Stephen Lote produced important tombs. For that of the King and Queen in Westminster Abbey, the two masons were paid £20,000 in a period of five years, or £2,000 each per year, of which 5 per cent represents another £100 a year. In 1387–88 Yevele was paid £5,866 for contract work at St. Paul's Cathedral, implying an income from this source of £293, which certainly continued for several years, as the total amount of the contracts was £24,528. For the shops in which he carried on business as a monumental mason in St. Paul's Churchyard he was able to pay a rent of £400 a year, but from one only of the many properties he owned in London and Southwark he received a rent of £267. During the last twenty years of his life his income cannot have been less than £3,000, or more than four times as much as the £720 earned by each of the skilled masons who found full-time employment under him on the works of Westminster Abbey. The proportion of four to one also occurs in Scotland, where the master mason of Roslin Chapel, begun in 1446, was paid 40l. Scots yearly, the ordinary masons 10l. each.

The figures quoted by Mr. Briggs for France, and adjusted to present values, tell a similar story, though fees and wages seem to have varied more widely in France than in England, and were at a particularly low level in the fifteenth century, the skilled worker's rate (on the basis of 300 working days) amounting only to about £300 a year, as against double that sum in England. But in France, as in England, the artist could command up to three or four times as much as the artisan. In the thirteenth century Eudes de Montreuil, the King's chief mason, drew pay and allowances equal to £2,100; in 1388 at Rouen a mason of architect's standing received £1,300, while at the Collegiate Church of St.-Quentin in the fifteenth century the resident master took £444 and a daily loaf of bread. In the sixteenth century the principal architects at the French Court were being paid sums equivalent to £1,400 and upwards to £2,800. During the English occupation in 1424, Maître Jacques Le Vaillant, master of the works of the King (Henry VI) and Regent (John, Duke of Bedford) was paid 120 *livres tournois* for the year in fees, and Jehan Smyth the Regent's carpenter had half as much. At that time the *livre tournois* was worth approximately 2s. 6d. sterling, making these salaries worth 15*l.* and 7*l.* 10*s.* respectively in contemporary English money, or £1,200 and £600 now.

I have dwelt at some length upon this question of differential pay, even at the risk of becoming tedious, for nothing else reveals so plainly, and with so little scope for the intrusion of personal opinion, how false is the notion of the master as a sort of builder's foreman, a craftsman like his fellows, just one of the lads, and the rest of it. Such evidence of the outstanding importance of the chief masters would be convincing at any period, but more especially since it comes from the Middle Ages, devoted as they were to the ideal of the just price and the "rate for the job". With the exception of the fifteenth century, a period of depression in England and also abroad, the disparity between the incomes of masters and of men remains fairly constant throughout the Gothic age, which again supports the literary and other evidence as to the high status of the early Gothic masters in the twelfth and thirteenth centuries.

For the late fourteenth century we get a brilliant picture of the different ranks of craftsmen in the portraits painted by Chaucer of three carpenters in the *Canterbury Tales*: he of the *Prologue*, member of the London Livery Company, "shaply for to been an alderman"; the well-to-do carpenter of Oseney Abbey, in the *Miller's Tale*, who "Knew nat Catoun, for his wit was rude", and took in a lodger to his sorrow; and the Reeve, typical of the village wright who could make ploughs and put up frame houses, but by the nature of his office, of villein status. Exactly contemporary is evidence from the archives: the Hall-Book of New College, Oxford, shows that on the 25th of March, 1389, Master Henry Yevele, Wynford and Herland, the great masons and carpenter, sat at the high table; an assistant of Yevele sat with the fellows; and a servant of each of the three masters with the household. Again in February 1391, Wynford and Herland sat at the high table, and their servants below; and in September of the same year Wynford again at the high table, with one assistant, and his servant among the College servants. In March of this same 1391, a Court was being held in Oxford under the Statutes of Labourers, and dismissed the case against John Sampson, accused of taking excessive wages, on the ground that "he is a master mason of freestones and highly capable and cunning in that art and in carving and that the pay of such masons cannot be rated with the pay of other masons of another degree and station, on account of the depth of discretion and knowledge in that art". (*non potest assederi cum capcione aliorum lathomorum alterius gradus et status pro altitudine discrecionis et sapiencie artis illius.*)

The social status of artists and craftsmen was nicely graduated, especially in the Royal Household, through a table of precedence which ranged everyone beneath the nobility in one of the six degrees, knight, esquire, yeoman, groom, page and child. Among the yeomen were those of the King's "serjeants of craft" (*Valletz de Mistere*) who were not chief masters, the latter taking place as "esquires of lesser degree", next after the esquires of gentle blood and coat armour. Some of the great masons even adopted coat armour, as for example Master William of Rameseye, chief mason to Edward III from 1336 until his death in 1349, whose exquisitely cut seal contains a shield bearing the canting arms of a compass between two rams' heads in chief and a gate (possibly referring to his dwelling by Aldersgate) in base. The royal precedence was less pedantically followed elsewhere, and numerous contracts and other documents provide that master craftsmen shall have their meals, dress and other allowances as esquires or gentlemen, while their assistants shall be treated as yeomen or grooms. A particularly interesting distinction is drawn in the case of two corrodies granted by Winchester Cathedral Priory to their chief masons, William Wynford in 1399, and his successor Robert Hulle in 1412. Each, if he wished, was to take his dinner and supper in the Prior's Hall at the prior's own table "unless great numbers or the presence of important and distinguished magnates of the country should supervene". (*nisi maior multitudo populi impedierit vel principaliores aut valenciores de patria supervenerint.*) Wynford's "yeoman" (*valectus*) and Hulle's "groom" (*garcio*) were to take their meals at the lower tables with the prior's servants of their own station.

In addition to the evidence from New College, it is fortunate that there also exists a Household Roll of William of Wykeham himself, in which the late Mr. Herbert Chitty discovered the names of Yevele, Wynford, Herland, and Simon Membury the clerk of works, among the marginal lists of guests in the summer of 1393. Yevele's visits took place at Southwark, of Herland both at Esher and at Winchester, of the other only at Winchester. In connexion with the relative positions of clerk of works as administrative chief, and of master mason as technical head of operations, it is of particular interest to note that while Membury attended on eleven occasions, Wynford was also present on every one, and also on two other days, while all seven of Herland's Winchester visits coincided with meals at which Wynford was present, but only five times with the visits of the clerk of the works.

The splendid tombs and grave-slabs of the great architectural masters, some of which are known by record or drawing, while others still exist, have often been instanced as proof of the high standing of the men commemorated. The inscription on the tomb of Pierre de Montreuil, formerly in the Abbey of St.-Germain-des-Prés, deserves quotation in full for the striking epithet, *doctor latomorum*, which it applies to this great architect, who died in 1266: "Weep, for here lies buried Pierre, born at Montreuil, a pattern of character and in his life a learned doctor among masons. May the King of heaven lead him to the skies: he died in the year of Christ the thousandth, two-hundredth, with twelve and fifty-four." Of the early fourteenth century there remains the splendid slab of Master Richard of Gainsborough, at Lincoln Cathedral, and at Strassburg is the memorial statue of Erwin "von Steinbach", who died in 1318; Thomas Wolvey's tombstone at St. Albans (1428) described him as mason and Esquire of Richard II; in Scotland there are two memorials at Melrose and Paisley Abbeys to John Morow, who died in 1485, master mason of both, and also of the Cathedrals of St. Andrews and Glasgow, as well as of Nithsdale and Galloway. Mr. Briggs gives an extensive list of such memorials and other inscriptions in England, France, Spain, Germany and Italy, and Dr. Pevsner quotes the tombstone of Burkhard Engelberger in St. Ulrich's, Augsburg, naming the mason as *Architector* (1512).

Social status is also indicated by the clothing presented to masons and other artists and craftsmen. This was of great value, but differed according to the rank of the recipient. Members of royal and other households received livery on one or more occasions in the year, and in England very extensive records of the Royal Wardrobe, the issuing department, survive, enabling the various garments and cloths, with their prices, to be identified. The Pipe Rolls show that robes and "cloths" were already being issued in this way to the royal craftsmen in the twelfth century, and by the time of Henry III there was a definite list of royal artists who received this livery, consisting of the clerk of the works, the chief mason and his assistants, the chief carpenter and his deputy, the smith, the plumber, the glazier, the sculptor of the King's images, and the King's painter. In some cases the artists' wives also received presents of clothing. Craftsmen attached to private households also received liveries.

Mediaeval lay artists were certainly not always illiterate. Throughout the Gothic period inscriptions and *graffiti* occur which are clearly the work of crafts-men, and from the internal evidence of Villard de Honnecourt's album Hahnloser has shown that Honnecourt himself, and two later technical possessors of the book during the thirteenth century (presumably the next two masters of the lodge) were literate in Latin and French. Indirect evidence of literacy is found in the appointments of master craftsmen as keepers of building works conjointly with clerks: from 1243–48 Master Simon the Carpenter was a keeper of the works at Windsor Castle; in 1245 Master Henry the Mason was one of the keepers at Westminster Abbey, as also was his successor, Master John of Gloucester, mason, in 1254. In 1259 the Sheriff of Lincoln addressed a letter, still preserved at the Abbey, to his friend, Master John "Le Mazun", concerning the supply of lead, and another letter from a Purbeck quarry-owner to John's successor, Robert of Beverley, came about 1261. At the end of the century, as we have already seen, the chief mason at Exeter Cathedral was keeper of the counter-roll, as was Hugh Herland the carpenter at the repair of Rochester Castle and again at the building of Westminster Hall roof late in the fourteenth century. In 1390 Henry Yevele, in his capacity as Warden of London Bridge, received a letter written in French from an English chaplain then in Rome, and in 1421, as we have seen, the master mason at Calais wrote a detailed letter to Henry V. Towards the end of the period actual signatures exist of a number of craftsmen, but it is important to notice that the absence of earlier signatures is proof only of the general custom of sealing documents, but leaving them unsigned.

The children of master craftsmen, if not the craftsmen themselves, sometimes had good academic careers: William Herland, almost certainly son of the great carpenter, was an original scholar of Winchester and proceeded to New College; a son of William Orchard, the fifteenth-century mason-contractor, took the degree of B.C.L. at Oxford after being a chorister at Magdalen in 1484–5; Richard Bertie, son of Bishop Fox's master mason, had a most brilliant career at Corpus Christi College, Oxford, and later married the widowed Duchess of Suffolk. A much earlier record is the letter dating between 1192 and 1203, printed by M. Deschamps, sent to the abbot of St.-Bavon at Ghent to request him to take into the monastery the son of Master G., an artist of Tournai "whose merits are in high repute not only here, but also in many other places and churches on account of his magnificent works and the outstanding examples of his skill; these, in addition to his honour-able and gentle character, for which he is noted, will keep his memory ever green". (*magistro G., cujus, preter honestatem et mansuetudinem, quibus preeminet, non solum apud nos, sed et in locis pluribus et ecclesiis ex magnificis operibus et insignibus artificiis merita vigent, et in perpetuum sui memoriam dereliquunt.*)

In addition to some Latin, and in England an acquaintance with French as well until the end of the fourteenth century, we may suppose the more important craftsmen to have had a good knowledge of arithmetic, and of course an out-standing eminence in practical geometry. The English masons before 1400 described their craft as "according to Euclid", and the poet Lydgate early in the fifteenth century echoed this with "by crafft of Ewclyde mason doth his cure"; while by the end of the century Henry Bradshaw in his *Life of St. Werburge of Chester* thus described the building of a church in her honour:

> "They sende for masons upon every syde,
> Connynge in geometrie the foundacion to take
> For a large mynstre, longe, hie, and wyde,
> Substancially wrought, the best that they can make,
> To the honour of God, for Saynt Werburge sake."

As to their training in craft skill, apprenticeship began in some trades early in the thirteenth century, but a mason's apprentice seems not to be mentioned before 1364–65, when the Westminster Abbey accounts contain a payment of 13*s.* 4*d.* "for the wages of the fourth mason, apprentice, for 13 weeks and for the previous quarter he took nothing because he was learning" (*quia fuit in addiscendo*). At Rodez Cathedral in 1293 there is mention of Master Stephanus and of Ponsetus "*scolar suus*", and before the days of regular apprenticeship there must have been some system of learners; the arts were handed down in families and from father to son all through the period, and this may have been even more common before the practice of taking apprentices began. Contracts of employment sometimes specify that a master shall train the men under him, or one or more apprentices.

Something may here be said on clerical artists and architects. While the earlier notion that monks were commonly architects has now been finally exploded, there is a certain amount of evidence in favour of artistic, though but rarely architectural, work by secular clerics, and at an early date by Cistercian lay-brothers. In 1227 Brother Ralph of Northampton, a lay-brother of St. James in that town, was sent to repair the King's fishpond at Woodstock, and the clergyman, Elias of Derham, himself a sculptor and metal-worker, was frequently instructed by Henry III to direct, dispose, or give his counsel concerning artistic work, though at the great cathedrals where Master Elias was a canon, and has been credited with the position of "architect", master masons of distinction were also employed, as Nicholas of Ely at Salisbury, and Adam Lock at Wells. In 1241 Nigel the chaplain, painter of the King's hall at Winchester, was to have 16*s.* (£80!) for a "robe", i.e. a complete set of garments. From 1248 an artist who actually was a Benedictine monk, Brother William of Westminster, was painting the King's chapel at Windsor, but seven years earlier a layman, Thomas the painter of Chertsey, had been paid 10 marks for "making images" in the same chapel. Between 1272 and 1298 the goldsmiths Nicolas of Douai and Jackemon of Nivelles made the shrine of St. Gertrude for the chapter of Nivelles, according to a "pourtrature" by Maître Jacques, Benedictine monk of Anchin (**25**). M. Stein states that in 1340 Brother Gérard of the Cistercian Abbey of Vaucelles, built the crossing-vault, and in 1353 and 1365 one John, a canon of St. Catherine's, described as "the King's picture painter", was painting images for Edward III's chapel in Windsor Castle. At the same time, 1355–60, Edward III was also employing Edward of St. Andrews, a canon of Newstead Priory, as master of the carpenters' work for the stalls in St. Stephen's Chapel, Westminster. At the earlier date the Sheriff of Nottingham was ordered to send the tools of Edward and his carpenters southwards, and in 1360 Edward was given power to hire carpenters for the work. Finally, Professor Hamilton Thompson has discovered two instances in the mid-fifteenth century of members of religious orders who had some knowledge of building, though how far this was technical knowledge is not clear. In 1440 Brother John Gowselle of the Austin Priory of Torksey was stated "not to take heed to the works of the church and priory, albeit he is learned in the art of stone-masonry"; and two years later the Prior of the Benedictine House at Daventry was said to be "of no account in matters temporal . . . albeit he has some degree of experience in the craft of

23 MALINES: Maison Échevinale. Carving by *Jan van Mansdale*
(*Keldermans*), 1377–85.

24 ROUEN CATHEDRAL: north porch,
c. 1280, by *Jean Davy*.

25 NIVELLES: Shrine of St. Gertrude, 1272–98. Designer *Maître
Jacques*, monk of Anchin.

GOTHIC DETAIL

26 (*above left*) HAL: Church of Notre-Dame. Virgin and Child of the south porch, *c.* 1390–1400.

27 PILSEN: the Madonna of the Church of St. Bartholomew, *c.* 1375.

28 NOUSIAINEN: Madonna from Gotland (now in the Finnish National Museum), fourteenth century.

GOTHIC SCULPTURE

stone-mason and carpenter". It is perhaps of some significance that in both cases the monastery was a small one, where at this late date the poverty-stricken inmates might try to save money by doing their own work. Of the arts, the only one which was in any degree a preserve of the monasteries was illumination, and that for very obvious reasons.

Except in a few cases, there is little evidence that clerics took any active part in design, while there is abundant proof that the master masons and other chief craftsmen made designs, drew them or had them drawn out, and exercised "ordinance and disposition" over the task of putting them into effect. Their function of supervision is constantly mentioned: in 1299 in France a furnace was to be built, according to the ideas (*ad cognitionem*) of good masters of that craft; fabric rolls record payments to masters "for supervision of the workmen" (*pro supervisione operariorum*) as to Robert Wadherst at Norwich in 1385–86, to Henry Yevele at Westminster Abbey from 1387 onwards, and to his deputy Walter Walton at Portchester Castle from 1396 to 1399. Walton visited from time to time "ordaining and supervising the work" while the day-to-day charge of the works was in the hands of Walter Weston the sub-warden, who resided at Portchester. In 1469 at King's Hall, Cambridge, John Wolryche had 8s. 4d. for supervision of the other masons. Similarly, at Ripon Minster in 1520–21, Christopher Scoign was given a reward of 10s. (£27 10s.) for his good diligence in supervising the masons working about the fabric of the new nave; Robert Squyer, mason, had 6s. 8d. (£18 6s. 8d.) for his good diligence about the works of the church, and William "Corver" had 6s. 8d. for supervision of the other carpenters.

The Middle Ages definitely recognized the individuality of the master: Coulton quoted Benvenuto da Imola's commentary on Dante with much point. Imola states that "some men marvelled that Dante should have immortalized (the miniaturists Oderisi and Franco, types of the fickleness of fame), for they were men of unknown name and a low type of art". (*homines ignoti nominis et bassae artis*.) But Dante here showed his genius "for thereby he giveth silently to be understood how the love of glory doth so fasten upon all men indifferently, that even petty artisans (*parvi artifices*) are anxious to earn it, just as we see that painters append their names to their works". One could hardly describe the architects of the great Gothic cathedrals as petty artisans, and a due respect for past work was inculcated at any rate by the ancient usage of the German masons, which laid down that "When a Master dies and another comes, he shall not remove the first Master's masonry already set, nor throw away the unset but hewn stones, that the Master whose work has been interrupted by death may not be put to shame."

Intentional collaboration undoubtedly took place, just as it does to-day, though perhaps not with great frequency. It was necessary for masons and carpenters to collaborate, and the evidence rather suggests a certain degree of collaboration by Henry Yevele in William Wynford's works for Wykeham. Honnecourt and Pierre de Corbie amused themselves by working together on an ideal plan, and throughout the Gothic period masters were called together to make suggestions regarding points of construction. These conferences of masters are particularly interesting, not only for the records which sometimes survive of the views expressed, but for their evidence of wide communications. In 1091 an accident befell the wooden steeple of St.-Pierre at Oudenbourg near Bruges, when the inhabitants speedily called together *architectos*, and promised them rewards if they could set matters right. Gervase of Canterbury in his famous account of the rebuilding of the choir at Canterbury Cathedral after 1174, states that French and English artificers were summoned, and that after they had differed in opinion, Master William of Sens was appointed to carry out the work. In 1243 the town statutes of Avignon proposed that the sworn masters of stone-masonry should study the emplacement of a fort for defence; at Chartres Cathedral in 1316 a meeting took place attended by the Master of Notre-Dame at Paris, the Master of the King's Works, two other masons, Simon the carpenter, and Berthaut the *maistre imagier*.

A commission on the works of Siena Cathedral took place in 1321; in 1336 the Tower of London was structurally surveyed by a commission of four masons, four carpenters, and two each of the trades of plumbers, glaziers, tilers and smiths; in 1366 there was a great conference at the Duomo of Florence; in 1390 Yevele, Wynford and Herland were appointed to see to the repair of Winchester Castle; and in 1392 there were the famous conferences to decide upon the proportions of Milan Cathedral. At Gerona Cathedral in 1417 twelve masters assembled to give their advice on the resumption of the works, two each from Barcelona, Tortosa and Tarragona, the master at Gerona, and others from Urgel, Manresa, Castellon de Empurias, and as far off as Perpignan and Narbonne (**144**). According to Vasari, though Guasti doubted the tale, the Florentine merchants in 1417 were ordered to spend large sums to persuade the principal, most experienced and gifted masters of France, Germany, Spain, England and Italy to come to Florence to give their advice upon the construction of the dome of Santa Maria del Fiore, and in 1420 they actually met. In the Westminster Abbey accounts for 1479–80 rewards are recorded to three unnamed masters of masons who came to survey the old and new church and to give their counsel as to the work about to be undertaken, and at Clermont-Ferrand a conference took place in 1496 to determine on the completion of the Cathedral, and the necessary repairs after the earthquakes of 1477, 1478 and 1489.

Quite apart from the instances where conferences of masters were called together from distant places, mediaeval architects travelled far and wide. It is well known that Villard de Honnecourt, before 1250, had business which took him through the north of France, Switzerland, Germany and Hungary; even in Romanesque times there are records of sending considerable distances for craftsmen, as in the case mentioned, when Walter Coorland was brought from England to build at Poitiers in the eleventh century. In 1153 English glass-painters were employed on the windows of the abbey at Braine-le-Comte; in 1175 the bishop and canons of Urgel in Spain sent for Raimond le Lombard who with four other Lombards and other masons was to roof the whole church and to build towers and a cupola in seven years; in 1190 William, an English mason, accompanied Richard Cœur-de-Lion on crusade and later built a church at Acre; and in 1224, Durandus, a mason from Rouen, was called in to work on Beaulieu Abbey. In 1241 Master Baldwin de Araz, mason, was granted a fee of 10 marks yearly (£667) by Henry III, and in 1267 the King undertook that he should be paid arrears of these fees from the time when he was in his service. Henry III also sent his chief mason and carpenter from London to view the defences of York Castle in 1244. The northern style of French Gothic was carried to the Midi by Jean des Champs, who began the work of Clermont-Ferrand Cathedral in 1248, and is again found at Narbonne, where the Cathedral was begun in 1272 (**62, 74, 75**); Eudes de Montreuil, St. Louis's master mason, accompanied his master on crusade and built the towers of Jaffa, in the mid-thirteenth century; and the collegiate church of Wimpfen near Heidelberg was built in 1268–78 "in the French manner" by a mason of great skill in architectural craft (*peritissimo architectoriae artis latomo*). We have seen the Norwich mason and carpenter setting out for Caen and Hamburg in 1274, and in 1287 Étienne de Bonneuil, mason, master appointed to build the church at Uppsala in Sweden, travelled thither accompanied by "companions and bachelors" of his craft. Lorenzo Maitani, appointed master builder at Orvieto in 1310, went on living in Siena for another twenty years, and during that time also worked at Perugia and Todi as well as in Siena itself; Nicholas de Chaumes, master at Sens Cathedral in 1308, also became master of the

29　COUTANCES CATHEDRAL from the north-east, *c.* 1220–50.

30　NARBONNE CATHEDRAL from the south-east, 1272–.　Designer, *Jean des Champs*.

CATHEDRAL GOTHIC

31 ABBEVILLE: Church of St. Wulfran, 1488–1539.

32 SENS CATHEDRAL: front of south transept, 1494. Designer *Martin Chambiges*.

King's work at Paris, sat on the Chartres commission of 1316, and in 1326 provided a plan for the façade of Meaux Cathedral.

To name only a few of the more outstanding English instances, Richard de Felstede, a London carpenter, contracted to work on the great hall of Kenilworth

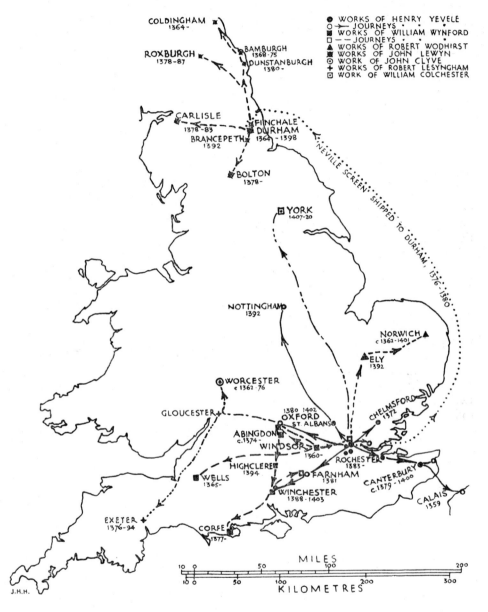

33   The documented journeys of English masons in the early Perpendicular period. An unnamed mason, possibly Lewyn, went from Durham to London for the Neville Screen in 1376.

Castle in 1347; in 1356–57 John Palterton, chief mason at Westminster Abbey, spent a year on pilgrimage; William Humberville, master mason for the library of Merton College, Oxford, journeyed with the Warden to Sherborne, Salisbury, Winchester and London to view libraries in 1371; a Ripon carpenter made a timber vault for Thornton Abbey, Lincs., in 1391; in 1407 William Colchester, master mason of Westminster Abbey, was sent to York Minster (**33**); Thomas Mapilton, whom we have seen laying a foundation stone at St. Stephen Walbrook, became master to Canterbury Cathedral in 1423, and in 1429 was called to Bury St. Edmunds to give his advice on the repair of the great western tower; in 1450 John Porter, mason of Lincoln, twice travelled to York to give his advice upon the Minster, and in 1456 took up a definite appointment there; and in 1472 William Hyndeley, a Norwich mason, became Minster Mason at York. Finally, Master Christopher Scune or Scoign, who was master mason of the new nave at Ripon from 1503 to 1523, was also master at Durham Cathedral from some time between 1508 and 1515 until 1519 or later, and for the building of the spire at Louth, Lincs., from 1505 until 1515.

The later French instances include Jean Auxtabours, who between 1345 and 1370 was concerned with the works of the churches of Mantes, Alençon, and Chartres, as well as the royal works; Hennequin or Hawkin Liège, who went to England in 1366–67 to make the tomb for Queen Philippa; Gilles Largent, the Duc de Berry's master, who worked at Hesdin Castle and elsewhere, in 1391 at Arras Cathedral, and also at the great Church of St.-Quentin; Pierre Perrat, who died in 1400 after working for the Cathedral and for the city of Metz, as well as on the Church of the Carmelites there, and on Toul and Verdun Cathedrals; and the great Raymond du Temple, who in addition to the old Louvre in Paris and other royal buildings designed the south portal of Mantes and the Church of the Célestins at Paris, in 1394. Jean de Dijon between 1389 and 1416 had charge of Reims Cathedral, and was also called to Troyes as an expert; Pierre Robin between 1421 and 1432 worked at Chartres Cathedral, Notre-Dame de Paris, and provided a plan for St.-Maclou at Rouen; and in 1499 Martin de Chambiges was called to Paris as consultant by Jean de Soissons, who paid him for advice in connexion with the façade of Troyes Cathedral.

Among the many Spanish architectural travels referred to by Street, in some ways the most interesting is the extensive journey made by Pedro Balaguer in 1414; invited to design the new bell-tower for Valencia Cathedral, he visited Lérida, Narbonne, and various other cities to examine their bell-towers in order to imitate the most elegant and fit form for his new work (**244**). In the German Empire, Wenzel, a son of Peter Parler, left Prague in 1399 to take charge of the new work on the great tower of Vienna Cathedral, and Heinrich Parler a few years earlier had gone to Milan; while Ulrich von Ensingen, who was also concerned with the work at Milan in 1391, worked at Strassburg Cathedral and also at Ulm (**257**).

In whatever light we consider these Gothic architects and artists, they appear as great men: their works have the classic poise of Greece together with a warmer, gentler spirit than Greece knew in her age of perfection. That keynote of Christian feeling, charity, grace, love, is infused into the stones of these prodigious works of men's brains and men's hands in a manner that might well be thought supernatural. Yet at the same time the buildings are rife with the satisfyingly pagan tradition of harmony with nature, with the ground and plants and with the sense of humour in man. Even the grim Cistercians had been infected by this warmer humour before the end, and in the whole gamut of the later Gothic there is no discordant note, save that introduced by the miseries and horror of the times, that morbidity which threatened to engulf the European spirit. Let us give all due credit to the Church, to the thinkers, the clergy, the Kings and the courtiers who made possible and encouraged so vast and whole-hearted an outpouring of all that is finest and most durable in the spirit of man. But in the end we must return to the craftsmen and the artists, and above all to those masters of design through whom flowed the inspiration of so marvellous works.

IV

Gothic Geography

CONTROVERSY has raged over the cradle of Gothic architecture, and is not yet at an end. No certain answer can be given to the question: where did Gothic begin? But the origin of certain factors has become clearer than it was a generation or two ago. The prime importance of the pointed arch is now seen to go beyond mere convenience in the practical arrangement of vault-ribs. It is a key motive accepted as the symbol of a new culture, and borrowed from the East. Pointed arches had been known in the Saracenic world for several centuries, and by the "Arabs" had been introduced to Sicily. But until the end of the eleventh century the Arabic Mediterranean and Romanesque Europe had been segregated, were worlds apart. Then within one lifetime the whole position was changed: in 1066, William of Normandy conquered England; between 1060 and 1090 Sicily was won by another Norman, Roger of Hauteville; in 1099 the new united energy of the West conquered Jerusalem. Again the impetus was provided by Normans, close relatives of Roger: Bohemund and his nephew Tancred.

By the year 1100 Norman dynasties were firmly settled at the centre and both ends of the world of western Christianity. And it is important to note that before this date there had been no occurrence of the pointed arch in the West. Yet within a generation it had begun its triumphal course, and in two it was established at the core of a new art. It can hardly be mere coincidence that the eastern arch appears first in the Norman realm of Sicily; the earliest combination of pointed arch and ribbed vault in Normandy and in England; the earliest flying buttresses, albeit hidden, again in Norman England; in fact, that the whole cultural movement that we know as Gothic should have followed immediately upon the great expansion of Norman power. Had the Norman realms ever coalesced into one political unit, this early primacy might never have passed from them. But as it was, after a few decades of keen competition, the leadership of the new civilization fell to the King of France and the area of his centralized government close to Paris. The identification of Gothic art with France is due to the capacity of the French Kings to pursue their policy over a period of generations, and to the corresponding disunity of the Norman princes, and their internecine conflicts, such as those between the sons of William the Conqueror.

In this limited sense, the development of Gothic belongs particularly to France, but by no means to a French national state, nor to the personified French people of chauvinist myth. The importation of such conceptions into the cultural history of the twelfth century is an utter anachronism. Besides, even the nominal Kingdom of France of that day differed widely from the France of our maps. While it included the county of Barcelona beyond the Pyrenees, it lacked everything east of the line of Meuse, Saône and Rhone, and much to the west too. Beyond this line was the Empire, a strange and loose union of Germany with northern Italy and with Provence. None of the three great monasteries, Cluny, Citeaux and Clairvaux, which were centres of cultural diffusion in the new age, was more than twenty-five miles from the frontier. But in speaking of frontiers we must remember that in the twelfth century the whole western European polity was a single unit in a way that it no longer is. Differences of vernacular language were of comparatively little significance when all learned men had a common language in Latin; a common ecclesiastical loyalty to Rome.

The significance of Paris and the domain of the French King is thus largely accidental; wherever the new art truly originated, it became concentrated around Paris by virtue of the continental movement of scholars to the teaching of Abelard and others at the schools of Notre-Dame. And though it is true that the main stream of Gothic flowed out from the early developments in metropolitan France, there were other streams. Only by juggling with definitions is it possible to confine Gothic in origin to the restricted domain, 150 miles long and less than half as broad, ruled by Louis VI and Louis VII. We cannot deny the name to the utterly different products of Provence and Languedoc before the Albigensian "Crusade", to the flourishing artistic schools of western France which grew up under Angevin protection, or to the independent union of Gothic elements which took place in England. We cannot speak of a positive Gothic art, even in architecture, earlier than 1150; yet by that year the first fruits were visible in several distinct areas covering nearly three thousand miles in total length, from Durham in the North-West, to Jerusalem in the South-East, where the Priory Church of the Holy Sepulchre was consecrated in 1149 (**34**).

While many details are still unsure, we may say that Gothic sprang into being from the impact upon the adventurous Norman (and northern) mind of Eastern symbols and knowledge. Its cradle included a large area of north-western, western, and Mediterranean Europe, notably England, geographical France, parts of Italy and the Near East. No such thing as Gothic, in thought, culture or art, existed in the year 1100; and by the year 1150 it was already ousting Romanesque within its cradle-lands. On the other hand, the vast number of great Romanesque buildings was such that nearly a century elapsed before the physiognomy of art became firmly Gothic. This brings us to the middle of the thirteenth century, by which time Gothic had reached the Rhineland and all western Germany, northern Spain, Cyprus and other places in the eastern Mediterranean, and in the North had spread to Ireland, Scotland and Norway.

A second great period of expansion followed in the later thirteenth and fourteenth centuries. Europe was realizing its dream of unity, and in spite of the loss of Palestine was sending out tentacles across the whole breadth of Asia to Peking. Further enriching contacts with Persian and central Asiatic art resulted. Before the end of the fourteenth century Lithuania, last of the pagan nations of Europe, had become officially Christian, according to the western rite. The boundaries of Gothic civilization were now those of the Roman Church: Scandinavia, Finland, the Baltic, western Lithuania and Poland, Hungary as far as the Carpathians and down to the Adriatic and Dalmatian seaboard, Italy, Spain, Portugal, and far-off Iceland were all included. This was the Golden Age of Gothic, the time of its greatest continental expansion, that of its fullest development without loss of force, that of its greatest purity.

There was to be one other ephemeral expansion in the very last days of the Gothic era, to America. Unlike Italy, Spain was slow in receiving Renaissance doctrines, and was still building exclusively in Gothic style when Columbus reached Hispaniola in 1492, when the town of Santo Domingo was founded four years later, and during the building of its cathedral, the earliest in the New World, between 1521 and 1527. Renaissance elements were already present at the time of the conquests of Mexico and Peru, but the earliest buildings were predominantly Gothic in construction, and Gothic vaults long persisted in churches otherwise of classic detail, as also happened at the other extremity of the Gothic region, the Baltic lands.

Not only trade but art too "follows the flag": through the whole history of Gothic it is closely linked to political movements. Its origin is due to Norman expansion and to the First Crusade. Its concentration and period of classic development followed owing to the capacity of the House of Capet. The later growth of

34   JERUSALEM: Church of the Holy Sepulchre. Portals
of main south front,   1140–44.

35   CHARTRES CATHEDRAL: portals of west front, *c.* 1145–50.

PRIMARY GOTHIC

36 NICOSIA CATHEDRAL: west front,
c. 1292–1326.

37 BELLAPAIS ABBEY: refectory,
c. 1324–39.

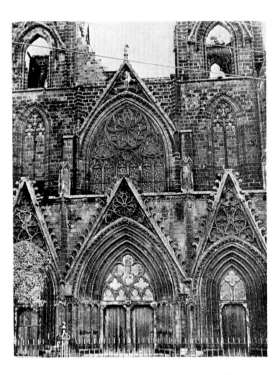

38 FAMAGUSTA CATHEDRAL: west front,
c. 1300–30.

39 NICOSIA CATHEDRAL: interior
looking east, *c.* 1200.

CYPRUS

strong national schools was in each case due to movements largely conditioned by geography. Just as the style of the Ile-de-France owed its predominance to the political centralization of the French Kings, steadily penetrating and "colonizing" geographical France, so other styles were founded in areas of relative unity. The only Gothic style which has a separate history largely independent of that of Parisian France, is the English; a history due to our position as an island, and to the unifying genius of our Norman and Plantagenet Kings. The Empire was always too unwieldy, too diversified, and too decentralized to yield a common style, though its wide adoption of the hall-church may be traced to the imperial status of Provence, and the common antipathy to Paris of the Empire and all southern Gaul. The very close links between the Provençal and Languedocian troubadours, and their German counterparts the minnesinger, point in the same direction.

The possession of flourishing indigenous schools of artists must be taken as the main criterion of artistic independence. Before 1300 such schools were only working in France and England; thereafter they rapidly developed in countries with a highly organized system of government. The chief continental example of such a country was Hungary, whose geographical unity was reflected in its centralized monarchy and at the same time in its county system, so similar in development to that of England. On a smaller scale Bohemia, with its dependency of Moravia, formed a comparable unit, and so did Aragon in Spain. Hungary, Bohemia and Aragon all owed their unity to geography: each occupied a river-basin surrounded by a defensive chain of high mountains. Less effective as an insulating medium than the sea-walls of England, these mountain defences were broken by river valleys, or in the case of Aragon by coastal and sea routes; in each case there was considerable importation of foreign specialists. Hungary and Bohemia employed many German artists and some Frenchmen; Hungary, thanks to its Adriatic seaboard and suzerainty over Dalmatia, cultivated relations with Italy as well. Aragon invited the assistance of both French and English artists.

England, on the contrary, was almost entirely self-supporting. After the end of the twelfth century continental building masters rarely worked here, and we have no transplanted major work later than the Canterbury choir of Master William of Sens. Receptive as the English architects and artists were of ideas from abroad, they invariably translated them into a distinctive vernacular idiom before carrying them into practice. Like the style of northern France, English Gothic was for export as well as for the home market. The earlier Gothic of Ireland is almost purely English, apart from the very earliest works of Cistercian inspiration, which preceded the English political conquest. The political and artistic conquests of Wales went hand in hand; conversely, the English failure to unite Scotland with the southern parts of Britain was followed by a marked independence of Scottish style. But in order to avoid reliance on English models and artists, Scotland had recourse to France and Flanders.

In the Peninsula, neither Castile nor Portugal had the coherence of Aragon until towards the end of the Middle Ages; both countries depended very largely on outside assistance, obtained by Castile from France and Germany, and to a less extent from England, by Portugal from England and from France. Norway was largely influenced by England, and Sweden also to a less extent, and rather more by France. Towards the end of the period Sweden, like Denmark, became a member of the Baltic artistic province which was penetrated through and through by artists and objects of art from northern Germany, and in particular from the Hanseatic cities. In so far as Poland, Lithuania, and the north-eastern Baltic lands became Gothic, it was as a province of German art. But it must be remembered that in this connexion the word German is used in its widest sense, implying not at all the influence of a single national state, comparable to that of mediaeval England; but on the other hand strictly analogous to the earlier outflow of "French" art (*ars Francigena*). It cannot be too often repeated that there is no organic connexion between either "French" or "German" Gothic art, and the modern national states bearing the names of France and Germany.

Two areas of very great importance have not been mentioned: Italy and Flanders. Italy was politically even more lacking in unity than Germany. At the beginning of the Gothic age the northern half of the country formed a nominal kingdom within the Empire, but this rapidly dissolved into a large number of constituent states and more or less independent cities. Venice was always independent, and preserved to some slight extent a sentimental loyalty to Constantinople; though it developed a Gothic art of its own, it never looked westward. Sicily and southern Italy had also had long contacts with and loyalties towards Byzantium; they went through periods of Saracenic, then Norman dominance; later passed to French and Spanish dynasties. None of the conflicting forces was strong enough altogether to counter the ecclesiastical power exerted by Rome. So it is that even in the middle of the thirteenth century, at the height of the Franco-English early Gothic movement, Rome preserved semicircular arches and a classic spirit. The Gothic that did reach Italy was reduced by the climate and this classic spirit to a curious effect of living in two dimensions only. Colour and surface take the place of northern sculptural effect and moulding, and the result tends to be flat, and thus non-Gothic.

The tale of Flanders is a very different one. The name is artistically applied to a much larger area than that of the political Flanders, precisely because diversity of control did not in this case lead to artistic disunity. Flanders proper and Artois at first belonged to the nominal kingdom of France, Hainault and Brabant to the Empire. These provinces, instead of looking away from each other, developed a common spirit closely bound up with the commercial interests of their great mercantile towns. Before the end of the Middle Ages something approaching political unity had been achieved between the units comprising the area of modern Belgium, Luxemburg and Holland, as well as the extreme north-east of France. They formed a distinct cultural province, with characteristics clearly marked off from those of the neighbouring territories, France, Germany and England. Great commercial prosperity is reflected in its enormous civic buildings, vast towered churches, and streets of massive stone and brick merchants' houses and factories. Owing its early Gothic impetus to France, Flanders was soon able, like England, to stand on its own feet. And even more than England it was able later to influence in its turn the course of art in France.

Now in this antithesis between the artistic lot of Italy and of Flanders a great deal is bound up: no less than the presumed identification of Gothic art with western Christendom. In face of the wide and lasting influence of Byzantium upon all the lands of the Orthodox Eastern Church, no one could attach Gothic to Christianity as such. And the extensive employment of Renaissance and Baroque forms for the churches of the last four centuries, both Catholic and Protestant, would in any case render doubtful the link between the Gothic style and even western Christendom. But to find, at the height of the age, that Gothic was at the same time accepted by the commercial centre, Flanders, and rejected by the religious centre, Rome, goes further. It suggests that the specifically Christian inspiration of Gothic art is a phantom; we must distinguish between the religion and the culture of Christendom during the vital centuries from the twelfth to the sixteenth. So far as any style in art ever typified the whole western Church, it was Romanesque; the coming of Gothic was not a peaceful development in organic succession to what had gone before. On the contrary, it was the opening of a new though hidden struggle for cultural domination within the West.

At the beginning I insisted that the opposition between Gothic and Romanesque is that between the dynamic and the static. The re-activizing of Europe into a dynamic age stemmed from the cultural explosion which took place when the Normans and the East came into direct contact. But there is another opposition which goes much further back in European and Mediterranean architecture, and which must derive from a very early antithesis of cultures. This is the conflict between circular and rectangular buildings: on one side the beehive hut and the dome; on the other the long house and timbered hall. Of all the positive Gothic characteristics the greatest is the pointed arch, the denial of the circle; its most decided negative is the rejection of the dome. Where concentric forms were desirable for practical reasons, Gothic shunned the circle and the dome, adopting faceted and polygonal shapes. Semicircular apsidal terminations became polygons or were eliminated altogether as in many Cistercian churches and almost universally in Britain.

The square east end of English churches was also normal in Ireland, in Scotland and in Norway, in spite of the general diffusion of Romanesque apses. It occurred occasionally in northern France, as at Laon Cathedral; Germany, Poland, and along the Baltic coast to Estonia. This ultimate denial of the circle and the dome is then typically north-western, and its centre is in England. This is not surprising, for England was (with the Baltic) the last European stronghold of northern paganism. Such deep cultural preferences and idiosyncrasies are maintained by the conservatism of religious practice and enforced by sanctions akin to taboo. Besides, we know that in England considerable care was taken to incorporate as far as possible the practices and forms of paganism in the new Christianity. Similarly, practices of southern paganism had amalgamated with the use of the Italian Church. The seeming paradox of the rejection by Rome of the typical "Christian art" of Gothic is explained. Within Christendom itself a secret and indeed subconscious struggle was in progress between the two basic cultures on which western Christianity itself was based: the Mediterranean or Classic, and the Northern or Gothic paganisms.

It is at this point that we can appreciate the justice of the appellation "Gothic": the latent forces behind the new outburst, though set free by an eastern stimulus, went back to the common cultural tradition of the North. That tradition, the property of many related peoples: Franks, Burgundians, Alamans, Saxons, Angles, Danes and Norse, got a name from one among them, the Goths. Allowing that the part may stand for the whole, the name adequately indicates the true background of Gothic art and culture. There is a continuity, albeit worn very thin at times, leading from the distant past of these northern peoples, and joining pre-Christian times to the present day. Like those of all other cultures, this continuum has been subject to periodic rises and falls; it is to the five centuries containing its main peaks of productivity that we give the name of Gothic.

All cultures are fundamentally religious; that is, they live and die with the beliefs and social practices of the community to which they are attached. Thus it is true that Gothic art is primarily the expression of religious feeling and faith. But it is clear from what has gone before that its basic religion is in no exclusive sense Christian. To be sure, the iconography of Gothic took on a largely Christian guise, due to direct control by the ecclesiastical power. But outside the controlled area, the Gothic artists were able to introduce the figures of an older mythology, and to demonstrate their underlying traditions which drew no hard-and-fast line between the religious and the secular. This indeed is the outstanding feature of Gothic art, the basis of its internal unity. Whereas the Christian ecclesiastics of the Middle Ages rigorously separated the sphere of the Church from that of the State, attempting to segregate all "clerics", the lay craftsmen who produced the buildings and most of their contents lived amphibiously in a world both religious

7

and secular. The churches at the same time served as assembly halls and theatres; the civic buildings were centres not only of material commerce but of the deeply religious and social work of the guilds.

This interpenetration of everyday life by religion is typical of the Gothic age, and explains basic similarities of treatment in buildings and works of art of all kinds. It is generally impossible to determine from internal evidence the destination of a particular motive, architectural or sculptural detail, or painting. With the exception of the Cistercian ban on work by lay-brothers for secular patrons (a ban not scrupulously obeyed), there is little evidence of exclusive classes of artists occupied with corresponding types of work. Against this we have noted the distinction between the German Lodge-Masons of the great minsters, and the Guild-Masons of the towns; but even in Germany the same man might work indifferently for church or lay patronage. Elsewhere this was common, and at least in England, universal.

In the Preface to this book the proposal was made that it should deal with the four questions; what, how, where, and when was Gothic art? The second has now been answered in considerable detail; the last two in general terms. The more detailed expansion of these answers, together with that to the first question, now lies before us. Neither a purely chronological, nor a strictly geographical treatment is possible. The first would become unwieldy in treating of the very diverse stages of development reached in different places simultaneously; the second is objectionable because it leads to confusion between past and present boundaries and conditions, and because there may be more than one main line of development within a given area at any one time. A compromise will therefore be followed. After a brief section upon the earliest Gothic there will follow the story of the cathedral art of the Ile-de-France and its expansion through Europe; secondly English art, with its outward influences; and thirdly the art of the single-naved and hall-churches, with their spread from southern France southwards into Spain and north-eastwards across Europe. Last will come the separate national styles of the close of the Middle Ages. By way of epilogue will come a general consideration of the Gothic age and its achievement.

40   CHARTRES, 1194–1212, and later.   41   AMIENS, *c.* 1258–70.
Flying Buttresses of early and mature Gothic.

42   REIMS CATHEDRAL: detail (the Knight's Communion) from the
internal screenwork of the west front, 1275–85.

GOTHIC FRAMEWORK

43   TROYES CATHEDRAL: looking east, 1208–1316. Crossing and eastern bays of nave by *Maître Henri*.

V

Cathedral Gothic

THE earliest origins of the various elements of Gothic art are hidden, and no absolute definition of the style is possible. Perhaps the best is that of the late Sir Thomas Graham Jackson: "the expression of a certain temper, sentiment, and spirit which inspired the whole method of doing things during the Middle Ages in sculpture and painting as well as in architecture". To this we might add: "and in music, poetry and the minor arts as well". Attempts to find a definition on purely logical grounds ended in absurdity when the American, C. H. Moore, proved that there had been no Gothic except in France, and very little of it even there. Similarly, attempts to trace the sources of pointed arch, ribbed vault, flying buttress, treatment of walls, spatial outlook and the rest, are inevitably unsatisfactory. The historical data simply do not exist.

What is quite certain is that there were pointed arches in use in Burgundy and sporadically across France within a very few years of 1100, if not absolutely at the opening of the twelfth century. This was during the rebuilding of the Abbey Church at Cluny, where also the western vestibule of the nave was built in the earliest style of Gothic transition between *c.* 1122 and 1135, though its vaulting may not have been quite so early. It was however finished by about the middle of the century. At Autun Cathedral (*c.* 1120–32) are pointed arcades and a pointed barrel-vault on cross-arches; on the tympanum of the portal the mason Gislebert left his name: *Gislebertus fecit hoc opus.* Other masons and carvers of the twelfth century recorded their names in this way, as did Brunus on the portal of St.-Gilles-du-Gard, Girbertus *cementarius* similarly at Carennac, Izembard who signed a capital of the Benedictine Abbey of Bernay, Umbert who did the same at the Abbey of Fleury-sur-Loire, Adam who put his name on a keystone at Poitiers. The number of really skilled stone-cutters was growing rapidly, but their accomplishment had not become mere matter-of-course.

Unfortunately we do not know, from signatures or records, the names of the great architects who before 1150 had produced a new synthesis, the basis of Gothic style. The leading works were St.-Martin-des-Champs in Paris, Sens Cathedral (45), the new Abbey Church at St.-Denis, the Abbey Church of St.-Germer, and St.-Maclou at Pontoise, all in or adjacent to the Royal Domain round Paris (44, 162). St.-Denis was the greatest abbey of the region, and under royal patronage; Sens was the metropolitan cathedral of the archdiocese. So closely do these churches resemble one another in plan and details that they seem clearly to reflect the mind of one master: "Gothicus I" we might call him. Accepting in principle the Romanesque plan of the greater church, as for liturgical reasons he was bound to do, he yet effected a considerable spiritual transformation, largely by means of thinning the supports, as better craftsmanship permitted. The arrangement of the supports as integral parts of an articulated system, of which the ribbed vaults were the crowning feature, imparted a new vitality and dynamic quality. The tall attached shafts supporting the cross-arches, already known in the great Romanesque churches such as St.-Sernin, Toulouse, were brought out and given much greater prominence and sharper outline, while between them, to take the diagonal vault-ribs, were inserted secondary shafts with bases and capitals set obliquely. This feature was borrowed from Norman practice, but considerably developed. The typical ambulatory, with apsidal chapels opening outwards, was

44 France in the Gothic period. The frontiers shown are those of *c.* 1460, after the expulsion of the English but before the acquisition of Provence. For north-east France and Flanders see **162**; for Germany see **9, 18, 200**; for Spain see **144**; for England see **33**.

transformed and unified by setting back the chapels into the ambulatory under a single series of vaults. The chapels, now much shallower, formed a continuous series of undulations in the outer wall. The general substitution of pointed for round arches and window-openings, and the crisper cutting of moulded and carved work completed the new picture.

The carving and sculpture of the new style were an integral part of its architecture; and from the twelfth century onwards to the fifteenth there is evidence that many if not most of the greatest architects were at the same time sculptors. In fact, while it is clear that the masters did not themselves labour at the banker cutting common ashlar, it is probable that many of them did carve at least specimen pieces and figures for the sculptural enrichment of their buildings. A special interest accordingly attaches to the signature of Rogerus, recorded by M. de Mély

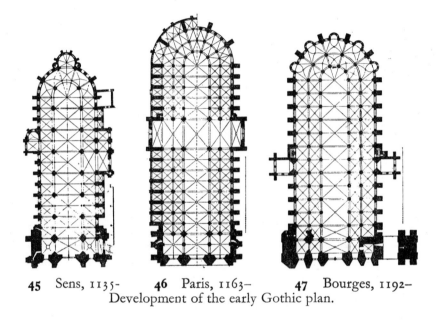

45 Sens, 1135-   **46** Paris, 1163–   **47** Bourges, 1192–
Development of the early Gothic plan.

from behind one of the statues of the Royal Portal at Chartres (**35**). Presumably identical with the "Rogerius artifex" whose obit was later commemorated in the Abbey of St.-Père at Chartres, this Roger was at any rate one of the very earliest Gothic masters. A master, for all the statues of the west doorways at Chartres are of the finest workmanship; and early, for the work began about 1145, only a year after the consecration of St.-Denis, and certainly with the same craftsmen. Even if the possibility that Roger was himself "Gothicus I" is a very faint one,* he must at least have known the inventor of Gothic, have worked with him or under his instructions.

During the second half of the twelfth century great cathedrals and churches of the new type spread rapidly through north-eastern France within a radius of little over a hundred miles of Paris. Noyon, Senlis, Laon, Soissons, and the Abbey Church of St.-Rémi at Reims, with Notre-Dame-en-Vaux at Chalons-sur-Marne were all begun within ten or fifteen years of 1150; all were to the north-east of Paris, where the first stone of the Cathedral of Notre-Dame was laid 1163 (**46**). A few years more saw work in progress at the new choir of Vézelay to the south-east, Le Mans and Tours to south-west, and Lisieux in Normandy. The early

* If the meaning of "*fecit*" were not so ambiguous, we might feel that a better Chartres claimant to the identity of Gothicus I was the "*Teudho qui frontem hujus ecclesie fecit*" of a twelfth-century cathedral obit.

Gothic, moreover, won its first success oversea when Master William of Sens in 1175 convinced the monks of Canterbury that he was the right man to rebuild their cathedral. This exportation of French architecture to England had surprisingly slight results, for it met with resistance from a native school already established. In France things went differently.

The story of Gothic development from this time onwards tends in fact to be overshadowed by the immense achievements of the cathedral builders of northern France. By means of modification, progressively adapting the methods and scheme of Sens and St.-Denis, they produced an export-style of greater church which found its way to Germany, to the Low Countries, to Spain, to Scandinavia, and to Cyprus in the eastern Mediterranean. Only Britain in the north-west, and Italy in the opposite direction remained little influenced by this evolution of the French cathedral. Without producing an effect of sameness, these great churches do conform very closely to one main type. Almost without exception they retain the plan of curving ambulatory and radiating chapels; a plan broad in proportion to its length, often with double aisles; transepts very short or even non-existent; and a main western front with three doorways below and a rose-window between twin towers above. The transeptal fronts often aimed at an importance nearly equal to that of the main front, and were similarly flanked by towers. On the other hand, a central tower was almost unknown in France proper, though frequent in Normandy and Flanders, as well as across the Channel.

Aesthetically, though these French churches were moving towards a new unity of articulated structure and of contained space, they were still far from achieving it. Every part still breathed memories of the Romanesque, and even the Classic: the heavy piers with attached shafts, the round columns with Attic bases and Corinthian capitals, horizontal string-courses and entablatures, bulbous mouldings. From all this top-hamper both France and England were to break free almost simultaneously, near the end of the twelfth century. So long as these details survived, the result remained unsatisfactory, as a mongrel must be. Each of these early, transitional Gothic monuments refuses to satisfy; confronted with a mass of unresolved problems, the mind is made restless and finds fault with the details piecemeal.

We shall deal with the English solution later; the first French cathedrals of the fuller Gothic were Bourges, begun about 1192 (**47, 48, 54**), and Chartres, rebuilt after a fire of 1194 (**35, 40**). The solution of Chartres, though the later, was much the less radical. A new form of compound pier was produced which cloaked the Corinthian column in a series of attached shafts, but did little to disguise its pedigree. The internal bay design was cut into horizontal layers by string-courses carried round the vertical shafts. That these defects pass unnoticed is mainly due to the supreme beauty of the windows of painted glass, and their almost perfect condition. The interior world of coloured light far outweighs in importance the material framework which allows it to exist. Strangely, it was this Chartres design which formed the basis for the somewhat later cathedrals of Reims and Amiens, the classics of their age. This is the more surprising, in that at Mantes, only a few miles away, the collegiate church had reached a more satisfying scheme a few years before the new work at Chartres was begun.

At Mantes, however, it was only the alternate piers that provided the solution of the future: multiple shafting from base to springing. Intermediately were Corinthianesque columns, and overhead were the old sexpartite vaults, covering square bays each equivalent to two bays in the side aisles. Still retaining the sexpartite vaults, but in other respects making a more radical break with tradition, was Bourges (**48, 54**). The plan, with its great sweep of ambulatory, and projecting apses of small size, goes back to Notre-Dame at Paris and to Sens, and the lack of transepts to the original disposition at Senlis. But the treatment is entirely new.

48 BOURGES CATHEDRAL: looking east, *c.* 1192–1225.

49 SÉES CATHEDRAL: looking east; choir, *c.* 1270–94; nave earlier.

50 ST.-DENIS ABBEY: looking east, 1231–81. Designer *Pierre de Montreuil*.

51 BEAUVAIS CATHEDRAL: looking east, 1247–72. Designer possibly *Eudes de Montreuil*.

FRANCE

52 COLOGNE CATHEDRAL: looking east, 1248–.
Designer *Gerhard*.

53 REIMS CATHEDRAL: nave looking west; west end,
c. 1275–85. Designer *Bernard de Soissons*.

CLASSIC GOTHIC

The cathedral is wholly interior. Of course, the inside of Christian churches had always outweighed the outside in importance, and the massive walls of earlier times had simply kept the despised (yet feared) outer world at bay.

But the new ideal was to make the whole church a thing of beauty, though concentrating study upon the problems of the internal arrangement. Gothic art, more than that of any other period in the West, was a search for unity, and the very complication of the traditional church arrangements made this search a difficult one. The provision of altars, aisles for processions or pilgrimages, and choir for the clergy in their conduct of the regular services, tended rather to serial treatment of a group of parts, interdependent but not united. The architect of Bourges, with a most brilliantly original conception, changed all that. By boldly suppressing the transept, he threw all the available space into one; and to prevent the arcades from interfering with this effect, he enormously increased their height and the attenuation of the supporting piers. The height of the piers was still further accentuated by surrounding them with eight very slender shafts, and by setting them upon low bases of new and graceful form. From the grand conception down to the smallest details everything was worked out afresh; Bourges is the first French work of pure Gothic.

As at the earlier Chartres, where we know only the name of the *artifex*, Roger, at Bourges a certain Giraldus left his name on the Porte de St.-Ursin of the west front, and we can probably identify him with the Girardus de Cornossa, named in 1224 as master of the images (*magister simulacrorum*); at the same date one Martin was the mason (*laptomus*). Whether one of these men was the actual architect is still uncertain. At the end of the thirteenth century other sculptors left their signatures: Aguillon de Droues carved the History of Noah on the jambs of the great central doorway of the west front, and one Niciel seems to have worked on the lateral porches. But even on the threshold of the thirteenth century the age of anonymity begins to pass away; historical records of individuals at last become sufficient to give some insight, at first only fitful, into the personalities behind style, and the links connecting building with building, workshop with workshop, over wide areas.

54 Bourges Cathedral: section, 1192–1218.

A separate Norman advance into Gothic was being made about 1200 at Caen, where the new choir of the Abbey Church of St.-Étienne was built by Master William. His tombstone tells of his pre-eminent skill in stonework: *"Guillelmus jacet hic petrarum summus in arte, iste novum perfecit opus."* His choir is as truly Gothic in a different manner as Bourges; here are compound piers made up of slender shafts of different sizes, and pierced spandrels of geometrical foils. His contemporary and fellow-countryman, Jean d'Andely, was beginning the nave of Rouen Cathedral at much the same time, *c.* 1201, and adopted similar piers, with even greater vertical emphasis on the main vaulting-shafts. At this time Normandy was still attached to England, but in 1204 it was lost by King John to Philip Augustus of France. Thenceforward for a century and a half the French Kings were to make a triumphal progress, acquiring one by one the great fiefs, and turning their kingdom from a nominal entity into a great power. The supreme triumphs of the northern French Gothic, the style of the cathedrals, royal palaces, chapels and castles, followed and expressed this political unification in the sphere of art.

A chain of French cathedrals stretched out across the north to Dol in Brittany, where work began about 1204; Mont-St.-Michel's marvellous fortress-monastery was building from 1203 onwards; a new choir was built at Bayeux Cathedral from about 1230. But before then there had been other notable results of the incursion of France into the erstwhile English provinces. The choir of Le Mans Cathedral was built between 1217 and 1254, in part at least by the Norman mason, Thomas Tostain, and in a style based on Bourges, yet incorporating valuable features from the Ile-de-France and Normandy (**55**). Its great achievement is the abandonment of the triforium, the logical outcome of the raising of the main arcade initiated at Bourges. Between 1220 and 1250 or thereabouts the whole cathedral of Coutances was built, especially noteworthy for its Norman insistence on a central tower in addition to the twin western towers with their spires (**29, 141**). As a work substantially of one generation, Coutances is almost

55   Le Mans Cathedral: internal elevation
and section, 1217–54.

unique among the greater Gothic churches, and it is also singular as a work of pure architecture; unlike its great contemporaries at Reims, Amiens and Beauvais, it owes practically nothing to statuary and enrichment, very little even to carving. As at Le Mans, there is no triforium, though its elimination is less complete. Of the noble central tower, known as Le Plomb, the seventeenth-century engineer, Vauban, enquired: "Who was the sublime madman who dared launch such a monument in the air?" We still do not know.

During the half-century the west front and towers of Notre-Dame at Paris were built from the ground to completion; the portals and gallery of kings between 1200 and 1220; the upper stage with the great rose in the next five years, and the towers in the twenty-five years from 1225, the southern being finished first. The front is of great geometrical regularity, being designed within a perfect square, and in spite of the long duration of the works it is clear that an original design was followed throughout. M. Marcel Aubert has shown that this design had been derived, along with those of its predecessors in the Ile-de-France and Champagne, from the Norman fronts of the great abbeys at Caen. Of all the early Gothic fronts that of Paris is the finest composition, the most striking example of the power of calculated design. There can be little question that the designer was the original architect of Notre-Dame, whose first stone was laid in 1163; and this architect should be the Ricardus *cementarius* who appears in the very next year as witness to a charter emanating from the bishop's chancery. The main work occupied three generations; after this were added the important transeptal fronts by Jean de Chelles between 1250 and 1270, and the chapels of the choir by Pierre de Chelles and Jean Ravy between 1296 and 1325. The upper part of the south front was completed after the death of Jean de Chelles (between 1258 and 1265) by the famous Pierre de Montreuil, architect of the refectory and Lady Chapel of St.-Germain-des-Prés and of the new nave of St.-Denis (50).

From Paris and Chartres we proceed to the most famous of French cathedrals, and in certain respects the most influential: Reims, the coronation church of the French Kings; Amiens, and Beauvais. The building dates and names of the first two were admirably recorded within the processional mazes laid out in the naves after their completion, though there are gaps in the information that has reached us. The chevet of Reims was begun by Jean d'Orbais in 1211, and the choir was finished by 1241. The works were continued by Jean le Loup and Gaucher de Reims c.1230–54, while the main part of the west front, including the great rose window, was built by Bernard de Soissons over a period of thirty-five years, from about 1255 to 1290. The towers were begun by Robert de Coucy, who died in 1311, but did not reach their present unfinished height until 1427. During the works on the choir the cathedral was visited by Villard de Honnecourt, who drew details and especially admired the windows with their early bar-tracery. Many other wandering architects must have taken away with them drawings or memories of these windows, which were the prime source for the future development of Gothic tracery of all forms. Another detail at Reims, less famous, but equally of future importance, is the decorative panelling inside the west wall, entirely made up of rectangular niches with trefoil-cusped heads, and intervening rows of squares carved with naturalistic leaves (42, 53). As panelling this points the way to all the surface decoration of later work, and in particular to the Perpendicular idea only fulfilled in England. This panelling was certainly designed by Bernard de Soissons, and Dr. Pevsner, who has emphasized the importance of the naturalistic leaf-carving, dates this work at about 1275–85.

At Reims, besides the cathedral, was the Church of St.-Nicaise, begun in 1229 by Hugues Libergiers, who died in 1263, and whose monument survives. The drawings of the "Reims Palimpsest" are quite probably by Libergiers himself or one of his associates (11).

At Amiens, the building began with the nave, under Robert de Luzarches, from 1220 to 1236, when the front was complete to the top of the rose window. The chevet chapels followed, c.1236–47, and the completion of the choir, after a pause, in the period c.1258–70. The transepts completed the main work by 1288. The eastern chapels seem to have been the work of Thomas de Cormont, the second master, and all the rest that of his son Regnault, who is mentioned in a deed of 1260, and was in charge to the end. The gallery above the great rose was vaulted, and the south tower built by Pierre Largent after 1366; and the north tower finished c. 1400–20 by Colard Brisset. Amiens stands as the model of a classic French cathedral; perhaps too much the perfect exemplar to be a sympathetic building, too proud to inspire the warmth which should be felt within a church; yet for all that unquestionably one of the greatest of man's symphonies in stone (41).

Even before the start of Reims, the capital of Champagne, Troyes, had begun work on its cathedral in 1208. Unfortunately, work proceeded slowly, and with many setbacks, and the choir and transepts were not completely finished until about 1316 (43). At the end of the thirteenth century, when the eastern arm was nearing completion, and the nave in progress, the master was one Henri; the name of the first architect is unknown. Maître Henri's work bears some striking resemblances to the contemporary nave of York Minster, and even closer likenesses between the aisle triforium of the Le Mans chevet and contemporary work at

Worcester and Lincoln Cathedrals have suggested to Mr. C. M. Girdlestone that the same master worked on both sides of the Channel. A more probable explanation is that English masons during their wander-years worked at some of the greater lodges on the Continent; this was almost certainly so with Master Henry "de Reyns" (probably Reims), the English chief architect of Westminster Abbey from 1245, and may have been so with Master Alexander, designer of the Worcester presbytery and Lincoln nave and chapter-house (the identity of the two Alexanders is all but certain), and Master Simon who had charge of the work at York around 1300.

The influences, however carried, were being widely diffused. We shall see shortly how the perfected type of cathedral, deriving from Reims and Amiens, was spread first through France and then across Europe. But during the progress of Reims, Amiens and Troyes a new influence entered the scene: the attenuation of supports and the replacement of walls by glass; and the introduction of skeleton construction and transparencies. It is difficult to be certain as to the first evidence of this new departure; the "transparency" produced by glazing the triforium and building a second, empty tracery plane within, was achieved both at the new nave of St.-Denis (**50**) and in the chevet of Troyes. The latter, as we have seen, was begun in 1208, but the triforium can hardly have been begun before 1228, and the date of 1240 assigned for the completion of the high choir is extremely uncertain. On the other hand, the high choir at St.-Denis was rebuilt from 1231 under the King's mason Pierre de Montreuil, though the nave was not finished until 1281, fourteen years after his death. Certainly the designer of the destroyed Lady Chapel of St.-Germain-des-Prés, and probably of the Chapels Royal at St.-Germain-en-Laye and the Ste.-Chapelle of Paris, Montreuil certainly had a particular love for enlarged window-area and for transparencies. M. Aubert finds these characteristics precisely in those parts of Notre-Dame which he completed shortly before his death, in details where he abandoned the design of Jean de Chelles; they recur at the nave of St.-Denis; and in after times underlie much of the finer detail of late Gothic.

One of Montreuil's favourite usages was the employment of a very tall slender shaft detached from the wall-surface; such occur supporting his flying buttresses at St.-Denis, and just one of the same form is at Notre-Dame. He may have derived the idea from the west front of Coutances, where three such shafts run the whole height of the south-west tower to the roof level, and others run in front of the stair-turrets of both spires. These shafts pass vertically in front of the staircase window openings, producing the transparency effect (**141**). The notion was still further developed by Montreuil to give cohesion to superimposed stages: the triforium and clerestory at St.-Denis are internally linked by shafts forming the innermost member of the mullions; and the same thing is done in his work on the south transept front of Notre-Dame, both inside and out. This design must be earlier than his death in 1267, and may go back some twenty years to his earliest recorded connexion with the work at St.-Denis. It is thus fairly certain that it precedes the pierced triforium and "long-panel" design at Amiens, which belongs to the work of Regnault de Cormont after 1258.

The Ste.-Chapelle, with its closely related but more developed imitation, the Lady Chapel at St.-Germer of 1259–66, stands at the beginning of a new phase of development, that of the glass-house church (**59**). Innumerable chapels built for royalty and noble families, isolated or projecting Lady Chapels, and especially in England, college chapels, followed this precedent. It is even possible that at least one cathedral, that of Albi, owes a good deal to this source. Fortunately there are precise dates for this vital design: it was projected in 1243, and consecrated five years later. Its lessons had certainly been well learnt by the unknown architect*

* Jean Langlois, master of the work, was a clerical accountant.

of St.-Urbain at Troyes, whose choir was completed between 1263 and 1266, and shows the hall-marks of the new style: immense windows, verticality in shafting, work in double planes ("transparency"), and the long-panel design (**61**). It also carries a stage further the additional transparency effect of the decorative lateral gables of the Ste.-Chapelle, spanning from buttress to buttress and piercing the parapets. These gables appear also on the high choir of Amiens, in the work of *c.*1258–70. One of the best examples of the long-panel and transparency design is the choir of Sées Cathedral (*c.* 1270–1300) (**49**).

The supreme attempt of High Gothic in France was the Cathedral of Beauvais, whose choir was built between 1247 and 1272 (**51, 57**). There is a tradition that the designer was Eudes de Montreuil, favourite architect and travelling companion of St. Louis, and possibly son of Pierre. Eudes certainly designed a number of

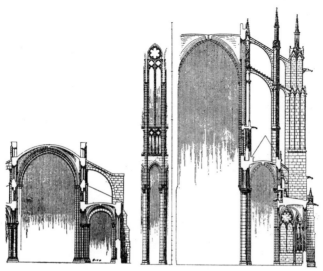

56 Sens, *c.* 1150.   **57** Beauvais, *c.* 1250.
Gothic aspiration, potential and achieved.

churches in Paris in his later life, and did not die until 1287. He was already active in 1248, when he travelled with the King to Cyprus and Palestine, where in 1250 he had charge of the fortifications of Jaffa. St. Louis had hoped to take Cairo, and build a cathedral there, and the completion of the great Church of Nicosia in Cyprus was the actual outcome (**36, 39**). This is a building of modest size, with simple round columns; apart from sharing the conventional plan of the Ile-de-France cathedrals it can hardly deserve comparison with them. On the other hand, it is quite possible that the visionary project of Beauvais, which was to surpass all other Christian churches in size, originated in the brain of a young man, brought up among the tracing boards and masons' lodges of the French cathedrals, and still too inexperienced to realize the impracticability of his dreams. At least the tradition of Eudes' responsibility has no inherent improbability, and deserves careful research. At any rate, the vaults fell from their height of 158 feet, and before they could be restored the design had to be profoundly modified by the building of intermediate piers in each bay. The fall took place in 1284, and the restoration lasted until about 1324, under the master mason Guillaume de Roye and his assistant Aubert d'Aubigny. The building of the transept and the abortive tower and spire, in the sixteenth century, belong to a later chapter.

Nothing as great as Beauvais was ever again attempted in France. But at

Cologne on the Rhine, one year after Beauvais, the foundation stone of a rival cathedral was laid in 1248. Though only completed in the nineteenth century, Cologne does preserve its mediaeval design, and shows the limit of what is possible in towering height (**52**). Its vaults rise to 150 feet, not appreciably short of Beauvais. There is no doubt that Master Gerard its designer was well acquainted with both Beauvais and Amiens on parchment or paper, and adopted details from both in the course of his work. In spite of its unfinished state during the Middle Ages, the designs for Cologne acted as important disseminators of the French cathedral throughout the Germanic area. In the second half of the fourteenth century the master, Michael, was closely related to Peter Parler who was invited from Schwäbisch-Gmünd to Prague to complete St. Vitus' Cathedral.

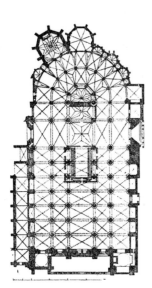

58 Toledo Cathedral, 1227–, plan by Master Martin.

Cologne is 250 miles from Paris as the crow flies; Clermont-Ferrand in Auvergne is very nearly as far. And it was in the same year that Clermont began its cathedral in the new northern style. In 1248 Maître Jean des Champs, a mason fresh from the building of the Ste.-Chapelle, travelled South to Clermont, taking with him sufficient drawings and notes to enable him to build a church on the model of Amiens, with certain modifications introduced from the plan of Reims and from the latest works in progress (**62, 74**). The works went on very slowly, but Maître des Champs cannot have been idle. For some twenty years we do not know what other works he may have conducted in central France; then quite suddenly he became the prime mover in a great artistic movement. It is possible that he had had something to do with the carrying of the Court style to the western Pyrenees, where the chevet of Bayonne Cathedral was founded about 1258. But Bayonne is more closely related to the work of a certain Maître Henri at Burgos and León in Spain. It is certain that Des Champs designed the Cathedral at Narbonne, the great metropolis of the middle South, begun in 1272, and where he was actually at work in 1286 (**30, 75**). Certain again is his connexion with Rodez Cathedral, where work started in 1277 (**77**). Two other cathedrals must certainly be credited to him on stylistic grounds: the new choir of Toulouse, begun in 1272, and Limoges, laid out a year later (**64**). His share in Albi, an astonishing brick structure with quite other relationships, begun in 1282, has been suggested, but is far from being proved. One other building of the new art in the South must here be mentioned: the new choir of St.-Nazaire at Carcassonne, begun in 1269 and not finished until c.1300 (**65**). At least the designs for this work had been seen by Jean des Champs when he made the plan for the chevet of Narbonne in 1272, as M. Émile Mâle has pointed out.

Before this time an earlier wave of French Gothic had reached the Peninsula, where the Cathedrals of Burgos, begun 1221, Toledo (1227–) and León (c.1250–) were all on French plans, and probably designed in the first instance by French architects. Burgos has considerable resemblances to Bourges and Le Mans, and to Norman works, notably Coutances; Toledo's plan is close to that of Paris and Bourges, and there are again links with Le Mans (**58, 71**). The first master at Toledo was named Martin; he appears in 1227, the year of foundation, and again in 1234; he was succeeded by "Petrus Petri", now generally considered to be a Spaniard, Pedro Pérez, who died in 1291. León very closely follows the plan and scheme of Reims (**70**), and its first architect was Enrique (perhaps Henri), who also

59　PARIS:　Ste.-Chapelle,　1243–48.
Designer probably *Pierre de Montreuil*.

60　CELLES-SUR-BELLE: Abbey
Church, fifteenth century.

61　TROYES: St.-Urbain, from the south-east, 1263–66.

FRANCE: LIGHT AND SPACE

62 CLERMONT-FERRAND CATHEDRAL: looking east, 1248–1325. Designers *Jean* and *Pierre des Champs*.

63 UPPSALA CATHEDRAL: looking east, *c.* 1270–1315. Designer *Étienne de Bonneuil*.

64 LIMOGES CATHEDRAL: looking east, 1273–1327. Designer *Jean des Champs*.

65 CARCASSONNE, ST.-NAZAIRE: transept, 1269–1300.

GOTHIC DIFFUSION

66 TOLEDO: cloister of San Juan de los Reyes, 1476–, by *Juan Guas*.

67 LAS HUELGAS: conventual church, 1180–1203. Designer *Ricardo*.

68 SANTES CREUS: south-east corner of cloister, 1331–41. Designer *Raynard Fonoyll*.

69 LAS HUELGAS: chapter house, *c*. 1200; by *Ricardo*.

71 TOLEDO CATHEDRAL: interior of transept, 1227–.
Designer *Martin*.

70 LEÓN CATHEDRAL: interior looking east, *c.* 1250–1303.
Designer *Enrique*.

SPANISH CATHEDRALS

continued the works of Burgos and died there in 1277. Mr. Bernard Bevan suggests that Enrique was responsible for the transept fronts of Burgos, which much resemble those at Reims. Both at Burgos and at León, Enrique was succeeded by Juan Pérez. The first architect of Burgos Cathedral is unknown, but he learnt much from the Cistercian Convent of Las Huelgas close to the city, built in 1180–1203 (**67, 69**). This was founded by Alfonso VIII and his Queen Eleanor, daughter of Henry II Plantagenet. Street remarked upon the close English and Angevin affinities of Las Huelgas, and Señor Julio Gonsalez has recently shown that the architect was a foreigner. In 1203 the King made a grant of property to the master, Ricardo, his wife Alda and their sons and daughters. This proves that the grantee was a lay craftsman, but more than this, the name Ricardo in Spain before 1230 invariably indicates an Englishman or an Angevin. This Maestro Ricardo was still living near Burgos in 1226.

French influences penetrated into Italy as early as to Spain or even earlier, but at first through Cistercian channels. At S. Andrea at Vercelli in Piedmont a French canon, Thomas from St.-Victor at Paris, was in charge of building the church between 1209 and 1221. But the most striking French influences were in such friary churches as San Francesco in Bologna, begun in 1236 and finished by 1260 (**104**), and those of the Frari begun 1250, and of SS. Giovanni e Paolo begun in 1260 in Venice (**102**); apart, that is, from the work of French architects in the South. These travelled in two waves, the first attracted to the magnificent court of the Emperor Frederick II, especially in the period 1230 to 1250. The chief of Frederick's French masons was Philippe Chénard, said to have been brought by the Emperor from Cyprus. Cathedrals at Cosenza and Lecce in Calabria and Apulia respectively, and a number of castles, are works of transplanted French Gothic belonging to the first half of the thirteenth century, chiefly modelled on the school of Champagne. The second wave of craftsmen followed Charles of Anjou, the son of St. Louis who became King of the Two Sicilies in 1266. At least four masters are known by name: Pierre d'Angicourt, Geoffroy de Bois-Guillaume, Pierre de Chaulnes, and another Pierre who had charge of work at the Church of St.-Maximin in Provence in 1295. To this period belonged San Lorenzo and other churches in Naples, San Francesco in Messina, and the Cathedral of Lucera in Apulia.

In the North, the artistic province of Parisian France merged imperceptibly into Flanders and the Netherlands. In going farther from Paris, more and more German influences are found, reaching a maximum in the north-eastern provinces of present-day Holland, which have always been a part of the northern coastal region of Germany. At the opening of the Gothic period, Rhenish influence was very strong as far as the Belgian coast, and even into France itself. The early plan with apsidal transepts, found in the Gothic Noyon and Soissons, derives in this region from the Cathedral of Tournai. Gothic versions of this plan in the Low Countries occurred at Valenciennes, *c.*1160–80, and at Cambrai Cathedral. Cambrai had a splendid Gothic choir with full chevet added between 1230 and 1250, possibly by Villard de Honnecourt himself. His position was probably that of chief master of the collegiate Church of St.-Quentin, whose choir was consecrated in 1257 in the presence of St. Louis himself. St.-Quentin and Cambrai had single western towers, a peculiarity often found in these provinces, and across the whole of the North to the head of the Baltic. It was later brought to perfection at Utrecht in the fourteenth, and at Malines in the fifteenth century.

The early thirteenth century saw the beginning of many greater churches of French plan, or following the French model. The greater churches which form perfect examples of the High Gothic sanctuary include St.-Gudule at Brussels, begun in 1220 (**72**), St.-Martin at Ypres, started in the following year, Notre-Dame at Bruges (1239–97) and the choir of Tournai Cathedral, built between 1242 and

1325. In Holland the choir of Utrecht was begun in 1254 and completed in thirteen years, and another thirteenth-century chevet was built at St. Servais in Maastricht. The choir of St.-Bavon, Ghent, is another example on a large scale, dating from 1274–1300. The French cathedral plan remained throughout the Middle Ages the dominant form in the Netherlands, and in some cases at least was introduced by imported masters such as the Nicolas de Soissons who directed the works of Liège Cathedral from 1281. The church was destroyed in the French Revolution, like those at Arras, Cambrai, and Valenciennes. The great Cathedrals of Malines, begun 1341, and Antwerp, 1352–1411 by Jean Amel of Boulogne, continue the tradition in Belgium, and in Holland even later it presided over the rebuilding of the choir of sHertogenbosch in 1419–39, St. Stephen at Nymwegen, begun 1456, and other churches such as Our Lady's of Breda, St.-Bavon, Haarlem, and Our Lady's in Dortrecht. Among the smaller Belgian churches built in French style is Notre-Dame de Pamele near Oudenarde, begun in 1235 by the Hainault mason,

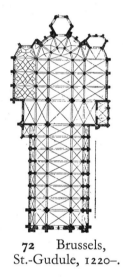 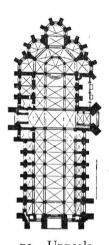

72   Brussels,
St.-Gudule, 1220–.

73   Uppsala,
c. 1273–1315, by
Étienne de Bonneuil.

Arnoul de Binche. This shows the Belgian triple lancets, so like contemporary English work. Later developments in the area of greater Flanders belong to the story of the national styles. In Scandinavia the one outstanding example of the French cathedral was at Uppsala in Sweden, and this was due to the direct importation from Paris of Étienne de Bonneuil in 1287, with a number of assistants, to carry out the work (63, 73).

The last and most romantic of the missions which carried the French cathedrals across Europe was that of Maître Mathieu d'Arras, called from Avignon in 1344 to design the new Cathedral of Prague for the Emperor Charles IV (76, 110, 186, 266). Charles, son of John of Luxemburg, the blind King of Bohemia who died at Crécy in 1346, was educated in France and had married a French princess. Regent of Bohemia during his father's life, he successfully negotiated with Pope Clement VI for the erection of Prague into an archbishopric. Maître Mathieu, who was evidently of northern origin, must have been attracted to Avignon by the great works of the Papal Palace, as were so many other artists and craftsmen. He equipped himself with plans of French cathedrals of suitably up-to-date type, notably those of Narbonne and Rodez (77, 243). During the eight years between his arrival at Prague and his death in 1352 he was able to complete the five radiating chapels of the chevet, and four more chapels to the west. As first architect, his bust appears in the triforium next to that of his German successor, Peter Parler (**22**), and in series with those of the Emperors, Archbishops and clerics who had control of the works.

The story of French Gothic art was very far from the end; but the building of Prague was the end of the story begun at Sens two centuries before. Gothic

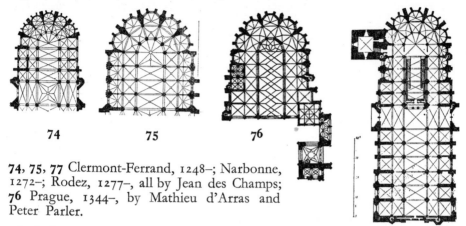

74, 75, 77 Clermont-Ferrand, 1248–; Narbonne, 1272–; Rodez, 1277–, all by Jean des Champs; **76** Prague, 1344–, by Mathieu d'Arras and Peter Parler.

cathedrals there would still be, some to be completed, others even to be begun; but they would have another lineage. While a French master was setting out foundations in Bohemia, the Bohemian King was dying on the field of Crécy; and with him not only the hopes of France, but of the international High Gothic of the French Royal Domain.

VI

Gothic in the British Isles

IT has earlier been remarked that the union of Gothic elements took place in England independently of developments in France. To speak of independence would be misleading without the qualification, already emphasized, that all Gothic art springs from a common source in the new European society of the late eleventh and early twelfth centuries. As we have seen, the new society was largely dominated by the vigour and enterprise of the Norman dynasties, who held strategic positions well distributed across the area of western life. It is not without significance that the one country which retained, more or less permanently, the Norman stamp should be England. Unlike Sicily, where the earlier traditions were incompatible, England was not merely an island, but an island with a single dominant culture closely related to that of the Normans themselves. Though London could not compete with Paris as a centre of intellectual life, its mercantile importance was far greater. Even in the Saxon period, London was the richest city of the North.

Immense prestige belonged to the King of England; and it was for this prestige that the Norman dukes endangered and finally lost their homeland. And because of this same prestige the elements of the new art found a more congenial soil in England than they did in Normandy. It is commonly forgotten that by the time the greatest Norman churches were built, in the Romanesque style, the true centre of Normandy had become London. Norman kings had reigned for more than a generation, and owing to the statesmanship of the Conqueror, their hold on England was much tighter than that they exercised across the Channel. In consequence of this the English Norman architecture greatly outweighed in importance the continental output. In the first place, there is the vast number of Norman foundations in England; in the second, their individual size. It was long ago pointed out by Professor Prior that the Abbaye-aux-Hommes at Caen covered less than half the area of such Anglo-Norman churches as Winchester Cathedral, St. Paul's in London, and Bury St. Edmunds. Only Cluny among the very largest Romanesque churches abroad: Spires, St.-Martin at Tours and St.-Sernin, Toulouse, could barely equal Bury. It is unquestionable that in the year 1100 there were in England both greater buildings, and more of them, in progress than anywhere else.

To build on such a vast scale, in a country which had previously known no large-scale structures, implied a technical revolution. We can still see the importance of the change at such buildings as Winchester Cathedral, where early and later Norman work stand side by side. Fifteen years before the end of the eleventh century all masonry is of the crude, wide-jointed variety, incapable of refinements. Fifteen years after 1100, and William of Malmesbury was amazed to see "stone being so correctly laid that the joint deceives the eye, and leads it to imagine that the whole wall is composed of a single block". So closely did the cultural and the technical revolutions go together, that it has been possible to suggest that the material improvements in technology were responsible for the awakened spirit which gave them birth. We must make no such mistake. Design precedes execution, and William Rufus's great hall at Westminster fell so far short of his imagination that he said it was fit only to be the kitchen for the hall he meant to build.

The main building technique in Saxon England had been carpentry, as for centuries it continued to be in Scandinavia. Saxon masons had not the ability to build the great minsters and halls required by the Norman Church and Court. Hence skilled craftsmen were imported from Normandy, and it took England a century to reach technical independence. Thus the continental masons could use England as a workshop and even laboratory, and then return with the knowledge gained from their large-scale experiments. Besides, owing to the mixed following of the Conqueror, and to his own marriage with the daughter of the Count of Flanders, the craftsmen were Picard and Fleming as well as Norman. So when the demand for the new Gothic art arose in and close to Paris, a high proportion of the masters attracted to the French Court, to Sens, St.-Denis and Chartres, had acquired their skill in or from England. And it is recognized by French anti-quaries that as late as the building of Notre-Dame in Paris between 1163 and 1196, design adhered largely to the Anglo-Norman school. In 1153 English glass-painters produced the coloured windows of the Abbey of Braine-le-Comte in Hainault.

Not all the continental masters who worked in England can have returned to their homes; some of them were rewarded with grants of land in England, and set up new homes here. It did not take them long to become, in the persons of their partly Saxon children and grandchildren, the thoroughly acclimatized leaders of a national art. For, much as English Gothic was to owe to France, it had from the beginning its own distinct spirit, which was to develop quite apart. A sharply linear quality, shown in the length of the greater English churches as well as in all the details of carving, painting and decorative work, is the keynote of this separate idiom. We may suspect the far-off influence of those linear patterns which were so deeply rooted in the art of early Britain that they survived four centuries of Roman occupation and sprang into new life in Saxon times. Again, though foreign masons had to be imported under the Normans, there were Saxon carpenters, and throughout the Gothic period England was to excel in her timberwork. The wooden roofs and vaults of English churches and halls were not the negative outcome of caution or incapacity, but the expression of a positive preference for the native material and method.

English mediaeval art is therefore dominated as much by the carpenter as by the mason-architect. In the twelfth and thirteenth centuries the term "engineer" certainly covered many men with both crafts at their finger-tips, and until the time of Henry VIII carpenters shared with masons the topmost places in the artistic hierarchy. It is indeed a fallacy to suppose that timber constructions are notably less durable than those of stone; while it is true that stone walls sometimes survive the burning of timber roofs, other roofs have been dismantled and re-erected, outlasting the walls first built to receive them. Carved screens and choir-stalls exist in plenty from churches otherwise totally destroyed. Stone decay can be as severe as the effects of beetle or fungus, and while much of the oak roof of Westminster Hall is still the work of 1394–99, in spite of the death-watch and the incendiary bomb, almost the whole of the masonry has been renewed. The English use of timber differs from the French preference for stone; but its results are in no way inferior. Moreover, the appearance of the English buildings bene-fited enormously from their at least relative lack of flying buttresses.

The course of Gothic development in England and in France presents at first sight a series of curious discrepancies. At one time France, at another England, is seen to be leading the fashion. England, which at Durham in the first quarter of the twelfth century had reached the synthesis which gave rise to the new architecture, then took a retrograde step. For two generations more our buildings remained Romanesque, apart from isolated introductions of the pointed arch at Cistercian monasteries. Meanwhile France was producing the matured architecture which might have been expected to arise from Durham. Next, the palm passed to England when, in the last decade of the century at Wells and at Lincoln she produced the first architecture which wholly rejected the old arrangements and forms. In a few years it was once more France that led the way with the bar-tracery of Reims and the first glass-house architecture of St. Louis's Sainte-Chapelle at Paris. This was to be dominant until nearly the end of the thirteenth century, when England rapidly forged ahead with its whole-hearted acceptance of the ogee curve. The resulting English Curvilinear style invaded France, and became by virtue (or vice?) of French logic Flamboyant, when England had abandoned curves for the insular right lines of Perpendicular.

This long ding-dong battle of the styles reflected, a few years late, the political fortunes of the two countries. The early achievements at Durham sprang from the strong rule of William the Conqueror. But at the crucial period, 1135–40, the Norman realm was dissolving into anarchy, while the France of Louis VII was increasing its prestige. Between 1154 and 1180 the Angevin Henry II had built up the strongest empire the West had seen since the days of Charlemagne; and during those very years England saw its first tentative works of Gothic: the new Church of Ripon and the nave of Worcester Cathedral. A few years after Henry's death, while England was in fact poised on the brink of decline, the full harvest of the first Gothic was reaped. The ensuing French advance reflected the conquests and unification of Philip II Augustus; the similar work done for England a century later by Edward I had its results in the rapid advancement of the Decorated style into its Curvilinear phase, beginning with the Eleanor Crosses and such great churches as Holy Trinity, Hull, and the Greyfriars of London. English invasion of France under Edward III, and simultaneous fostering of the Netherlands, led to a pause in French development, and to a growing dependence of France upon Flemish artists.

At the opening of the Gothic period in England, it is perhaps significant that at Ripon the one mason known from the documents should bear the British name of Arthur. Moreover, throughout the reign of Henry II the King's chief engineer, mentioned yearly on the Pipe Rolls, was the Saxon Ailnoth. The fact that there were by this time English masters of the first rank is again shown at Canterbury. Although the Frenchman, William of Sens, was brought in to design the new choir in 1174, his English assistant was able, only three years later, to take over the work, and to continue it in a more advanced Gothic style than that adopted by the foreigner. But even so, this Canterbury of French inspiration was only half Gothic; it still retained the massive wall surfaces and solid, Corinthianesque piers of Romanesque. Quite as early as Canterbury, it may even be earlier, was the western nave of Worcester Cathedral, which made a close approach to the new aesthetic, and foreshadowed both verticality and the clustered Gothic pier. Finally, while the work at Canterbury was in progress, and quite uninfluenced by it, an unknown but certainly English master at Wells had produced the first design in the world to rank as pure Gothic.

The complete substitution of pointed for round arches, their acute points and the steep pitch of the vaults, the perfected clustered piers and refined mouldings, all are entirely of the new world. Lastly, the carving marks if possible an even greater advance from the conventions of the Romanesque and the stiffly archaic productions of contemporary France. Regarded simply as examples of the Gothic spirit, there is no comparison between the sculptures of Chartres, splendid as they are, and the foliage capitals of Wells, with their abundance of humour and incident (**78, 79**). Setting aside the major figures, which have no counter-part in the first work at Wells, the foliage and minor scenes at Chartres are, relatively speaking, lifeless. At Wells, every single capital, eight to a pier, well over two hundred altogether, besides corbel-heads and bosses, is a most brilliant improvisation, exquisite both in conception and execution. The Wells master

78, 79 WELLS CATHEDRAL: details from the work of 1192–1206.

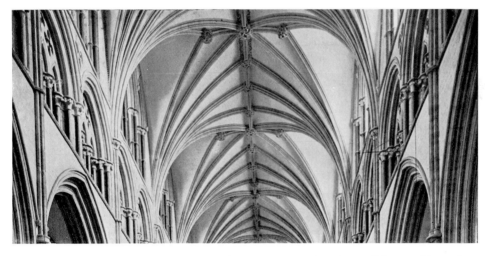

80 LINCOLN CATHEDRAL: nave vault, *c.* 1230–35. Designer *Master Alexander.*

81 WELLS CATHEDRAL: vault of Lady Chapel, *c.* 1310–19.

ENGLISH DETAIL

82 WALBERSWICK CHURCH: tower 1426–
50, by *Richard Russell* and *Adam Powle*.
Photo. *c.* 1896.

83 KESSINGLAND CHURCH: tower, *c.*
1430–54. Note change of pattern in
second stage of buttress.

ENGLAND: TOWER DESIGN

himself must be responsible for the best of them. These carvings are one of the supreme miracles of Gothic art.

After Wells followed the first Gothic Lincoln of St. Hugh. This was distinctly affected by Canterbury and by developments in south-eastern England under French influence, but at Lincoln again the actual result was triumphantly English, and purely Gothic. Geoffrey de Noiers, the master of the work, and Richard the mason, were responsible. In some ways of greater significance was the second major work at Lincoln, between 1220 and 1250, under Master Alexander. This included the nave, upper west front, galilee porch, chapter-house, and the lower stage of the central tower. On all this work is the stamp of a great personality, and there is little doubt that it was the same Alexander who was master for the choir at Worcester a little earlier. From Worcester's circular chapter-house he acquired the idea of the great polygonal venture at Lincoln, which was to be the unsurpassed standard for England. In the nave vault, with its truncated transverse ribs, he opened the way to an immense future (**80**). The enrichment of the Gothic vault to the reticulated and stellar patterns which it was to take in almost every country but France, and even there at last, owes its origin to the step taken by Master Alexander about 1230–35.

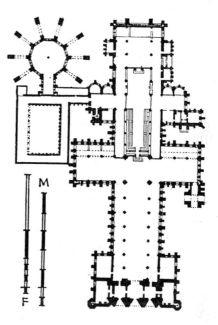

Roughly contemporary with the first work of Lincoln, and entirely different, is the west front of Peterborough, with its immense arches. Before its completion, another front, supreme in its own way, had been started at Wells. There the west wall of the church was made to spread across nave, aisles, and external towers, until it filled a great double square. Unlike the fronts of France, where the entrance doors were always emphasized, the porches at Wells are almost insignificant. The whole façade, designed by Master Adam Lock some years before his death in 1229, is one

84   Lincoln Cathedral, 1192–; plan by Masters Richard, Alexander, and Simon of Thirsk.

great gallery for sculpture from top to bottom. It is as though Lock had visited Chartres, Laon and Paris, perhaps even saw the drawings for Amiens, and then came back to design a radically new creation which should excel them, not simply as an architectural composition, but as an iconographical hoarding. The specifically English external towers beyond the aisles derived from the Norman old St. Paul's in London, possibly designed by Andrew the mason, who appears there in the second quarter of the twelfth century. The plan was followed at Peterborough, c. 1177, at St. Albans, c. 1195, and at Rouen Cathedral, begun by Jean d'Andely c. 1201, before the English were beaten out of Normandy by Philip Augustus. They occur also in the Cathedrals of Poitiers; León and Sigüenza in Spain; and Trondhjem in Norway.

Scarcely later than the beginning of the Wells front was the foundation of the new cathedral at Salisbury in 1220. The King's clerk, Elias of Derham, had much to do with the building, and probably collaborated in its design with the master mason Nicholas of Ely. In spite of imperfections of detail, unduly heavy horizontal mouldings and internally a wretchedly cramped triforium, Salisbury has great perfection in its proportions and stands as the examplar of a new English type of cathedral. Carving is abandoned: shafts and mouldings are left to tell their story by purity of line and admirable composition. The result, remarkable as it is, is too austere and cerebral; it is saved from insipidity by the fantastic addition in the next century of an enormous tower and spire. Salisbury shows in perfection the south-western type of English east front, where beyond the high gable of the presbytery is a cross aisle and Lady Chapel of less height. This type became universal in the one half of England, while in the north-east its place was taken by the high eastern gable, rising from the ground to its full height.

Both types of eastern termination agreed in being square, and this square-ended English plan goes back in the greater churches at least as far as the rebuilding of Old Sarum Cathedral, c. 1113–39. This is too early for it to be due to Cistercian influence, and it certainly springs from British tradition. This tradition was based on a demand for proper orientation, almost certainly of pagan origin, and a corresponding love of brilliant lighting of the High Altar. This lighting, denied by the French chevet, but secured by the great east windows of English churches, was reinforced by the provision of eastern transepts in line with the altar, a feature extremely rare abroad, though it occurs at St.-Quentin. The square presbytery was introduced at Lincoln after 1256, when the Angel Choir was built. Deriving its angels and certain other features from the new Francophil Westminster Abbey of Henry III and his Master Henry of Reyns (Reims?), the Angel Choir converts them to typically English guise. The designer was probably Master Simon of Thirsk. By the last quarter of the thirteenth century the greater English churches had acquired their main form. In sharp contrast to the French cathedral, they were long, not unduly tall, provided with transepts of strong projection, square east ends, central towers and spires (or the intention of spires). Their chief entrances were lateral, through elaborate porches such as those of Salisbury and Wells, while their west fronts became the opportunity for displays of virtuosity in design. The main tendency in these fronts was to develop a screenwork of niches for statues; later this was to become in some cases a low-level horizontal range of porches with tilted vaults, welcoming the passer-by.

The reign of Henry III encouraged all forms of art, and the King himself took an active part in devising iconographical schemes and in directing the royal works. He surrounded himself with artists of all kinds, to whom he extended most generous patronage, and it is largely to him that England owes the fulfilment of her early Gothic promise. A lover of beauty and no nationalist, though a stubborn defender of English rights, Henry imported French, Italian and Spanish artists on many occasions. There were at the same time no lack of opportunities for the preferment of the best English workers. The result was not only the production of an enormous body of work of the highest quality within a period of fifty years, but also a rapid assimilation of desirable foreign elements, and a rejection of forms incompatible with English practice. Though too much occupied with matters of state to equal his father as an art connoisseur, Edward I contributed very greatly to the development of English Gothic. This was less by way of direct patronage of artists (though he was responsible for the extraordinary series of Eleanor Crosses) than by his experiments in fortification and town-planning.

Returning from the Crusade with a wide knowledge of Levantine and Mediterranean buildings, and perhaps accompanied by foreign experts, Edward in 1274 set himself to the task of stabilizing and unifying England's administration. The whole of the later progress of English art towards unity, rested upon this fundamental work of Edward I. Specifically, such architects in Edward's service as Walter of Hereford, the designer of Caernarvon Castle, and probably inventor of the new type of great town church, were influential in spreading the latest ideas to the farthest parts of the country. Master Walter, for instance, travelled with his sovereign not only to Wales but to Edinburgh, built Edward's own foundation of Vale Royal Abbey, and for his second Queen brought masons to London to build the Church of the Greyfriars. At the same time he was architect in charge of Winchcombe Abbey, Gloucestershire, one of the chief western centres of architectural action.

Due to Edward's policy also were direct contacts with parts of Asia under Mongol control, notably Persia. The visits of Persian envoys to England, and of English expeditions to Persia, account for the sudden appearance in England about 1290 of the ogee curve, and of diaper patterns based on its use (**85**). It is also possible that the introduction early in the fourteenth century of the four-centred arch is due to observation of Persian originals. Knowledge of Persian domed and concentric buildings such as the mausoleum of Oljeitu at Sultaniya (1307-13) probably underlay the design of the octagon at Ely (1322) and the proposal to build a circular hall, 200 feet in diameter, for Edward III's Round Table at Windsor in 1344.

The spread of the ogee curve was very rapid in England, though it was scarcely used in France until towards the end of the fourteenth century. English ogees cannot with certainty be dated before 1291, and yet by 1331 or very soon after, at Gloucester and at St. Paul's in London, the Curvilinear motives based on the ogee were already giving place to rectangular and polygonal traceries. The west windows of York (glazed 1338) and Durham (*c.* 1341), and the east window of Carlisle Cathedral, perhaps designed before 1322, are the greatest achievements of English Curvilinear tracery. The enormous Perpendicular east window of Gloucester is not later than 1350. These rapid changes were mainly due to two families of masons: Michael of Canterbury who worked at Canterbury from about 1275 and was

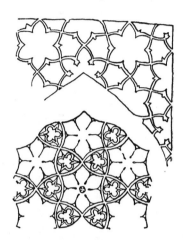

85 Diaper patterns: (*above*) Persian Mihrab, 14th century, Pennsylvania Museum; (*below*) Canterbury Cathedral, *c.* 1320.

settled in London by 1291, and his followers, Walter and Thomas of Canterbury; and the Ramsey family of Norwich, who migrated to London about 1320. The Canterbury's first made extensive use of the ogee and ogee-based diapers, and produced the so-called London type of canopied tomb; that of Edmund Crouchback, *c.* 1295-1300, was undoubtedly made by Master Michael (**87**). There is a close connexion between this work of Master Michael and certain monuments and decorative features in France, notably the south porch of St.-Jean-Baptiste at Chaumont in Champagne (**86**). There is no doubt that the English works were both earlier and, in using the ogee curve, more advanced in style. Within a few years Thomas of Canterbury was breaking up the undulating ogee patterns by introducing reversed cusps: thus forming a new, crystalline form of tracery known as Kentish. Master Michael of Canterbury was also master of the important St. Stephen's Chapel in Westminster Palace from 1292; Walter of Canterbury took up the work after a pause, *c.* 1320; and Thomas of Canterbury began the upper chapel in 1331.

The Ramseys produced the second transformation, the introduction of the Perpendicular style. Vertical elements had been present in Gothic from the beginning. We have seen that in France these elements were grouped in a special way by Pierre de Montreuil somewhere about 1250, in the triforium of St.-Denis and elsewhere, and that they were linked with increased areas of glass and transparencies, or double-plane tracery (**50**). Further developed towards the glasshouse church, these ideas found fuller expression at St.-Urbain, Troyes in 1263–66 (**61**). Separately, another expression of unifying pattern was reached by Bernard de Soissons about 1275 at Reims, when he designed the rectangular panelling inside the west front (**42, 53**). All these elements in France, though they represented the same movement towards unity which gave England Perpendicular, never reached a final synthesis. On the other hand, they were piecemeal introduced

86   Chaumont Church: south porch,
14th century; compare **87**.

to England, and found a more congenial atmosphere. Triforium linked to clerestory, and provided with an openwork screen, had been reached in the nave of York designed before 1300, and perhaps slightly earlier at Bridlington Priory on the south side of the nave, and at Guisborough Priory choir, both in progress from *c.* 1290. It is possible that this Yorkshire development came direct from a French source, most probably Troyes; on the other hand there had been similar ideas at work in the West even before the time of Pierre de Montreuil. Somerset masons working at Christ Church Cathedral, Dublin, about 1220, produced a linked triforium and clerestory in the nave, and within a few years another version was in being at Pershore Abbey; before 1250 this type was employed in the choir of Southwell. It is thus arguable that there was an independent line of English development, or that England received back from France in a perfected form a device which had originally been an exported native invention.

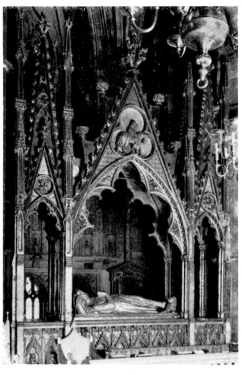

87 WESTMINSTER ABBEY: tomb of Edmund Earl of Lancaster, *c.* 1295–1300. Designer *Michael of Canterbury*.

88 TRONDHJEM CATHEDRAL: screen of octagon, after 1328. English detail of the Canterbury school.

THE CANTERBURY SCHOOL

89   KILKENNY: St. Canice's Cathedral from the south-west, *c.* 1210–.

90   GLASGOW CATHEDRAL from the south-west, 1233–58;
later nave; fifteenth century spire.

Whatever the precise course of events, it is beyond coincidence that the triforium screens of Bridlington and Limoges should be almost identical, and practically contemporary. There was certainly close contact between English and French masters, and so far as Limoges is concerned, this would be natural, as the whole of the Limousin had been ceded to Henry III by St. Louis in 1259. Both in England and in France, by the opening of the fourteenth century, there existed these parallel series of motives and ideas. In France, they led to no further development; in England they became integral parts of the new and highly distinctive style which we can see in its first, tentative form in the re-cased choir of Gloucester, built between 1337 and 1350, out of the offerings at the tomb of Edward II. Owing to this royal burial, it is likely that the King's masons would be responsible for the new work's design; but there is much stronger evidence that the inventor of the new style of Gloucester was William Ramsey, King's Mason from 1336 to his death in 1349. His colleague, William Hurley, the King's Carpenter, also deserves a share of the credit, for his contemporary timber framing and tracery in the lantern over the Ely octagon embody the same principles. Perpendicular also owes something to the strength of the English tradition of timber-framing, with its necessary rectangularity. But the link between Gloucester and Ramsey is to be found in the remains of the chapter house and surrounding cloister of St. Paul's in London, begun by Ramsey in 1332. Here there were the hall-marks of the new style: vertical treatment, the long-panel design carrying the mullions of the chapter-house windows down the walls, four-centred arches, rectangular panelling, tracery formed of straight lines and almost identical with that of Gloucester; above all, a new type of moulding profile.

91 Kilkenny Cathedral, *c.* 1210–.

Leaving Perpendicular, as a national style, for later treatment, we must examine briefly the effect of English art on the rest of the British Isles. Early Gothic in Wales is an extension of the western school: St. David's Cathedral and Pembrokeshire seem to have been a province exploited by the masons and sculptors of Wells, Glastonbury and Bristol. In North Wales the influence of Chester was felt, and Edward I finally brought the area into submission by planting it with fortresses and bastide towns filled with English settlers. The major art of these towns, castles, and churches was exported from England, and carried by official craftsmen. Native Welsh influence is so slight as to be negligible.

On the other hand, the earlier style of South Wales, though based on the western school of Somerset and the Severn Valley, developed certain minor peculiarities. These were carried to Ireland by the invasion of 1169, which was largely a Welsh exploit, under Anglo-Norman leadership. The first strictly Gothic buildings in Ireland were transplanted English buildings upon Irish soil. Before the English invasion there had been a prior wave of Cistercian monasteries, bringing with them sporadic pointed arches, but little more. Even the first of the English buildings were transitional in character; Christ Church, Dublin, begun *c.* 1172, only becomes fully Gothic with the nave, not started until 1213. St. Patrick's Cathedral, the largest mediaeval church in Ireland, followed in 1225, and bears a general resemblance to Salisbury, though differing in detail. In the south-east St. Canice's Cathedral, Kilkenny (**89, 91**), is closely related to work in Wales; it dates from about 1210, and similar again was the Collegiate Church of Gowran, now largely in ruins.

Between 1200 and 1400, when English influence in Ireland almost collapsed, the general style of architecture was English, but usually belated. Lancet windows give little indication of date, and were for long extremely popular, singly and in

79

combination. Since Irish chancels were normally aisleless, they gave opportunity for lateral series of lancets in addition to triplets or ranges of greater number in east and west ends. Kildare Cathedral, begun *c.* 1225 and soon completed, has the interesting feature of defensive machicolations running along the walls. These consist of a series of arches from buttress to buttress, slightly in advance of the main wall-face, and carrying a parapet. Similar machicolations occur in the fortified churches of Languedoc and Hungary. Few of the Irish cathedrals have escaped ruin or disastrous rebuilding. Old Leighlin is one of the exceptions, but dates largely from the second quarter of the sixteenth century. At Ardfert are ruins of the cathedral (**93**) and of the Franciscan church, both begun soon after 1250; on the Rock of Cashel stands the thirteenth-century cathedral in ruins, beside the earlier Cormac's Chapel. The artists employed in Dublin, such as John of Corfe, King's mason there from 1334, were almost all of English extraction, but very few names have survived in connexion with buildings now identifiable.

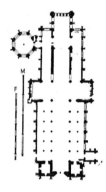

92 Elgin Cathedral, 1224–, by Master Gregory; choir *c.* 1270.

To the closing Middle Ages belongs Ireland's own Gothic, a simplified compound of Flamboyant and Perpendicular characteristics, with recrudescent Celticisms. This must be briefly touched upon later. Parallel with developments in Ireland were those in Scotland, which was similarly an English architectural province through the earlier Gothic period, only to achieve with its political independence a separate national style, again compounded with Flamboyant designs from France and Flanders. The English influence in Scotland, before the wars under Edward I, was immense, for not only was a large proportion of the nobility Anglo-Norman, but the Scottish religious houses were daughters of English abbeys. Style was later in development, being for the most part transplanted from the South. It was, however, chiefly the local variant of Yorkshire and Northumbria that ruled in Scotland until the end of the thirteenth century. Dunfermline Abbey, whose eastern arm (now destroyed) was begun in 1216, and completed in 1250, was closely linked to Canterbury and to Durham. Coldingham Priory was, almost until the end of the Middle Ages, a cell to Durham and administered from England; its chancel also was begun about 1216, and still remains.

Dryburgh Abbey was founded in 1150 for Premonstratensians from Alnwick; Melrose in about 1136, and Dundrennan about 1142, were Cistercian colonies from Rievaulx. Other abbeys of great importance, in a mainly English style, were Arbroath, built between 1176 and 1233; Holyrood, and Kilwinning, both of the early thirteenth century; and Inchcolm, which towards the end of the century built a small octagonal chapter house in imitation of English work, as, much later, did Elgin Cathedral (**92**). St. Andrews Cathedral was started about 1160, and most of it was finished by the middle of the thirteenth century. The west front, which survives, was a rebuilding of 1272–79. Dunblane Cathedral, still in fairly complete preservation, dates from 1240–1300 (**95**). Elgin Cathedral, now in ruins, preserves the noble west front and portal designed by Gregory the mason (**94**), master of the first work begun in 1224, and parts of the later choir of *c.* 1270. Of all the great Scottish churches, that in most perfect condition is Glasgow Cathedral, with a lower church and choir built in 1233–58, and later nave and added central tower, spire and chapter-house of the fifteenth century (**90**).

In both Ireland and Scotland the normal eastern termination was square; while in Ireland chancels were rarely aisled, the Scottish plan was to have aisles

93 ARDFERT CATHEDRAL: east end, *c.* 1253–.

94 ELGIN CATHEDRAL: west front, 1224–. Designer *Master Gregory*.

95 DUNBLANE CATHEDRAL: interior of nave looking west, 1240–1300.

96   AMIENS CATHEDRAL: choir stalls, 1508–19, by *Jean Turpin*.

97   ULM CATHEDRAL: choir stalls, 1469–74, by *Jörg Syrlin the elder*.

98   BRUGES CATHEDRAL: choir stalls, *c.* 1430.

GOTHIC STALLWORK

in the western bays only, leaving an unaisled projection at the east end. This has an English ancestry going back to Oxford (Cathedral), *c.* 1160, and found in Rochester, Worcester, Southwell and Bristol Cathedrals at later dates. The square British termination also reached Norway, at Stavanger Cathedral begun after 1272, and rather earlier in the Norwegian Cathedral at Kirkwall, Orkney, where the apse belonging to the Norman church of 1137–52 was replaced by a great square-ended presbytery in the middle of the thirteenth century (**228**). Later still are the three doorways of the west front, and one in the south transept, built in recessed orders of polychrome masonry. These portals probably indicate a French influence.

Neither Ireland nor Scotland can show much domestic architecture of the earlier Gothic period, other than the domestic apartments of castles, and even these remains are very scanty. Of the military remains as such I cannot treat here, except to note that the forms of Irish and Scottish architecture, even in churches, were modified by the need for defence. We have seen this at Kildare Cathedral, and the sturdy towers of many churches bear a close resemblance to the tower-houses and castle keeps which studded these contested lands from end to end. The same architects were responsible for both, though beyond the virtues of noble composition they could make few aesthetic concessions among the stern needs of their military work. But if we reflect upon the stormy history of the border lands, we must pay tribute to the resilient temperament of these engineers, which permitted them to turn from their siegecraft and defensive works, and build a church or chapel exquisite in its very simplicity.

Beyond the British Isles, English art spread in part by the export of English productions such as embroidery, and later alabaster carvings; partly by the travel of individuals. Among travellers, Matthew Paris is noteworthy; during his visit to Norway in 1248 he may even have painted the Faaberg St. Peter upon an oak panel; at least it is a work completely English in character, and closely related to the "St. Albans school". Even France was to import English artists on occasion, and the tomb of Pope John XXII at Avignon is not merely based on English designs of a generation earlier. Much of its canopy-work was clearly carved by an Englishman, presumably the *Johannes Englicus* whose name is recorded from 1336 to 1341. An English mason, whose name appears as "Raynard Fonoyll", was from 1331 to 1341 in charge of building the south cloister of the Catalan Monastery of Santes Creus (**68**), and other English or Irish masons are said to have worked at Batalha in Portugal towards the end of the fourteenth century.

English influence was certainly paramount in breaking the spell which bound Gothic architecture to the monotony of the French "classic" solution of vaulting and tracery. Flamboyant tracery and vaulting with intermediate and lierne ribs were mainly developed from English patterns. These influences reached the Peninsula and Germany, had a great effect in Flanders, and to a certain extent reacted upon the later style of France. The highly complex vaults of late German Gothic, with those of other central and northern European lands, derived directly from the English experiments which were in progress at the beginning of the fourteenth century. The English work, in its turn, was closely connected with the building science of Poitou and other parts of the English possessions in south-western France. There the course of architectural change had been almost entirely insulated from the classic style of the northern cathedrals. And it was from this southern region that another main factor in the later Gothic was to take its rise: the treatment of space. With this we have to deal in the next chapter, and must here conclude with a brief summary of the English contribution to the synthesis of late Gothic.

The final phase of Gothic art became concerned chiefly with two things: space, and pattern. Spatial treatment was distinctively southern, as we shall see.

Pattern, the pattern produced by linear combinations, was in its highest development typically English. Some of its manifestations, such as the ridge-rib or inverted keel of the English vault, were almost exclusively insular. It was the historical accident of the Angevin Empire, linking England for so long with the southern centres of resistance to Parisian imperialism, that brought these two dominant motives together. It was England's mercantile importance, and the adventurousness of her sons, that made possible the diffusion of these conjoined elements, and spread a new art over England herself, and over most of Europe.

99   King Henry III and his masons.

VII

Spatial Gothic

IN describing the geographical features of Gothic Europe, I have stressed the opposition between the French Royal Domain on the one hand, and the surrounding fiefs and the Empire on the other. The growing power of the French Kings provoked enmity on the part of those who saw their own power and independence lessened. For two centuries from the opening of the Gothic period royal France was in constant danger of encirclement. Most formidable of the surrounding opponents was the King of England, and during those two hundred years the whole of the marriage alliances of the English Royal House tended to link it to the other powers on the perimeter of France. Thus Henry I's daughter married the Emperor Henry V of Germany; Henry II, though he refused the offer of the Empire, married a daughter to Henry the Lion, Duke of Saxony; John's daughter, Isabella, was the wife of Frederick II, and his second son, Richard, became King of the Romans. The second marriage of the Empress Matilda to Geoffrey Plantagenet not only brought the throne of England to the House of Anjou, but formed a direct link with Jerusalem, whose King was Geoffrey's father Fulk. Henry II himself married the heiress of Aquitaine, and thus came to control more of geographical France than the French King did; daughters married into the houses of Castile and Toulouse. John's two sons both married daughters of Raymond Berenger IV of Provence, whose uncle and cousins were Kings of Aragon and Counts of Barcelona. Edward I was to marry a princess of Castile, and his brother Edmund of Lancaster, the widow of Henry III of Navarre.

The political significance of this great area surrounding the French Royal Domain was enormously strengthened by the fact that it contained the territory of the first literary vernacular of Europe: Provençal.* Almost the whole of France south of the Loire as far east as Savoy, and Catalonia beyond the Pyrenees, formed one great linguistic province. Long before the emergence of northern French, English and Italian as the languages of important cultures, the Langue d'Oc had been the vehicle of a great poetic tradition. Both the trouvères of northern France, and the minnesinger of Germany learnt their craft from the troubadours of greater Provence. Thus the formation of the Angevin Empire by the marriage of Henry of Anjou and Eleanor of Aquitaine in 1152 had implications that went far beyond the political sphere.

Henry was already Duke of Normandy, and in two more years was to become King of England. Angers, Poitiers and London became the three capitals of a realm nearly a thousand miles long, from the Cheviots to the Pyrenees. London was the centre of a firmly established Anglo-Norman tradition of building; Angers and Poitiers now became the sources of a new form of art. At Angers Cathedral, begun in 1149, the outer walls of the earlier church were retained, the arcades swept away, heavy external buttresses added, and an enormous vault built in a single span. Romanesque aisleless naves, some of them covered with a series of domes, had been a normal type in southern France, and at first their Gothic counterparts had "domical" vaults rising at the centre. These domed vaults were to reappear in late Gothic in the Baltic, Spain and America. The example of Angers was almost immediately followed at Bordeaux, and later at Toulouse,

---

* Old English literature was still earlier, but was broken by the Conquest.

where the vault of the cathedral nave was being set during the siege of 1211. Bordeaux, now greatly altered, was significant because it incorporated recesses in the side walls, already known in the Romanesque period, and later to become so characteristic of the aisleless churches of Catalonia and elsewhere. Romanesque again in origin was the third type of southern church, with aisles of great height and no clerestory. This existed at Valence Cathedral by *c.* 1100, and on the western side of France at St.-Pierre, Chauvigny, close to Poitiers. The first large-scale Gothic application of this system was at Poitiers Cathedral, begun *c.* 1161 under the patronage of Henry II of England and his Queen, Eleanor of Aquitaine (**100, 103**).

Valence and Chauvigny and Notre-Dame-la-Grande in Poitiers itself, like the domed aisleless churches such as Angoulême Cathedral, were additive; built up lengthwise of bay after bay. The Gothic spirit demanded that these churches should have unity, not merely in cross, but in long section. The thinning of the piers, as at Poitiers Cathedral, was the first step towards unity, here as elsewhere.

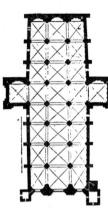

100 Poitiers Cathedral, *c.* 1161–.

We have already seen what this concept of unity was to achieve at Bourges before the end of the twelfth century. And by comparing Bourges with Poitiers we can see what makes Bourges so exceptional among the great cathedrals of the northern type. It results from a brilliant marriage, a compromise of genius, which allied the vertical thrust and clear line of the North to the southern space.

The hall-church, as the aisled type without top-lighting has come to be called, is in fact derived from the pillared hall. It is, as might be expected from the courtly Midi, a secular motive in contrast to the hieratic basilica. Its adoption for the great cathedral of Poitiers by the Angevin Court shows most clearly the humanist spirit at work in the very beginnings of the Gothic movement. Furthermore, in the expansion of the spatial idea to the church art of other regions, we find additional manifestations of the same underlying spirit. While one symptom of the Gothic age was the increasing influence of the lay craftsman, on the other hand the Church itself was being penetrated by a different kind of humanism, giving rise to the orders of Friars. The great movement of the Albigenses was essentially a reawakening of the Mediterranean pagan culture, a revolt against the dead hand of Romanesque sacerdotalism. But it was a Mediterranean culture with a difference, revitalized from eastern and northern sources. And though this great culture perished, it succeeded all the same in effecting a radical change in the outlook of its persecutors. The lives and work of St. Dominic and St. Francis of Assisi, and the orders they founded, looked away from this world, it is true. But their ends were only to be attained by bringing the Church into daily touch with the lives of the great masses of men and women.

So it is that another most important influence was brought to bear on the design of churches. Besides the general desire for unity of spatial composition, there was now the particular demand of the friars for open churches in which sermons could be preached to large congregations. The idea of the church as a preaching space was the practical outcome of humanized, almost vulgarized religion. The mother-church of the Franciscans at Assisi, built in 1228–53, adopted the simple plan of a single nave from the tradition of Angers (**101**). It is customary to reject Vasari's definite statement that the architect was Jacopo da Alemannia, on the ground that no German could have designed a pure Gothic church at this period; but Alemannia in its strict sense covered not only Swabia but Alsace and northern imperial Burgundy. Messer Jacopo was presumably a Burgundian, or even by political extension of a geographical term, a Provençal.

101 ASSISI: Upper Church of
St. Francis, 1228–53. Designer
Jacopo da Alemannia.

102 VENICE: Church of SS.
Giovanni e Paolo, 1260–1385.
Designer possibly *Giovanni Pisano.*

103 POITIERS CATHEDRAL,
looking east, 1166–.

104 BOLOGNA: Church of San Francisco
from the east, 1236–60.

POITOU AND ITALY

106 WINCHELSEA: choir of St. Thomas's Church, *c.* 1300–05.

ENGLISH SPACE

The Dominicans in their great Church at Toulouse, still known as the Jacobins, begun in 1260, adopted a different plan, that of the double nave. Here again was a scheme with no top lighting, though divided down the centre by a line of pillars. Though it might be thought to have distinct disadvantages for an order of Preachers, this double-aisled plan was distinctive of the French Dominicans, and repeated at a number of their houses. It occurred later across central Europe, notably at friaries in Bohemia and Poland. Owing to the clever planning of the east end, with a wide span giving additional space before the altar, and the plain cylindrical form of the columns, almost every member of the congregation would get a clear view of the altar itself. Many refectories of the earlier orders in France had taken this twin form; just as the great hall of the Hospital at Angers founded by Henry II in 1177 took the same plan as the three-aisled hall of Poitiers Cathedral. In other countries the friars' churches took different forms, but always with the idea of open space strongly emphasized. In England they omitted transepts, in Ireland were generally aisleless. By way of the churches of the popular Orders, spatial Gothic began to exercise a wide influence on the architecture of the normal parish churches, and both reacted upon the main stream of art.

Poitiers Cathedral may be considered as the first Gothic hall-church; though its design was settled by the middle of Henry II's reign, it was not completed until after 1271, and the west end and final dedication bring us to 1379. Still, its square east end, and probably the plan of its western towers, outside the aisles, are signs of English influence. Lying at the very centre of the Angevin Empire, Poitiers combines northern with southern elements to form a style Gothic, but very different from the Gothic of the French King's Domain. Long after the disappearance of the empire of the Plantagenets, this spatial Gothic architecture was to persist in its home region. Soon after 1200 the Church of St.-Serge at Angers exhibited the hall-church in fully Gothic guise (**107**); later came the Abbey Church of Solesmes; at the very end of the age, the splendid Church of Celles-sur-Belle, with clustered shafts branching out into vault-ribs without the intervention of any capital (**60**). But the defeat of the Albigenses was also the defeat of southern Gothic in France; save for these sporadic survivals, the future of spatial art was to lie mainly elsewhere, in Spain on the one hand, and on the other in Germany and central Europe. All the same, it was the spirit of space and unity which in the end won everywhere, and infused itself into the whole of later Gothic art.

In England it was this spirit which was ultimately to produce the national style of Perpendicular, but long before that achievement it had won recognition in the newer types of parish church. Crossing, transepts, chancel arch, all tended more and more to be suppressed. Eventually there was even to be a movement to abolish existing central towers, and to build new ones at the west end, where their whole height would tell in independent composition, while the interior would be disencumbered of its heavy piers. More direct results of the southern style can be seen in the aisled retrochoirs of several English cathedrals, notably those begun soon after 1200 at Winchester and Southwark; still more in the hall-church choir added to the Temple Church in London and finished by 1239 (**105**). At the same time the single-unit design was represented by the Chapel of the Archbishops of Canterbury at Lambeth Palace, in progress in 1240. There the triple lancets of the sides have come to fill each bay, and five graduated lights span the east end. Here is the English original of the glass-house chapel, which within a few years was to be spurred on to emulation of the Ste.-Chapelle of Paris, and was to culminate in the glories of Eton, King's College, Cambridge, and Henry VII's Chapel at Westminster.

The hall-church tradition, though never of primary importance in England, was carried from the Temple to such churches as that of St. Thomas in New Winchelsea, laid out about 1300, though here the omission of a clerestory may be due to the same lack of funds that prevented the building of transepts and nave (**106**). A better example of the designed hall-church in England might be the former London Austin Friars, built in 1354. Of much greater size and significance is the choir of St. Augustine's, Bristol (now the cathedral), begun after 1298 (probably *c.* 1311), and finished by 1340. This is a complete and stone-vaulted hall-church, with remarkable skeleton vaulting construction in the aisles and again, of a different pattern, in the sacristy. Perhaps derived from the curious buttressing traceries in Pierre de Montreuil's lower chapel of the Ste.-Chapelle (**108, 109**),

107   Angers: St.-Serge, *c.* 1205.

this English skeleton vaulting is itself the source from which the German masons of the Parler family must later have derived their designs for such a vault as that of the south porch of Prague Cathedral (**110**). In England the only vault of large size with skeleton ribs is that of the chancel of St. Mary's, Warwick, built 1381–91, perhaps by Robert Skillington (**111**). Skillington was the architect of John of Gaunt's extensive works at Kenilworth Castle, close to Warwick and in the same style and with similar mouldings. Before leaving the subject of the English hall-church, it is proper to mention that the Temple may have obtained the scheme of its choir from that of the Hospitallers at St. John's, Clerkenwell, where the new choir was consecrated in 1185. If the hall arrangement does in fact go back to this twelfth-century work, a direct connexion with Poitiers would be almost certain. At any rate, the hall-church in England was closely connected with the Court.

108 BRISTOL CATHEDRAL: vault of choir aisle, *c.* 1311–40.

109 PARIS: Ste.-Chapelle, 1243-48. Skeleton buttresses in lower chapel.

110 PRAGUE CATHEDRAL: south porch vault, *c.* 1396. Designer *Peter Parler.*

111 WARWICK: St. Mary's Church, choir vault, 1381–91. Designer perhaps *Robert Skillington.*

SKELETON FRAMEWORK

112 PALMA CATHEDRAL: choir vault, *c.* 1280–. Designer possibly *Jaime Fabre*.

113 BARCELONA: Church of Sta. Maria del Mar, 1328–85. Designer probably *Jaime Fabre*.

114 GERONA CATHEDRAL: looking east, 1312–47. Designers *Enrique* and *Jacques Favran*.

115 PALMA CATHEDRAL: looking east, *c.* 1280–1406.

CATALAN SPACE

Similarly in Catalonia the early hall-churches were often under royal patronage. The earliest in Gothic style are thought to have been those of the orders of friars in Barcelona: St. Catherine of the Dominicans, begun about 1225, and St. Francis, some few years later, but completed by 1247. These had simple polygonal chevets with no chapels, and cellular naves with a single span and side chapels between internal buttresses. The system spread, still as that typical of the friars' churches, to St. Dominic's at Gerona (1253–), and St. Francis at Palma in Majorca (1281–1317), with hexagonal chevet chapels. From 1296 the church of the Dominicans at Palma was in progress, and its great mason, Jaime Fabre, was chosen by the King of Aragon and Bishop of Barcelona to direct the works of Barcelona Cathedral. Also at the turn of the century the Chapel Royal of Sta. Agueda in Barcelona was being built, with a single nave and a timber roof supported on transverse stone arches, made by Bertrand Riquer before 1309. A rich harvest of churches followed, some of the cellular type, others, like Barcelona Cathedral, of

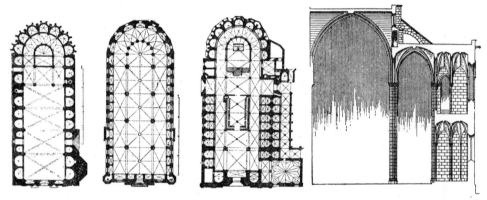

116 Gerona Cathedral, 1312–; plan by Master Enrique and Jacques Favran.
117 Barcelona Sta. Maria del Mar, 1328–; probably by Jaime Fabre. **118, 119**
      Barcelona Cathedral, 1298–, by Fabre.

three aisles with a very low clerestory. In Barcelona are Sta. Maria del Pino, begun 1320; the Church of Pedralbes, completed in a single year, 1326–27, under royal patronage; and the lost Church of the Carmelites, which was somewhat earlier, all of the single-naved type, with side chapels. Three-aisled are the Cathedral (**118, 119, 150**), whose first work from 1298 to 1356 was directed by Jaime Fabre, and Sta. Maria del Mar, built between 1328 and 1383, and also probably designed by Fabre (**113, 117**).

Architects were not limited to the use of a single system, for the Barcelona mason Berenger de Montaigut began the Carmelite Church at Manresa on a cellular plan in 1321, and a year later started work on the cathedral in the same city, designed with three aisles. Foreign influences were welcomed: the Church of Sta. Maria at Montblanch was begun in 1352 by the English mason, Raynard Fonoyll, whom we have met at Santes Creus, while Gerona Cathedral from 1312 employed architects from Narbonne, a certain Enrique or Henri, and after 1321, Jacques Favran, the master in charge of Narbonne Cathedral. Favran seems also to have designed the cellular cathedral at Perpignan (then a Catalan town), begun in 1324. Here again the same master was ready to turn from cellular to three-aisled naves and back again. The original plan for the immense single nave of Gerona probably goes back to Favran, who was in charge until 1330; it was already an old scheme when Guillermo Boffiy at last received permission to build it in 1416 (**114, 116**). At Tortosa there may have been a regular architectural competition to design the cathedral, for a plan by Antonio Guarch survives, dated in 1345, differing entirely from the actual plan begun in the next year by the mason Benito Dalguayre.

Apart from the nave of Gerona, which with its span of seventy-three feet has the greatest of Gothic stone vaults, the chief monument of the Catalan style of spatial church is the Cathedral of Palma, Majorca (**112, 115**). The Royal Chapel at the east end was begun in 1232, and the main choir behind about 1280. This choir has the unusual feature of square end walls to all three chapels, converted at a higher level to the normal pentagonal shapes. The great body of the church was not begun until the early fourteenth century, work on the nave was still in progress in 1406, and vaults were erected in 1529 and 1609, while the consecration only took place in 1613. It is at least possible that Fabre was the original designer of the main church, with its immense width and height, and slender octagonal pillars, like those of Sta. Maria del Mar in Barcelona. At Barcelona Cathedral, on the other hand, are clustered piers derived from French practice, and reminiscent of Bourges and Le Mans.

The course of Catalan Gothic has been traced in detail by M. Pierre Lavedan, and it is unnecessary to dwell longer on the history of individual churches. But there is one major point concerning these southern spatial churches that deserves consideration. In midland France, in England, and in Germany the development of spatial architecture was directly linked to an increase of light. We have seen the growth of transparencies in the French cathedral style, and the introduction of glasshouse architecture at the Ste.-Chapelle of Paris, at St.-Urbain, Troyes, and in a rudimentary way even at earlier English buildings such as the Chapel of Lambeth Palace. The same enlargement of window space at the expense of walls was to become typical of the later building of Germany and central Europe: indeed, large expanses of stained glass are a leading characteristic of Sondergotik as they are of French and Flemish Flamboyant and English Perpendicular. Obviously great floods of light, highly desirable in the North, were the last thing wanted in Mediterranean countries. And in fact the interiors of Barcelona and Gerona Cathedrals, even on the most brilliant day, are intensely dark. The sense of entering a new world of flowing and moving space is there; but not the sense of an interpenetration of the internal world and the world without, achieved through the glazed windows of the North.

This fact of the darkness of the great churches of Catalonia is of importance in interpreting the aesthetic views behind spatial architecture. One of the crucial texts bearing on this subject is the well-known decision of the Chapter of Gerona in 1416. After hearing the individual views of the Commission of twelve architects they had summoned (**144**), they accepted their own master's proposal for a single nave on four grounds. Of these the third and fourth were that, in the opinion of many of the consultants, the single nave would be cheaper and more speedily finished. The first was that the church thus built would be more solemn, noble and better proportioned to the existing choir (*solemnius, notabilius et proportionabilius capiti dictae ecclesiae*). The second, and much the most interesting, was that such a work *multo majori claritate fulgebit quod est laetius et jucundum*. To translate this as: it will shine with much more light, which is more agreeable and delightful, makes nonsense of it. Not only is the nave built according to this design actually dark, but the universal darkness of the other great churches of the South proves that Gothic people were as anxious as those of the present day to escape from the piercing rays of the sun.

The apparent paradox is resolved if we turn back to the beginning of Gothic architecture, the new St.-Denis of Abbot Suger. Suger composed a number of inscriptions for his church, in which he set forth, as Dr. Panofsky has shown, not merely the facts and dates, but also the philosophic purpose on which he founded his endeavour. Again and again in these inscriptions he harps on the words "noble" and "clear". *Nobile claret opus, . . . opus quod nobile claret clarificet mentes . . . claret enim claris quod clare concopulatur, . . . claret opus nobile.* This noble work shining clearly which clarifies minds, which being brightly coupled with brightness shines brightly in nobility, does so not literally but metaphorically. It was no harsh glare of sunshine that the Canons of Gerona wished to embody in their cathedral for the benefit of worshippers, but the supernal splendour of the True Light. Northern men, even when like Suger they aimed at this higher reality behind appearance, could revel in the physical properties of light. The southern climate made this direct equation of the material and the spiritual splendour out of the question, and the search for *claritas* becomes a metaphysical rather than an aesthetic preoccupation.

The northern version of spatial architecture, like that of the South, was being developed in the thirteenth century. The first of the Gothic hall-churches of Germany was the nave of St. Elizabeth's at Marburg, begun about 1257 and completed by 1283 (**245**). Others followed rapidly: the nave of Minden Cathedral, *c.* 1267, and other churches in Westphalia; the Severikirche in Erfurt, about 1270 (**246**); and Meissen Cathedral by about 1300. The more remote Bohemia was reached within a few years of western Germany: Olomouc Cathedral (*c.* 1265) and the nave of St. Bartholomew at Kolín (*c.* 1270–90), are fully developed hall-churches (**120, 247**), and so is the choir of the Cistercian Monastery of Heiligenkreuz in Austria, consecrated in 1295. The choir of St. Stephen's, Vienna soon followed, and was finished in 1340.

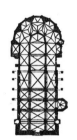

120 Kolín: St. Bartholomew; nave *c.* 1270–90; choir 1360–78, by Peter Parler.

In Germany proper the type soon began to displace the Romanesque and French Gothic models which had reigned for so long. It is at this stage that we reach the threshold of the late, national Gothic. A final and complete emancipation from Romanesque traditions is found in such works as the choir of the Barfüsserkirche at Erfurt (1291–1316), and Johann Schendeler's Wiesenkirche at Soest, a hall-church with three parallel apses, begun in 1331 and completed after 1376 (**248**). These east ends with enormously tall mullioned windows are closely comparable to certain Belgian churches such as Notre-Dame at Huy (**169**), begun in 1311, and the choir of St.-Paul, Liège, rebuilt in its present form from 1334. In England William of Eyton's Lady Chapel at Lichfield Cathedral (*c.* 1320–36) shows similar tall windows of impressive verticality. Rectilinear elements, a simple transom supported by cusping at St.-Paul, Liège, and a double transom containing quatrefoils at the Soest Wiesenkirche, are probably derived from the first works of English Perpendicular, though as we have seen there had been tentative movements in the same direction in northern France before the end of the thirteenth century.

The introduction of the spatial hall-church to the Germanic lands was one of the most fateful moments for the production of the later Gothic architecture.* This may have been connected with the Emperor Frederick II's marriage to Isabella Plantagenet, or simply the outcome of the great emperor's wideflung interests and southern education. But at the very same time another influence, tending in the same general direction, was entering Germany from France at Strassburg. Here the height of the church was governed by an earlier transept, but the principles of the new art of Pierre de Montreuil were being applied in the nave practically as early as they were at St.-Denis. So close is the identity of detail,

---

* There had been some German Romanesque hall-churches, but it is improbable that these were direct ancestors of those in Gothic style.

and so nearly contemporary are the two naves, that one must suppose the German master, Rudolf the elder, to have had access to Montreuil's drawings. It is particularly fortunate that a complete series of names has been preserved at Strassburg, proving that the architects were all Germans, however much they owed to France. From soon after 1230 Master Rudolf I was at work in the south transept, where the remarkable Angel Pillar survives from this period, and by 1250 at the latest work on the nave had begun. The vault was completed in 1275, and Master Rudolf died a year later. Breadth and light, and a foretaste of rectilinearity are all present.

In 1276 began the work of the west front (**121**) under the famous Master Erwin, whose surname "von Steinbach" is perhaps only traditional. Erwin himself is a sharply historical figure, and one of the very greatest of the Gothic architects. The primary design for the front had probably been drawn up by Master Rudolf I about 1250, and still exists as drawing A of the cathedral drawing office. This had been revised (drawing A 1) by 1275, also probably by Master Rudolf I. Further revision by Erwin yielded the existing front, which had reached the top of the great rose by the time of his death in 1318. His sons and nephews continued the work until the towers had reached their final height in 1365. The openwork octagon with its staircase turrets over the north tower was built in the twenty years 1399–1419 by Ulrich von Ensingen, while the spire took a further twenty years under Johann Hültz of Cologne. The great innovation of the Strassburg front is its wholehearted adoption of the transparency combined with vertical emphasis. What Pierre de Montreuil had done in a small way at the middle of the thirteenth century, and in its rudiments appeared in the front of Coutances Cathedral even earlier, was being done by Master Erwin on a grand scale, and with full mastery of his materials, at Strassburg about 1300.

It was with good reason that Strassburg was recognized by the German masters as having precedence over all the lodges of masons within the Empire. Not only in architectural composition and detail, but in the splendour of its sculpture, does Strassburg excel the other churches, not merely of Germany, but of the rest of Europe. The great inventions of the French masters were here united with a warmer humanity, a more direct observation of nature. Only in another German masterpiece, the western choir of Naumburg, begun in 1249, can figure sculpture of greater power be found (**122, 123**). Even so, the difference is largely due to the rigidity of the classical iconography at Strassburg. The Naumburg figures are conceived as portraits, and possess as no others, except the fragmentary remains of a few of the finest English works, the poignancy of first-hand psychological studies. But the marvel is that both at Strassburg and at Naumburg these humanized statues are not less, but more a part of the building than the classic works of Chartres and Reims (**124**). Here for the first time the art of Gothic reached, as near as human art may reach, its goal long sought. Proportion, composition, distribution of light and shade, arrangement of parts, detail, statuary, carvings; all share in producing a single, co-ordinate, integrated form. Goethe wrote more wisely than he could have known when he described Erwin as the Master who first out of scattered elements created a living whole.

121 STRASSBURG CATHEDRAL: west front. Bottom story and rose, 1276–1318, by *Meister Erwin*; towers completed 1365; northern octagon, 1399–1419 by *Ulrich von Ensingen*; spire, 1420–39 by *Johann Hültz*.

122, 123 NAUMBURG CATHE-
DRAL: statues in western
choir of Hermann and Rege-
lindis, and of Wilhelm von
Kamburg, 1249–.

124 REIMS CATHE-
DRAL: angel of the
Annunciation, c. 1255–.

GOTHIC HUMANISM

VIII

National Gothic

THE Gothic civilization of western Europe in the twelfth and thirteenth centuries was international. The dissimilarities between the various countries of Europe were mainly due to the varying extent to which they had acquired the new spirit, and forsaken the outlook of the Romanesque age. Owing to the near-monopoly of higher education possessed by Paris, the demands of art patrons tended to be standardized, wherever the patrons happened to find themselves. At first, lay craftsmen from France: Normans, Angevins, Picards, and Frenchmen in the strict sense, were imported by other countries to carry out work for which their home craftsmen were unfitted. But this stage began to pass away in England by the middle of the twelfth century, though it continued sporadically elsewhere until the fourteenth. From the mid-thirteenth century, Germany was becoming artistically independent, and so was Spain. Central and eastern Europe began to borrow from Germany rather than from France; so did the area of Germanic colonization towards the head of the Baltic. Scandinavia and Scotland were ready to accept help from France, Flanders, or Germany until the end of the Middle Ages.

At the centre of affairs, and speaking geographically that includes France, England, Flanders, Germany, and northern Spain, the international era was passing away by 1300. Vernacular languages had emerged, first Provençal, then French, then English, then Italian, German and Spanish. The idea of separate nations, each with its own government within a distinct ring-fence, and each marked by its own language, had displaced the theoretical comity of Christendom under the rule of the Pope and using the Latin tongue. Some nations became organized much earlier than others. The first to reach unity was England, and England remained until nearly the end of the Gothic age the sole example of a self-supporting as well as self-contained structure. France, though self-supporting culturally, only achieved union about 1500. Christian Spain became united at about the same date, but never succeeded in absorbing Portugal. Throughout the Middle Ages the Peninsula (apart from the Moslem South) must be considered as the three separate states, Castile, Aragon, and Portugal. Italy likewise was threefold: the Imperial North; the Papal centre; and the Angevin and Aragonese South, the Kingdom of the Two Sicilies of a later age.

Hungary, surrounded by mountains as England by the sea, soon developed a self-contained structure. But its changes of dynasty and fluctuating political boundaries tended to make it dependent upon French, German and Italian artists. By the fifteenth century, as we have seen, its lodges of masons were under the jurisdiction of the Master at St. Stephen's, Vienna, and he under the final control of Strassburg. From Alsace in the west to the Carpathians, and from Trent in the south up to Linköping in Sweden, German masters were supreme in the later Gothic age, and they also carried out important work in Spain. Within this Germanic area, influenced by it, but to a considerable degree independent, were the Slavonic Kingdoms of Bohemia and Poland. Thus, apart from the minor local styles, we may count for the latter part of the Gothic age seven main regions, divided into not less than eighteen nations or provinces.* This excludes Italy,

---

* *Britain*: England; Ireland; Scotland; *France*: Northern; Midi; *Spain*: Aragon; Castile; Portugal; *Flanders*: Belgium; Holland; *Germany*: Central; North-Eastern with the Baltic settlements; South-Eastern with Hungary; *Slavonic Kingdoms*: Bohemia; Poland with Lithuania; *Scandinavia*: Denmark; Norway; Sweden.

which was rapidly becoming lost to the Gothic world, and relapsing into the Renaissance of Roman Classicism. Venice and Dalmatia, however, form for a time a supplementary province by themselves. Though hardly national, we have also to consider what Gothic developments took place on the fringes of Europe: in the Mediterranean, at Cyprus, Rhodes and for a short time in Greece; and after the expeditions of Columbus, in America.

Before considering each of these regions, we may sum up the position at the opening of the fourteenth century. The main elements of Gothic art had become common property, though as we have seen they were following three main currents: that of the Ile-de-France, that of the Midi, and that of England. The spatial outlook which sprang from the Midi was already branching into two divisions, that of the North where space was combined with light; that of the South where light had to be excluded. So far as architecture is concerned, these artistic currents had been developed mainly by the building up of traditions in the hands of great master masons. Thus the works of Anglo-Norman Romanesque, whose technical achievements made Gothic possible, included the St. Albans Abbey of Master Robert and the Old St. Paul's in London of Master Andrew. The earliest Gothic buildings of the French Royal Domain had among their architects Roger and Teudho of Chartres, Richard of Paris, and Girard de Cornossa of Bourges. William of Sens carried French style to Canterbury, and England produced Arthur of Ripon and Richard of Lincoln, Ailnoth the King's Engineer, Maurice the King's Mason who built the great keeps of Newcastle and Dover, and the nameless master of Wells. In the early thirteenth century England again found an architectural leader in Master Alexander, who perfected a national early Gothic, and introduced the first patterned vaults.

France once more took the lead with the sharply defined polygonal chapels of Jean d'Orbais at Reims, with their windows of the first bar-tracery. The classic example of the French cathedral form was produced at Amiens by Robert de Luzarches. Then came the great innovator Pierre de Montreuil, carrying to their logical conclusions the reduction of supports and the enlargement of window-space, the vertical emphasis of perpendicular members and the illusion of movement provided by the transparency. His pupil (at least in the wider sense), Jean des Champs, was to carry Montreuil's new style to the shores of the Mediterranean before the end of the century. Contemporary work on similar lines was in progress in England under Walter of Hereford and Michael of Canterbury, and Master Michael added another element of the greatest importance, the ogee curve. In western Germany Rudolf at Strassburg had been an able copyist of Montreuil, but his successor Erwin not merely accepted the separated elements which Des Champs was carrying through the South in the wake of the Albigensian Crusade, but succeeded in welding them into a new style.

Master Erwin was as surely the grandparent of Sondergotik as Michael of Canterbury was of both Flamboyant and Perpendicular. These two contemporaries, working through the last quarter of the thirteenth and into the fourteenth century, alike took the fateful step of rejecting the classic solution of France, reached by Robert de Luzarches, and raised to a higher power by Pierre de Montreuil. The inventiveness, the imagination, and the love of craftsmanship of the English and the German masters were all involved in this critical decision to break into new styles. It is important to distinguish clearly what is meant by "style" and "invention". We have seen that all the main elements of Gothic architecture were present in the Romanesque Durham Cathedral before St.-Denis was rebuilt by Suger. Yet it is not true that Gothic architecture was invented at Durham. It has been shown that England used all the elements of the Flamboyant style before they were current in France; yet Flamboyant was not an English invention. Neither, in spite of France's prior insistence on vertical and rectilinear elements, must we attribute the invention of Perpendicular to a French master. A style is not merely a collection of isolated elements and motives; it must have coherent unity. And it is the creative artist who first gives this unity to the elements of a new style that must be termed its inventor.

The first of the truly national Gothic styles was the English Curvilinear. Though no earlier than Master Erwin's work at Strassburg, it was the English development which first became a true style, represented in many buildings over a wide area. Starting in the decade 1290–1300, the Curvilinear style was already yielding to Perpendicular by 1340–50. It was a transitional period of relatively short duration, but in it was accomplished a number of most outstanding works. At Canterbury itself, and at the King's Court at Westminster, work of the finest quality was being produced by the masons of the "de Canterbury" family. The Eleanor Crosses of 1291–94, the Westminster Abbey tombs of Edmund of Lancaster (**87**) and his wife Aveline, and later that of Aymer de Valence; and the crypt of St. Stephen's Chapel in Westminster Palace, with its lierne vaults, are the outstanding London works which remain. At Canterbury are the new stone screens of the cathedral choir, the great gateway of St. Augustine's Abbey, and Archbishop Meopham's monument. Later came the great upper chapel of St. Stephen's, designed by Master Thomas of Canterbury, and in 1336 at Canterbury, the inserted window of St. Anselm's Chapel.

Winchelsea Church in Sussex is an outstanding production of the Kentish school of Court masters, belonging to the first decade of the fourteenth century (**106**). In the west of England the astonishing hall-church of St. Augustine's, Bristol, was built, and William Joy, a mason found at Bath, Wells and Exeter, was working in a style that already included distinctive Perpendicular elements soon after 1330. The retrochoir and re-modelled choir at Wells form his chief identified work, but it may have been in his time at Exeter that the decision was taken to alter the curve of the nave vaulting ribs to produce a greater effect of smoothly changing surfaces and moulded space. At Norwich, John Ramsey built the east walk

125 Gloucester Cathedral: detail of great south window showing "Kentish tracery" becoming "Perpendicular", *c.* 1337.

of the Cloister before 1325, while at York Minster the nave and west front below the towers were completed between 1291 and 1345 to the designs of Master Simon, who died in 1322, one of the greatest of the northern masters. The highly developed Curvilinear tracery of the York west window, glazed in 1338, also appeared at Durham and Carlisle in variants within a few years.

A close adherence to nature in the sculpture of the last quarter of the thirteenth century, which had found its highest demonstration in the chapter house at Southwell Minster, began to give way to rich and undulating mannerism. Many buildings were overloaded with carved detail, and the never-ending flow of ogee curves became tedious. This was remedied by the Canterbury school, who introduced split cusping, where the meanders were sharply interrupted by intrusive crystalline forms. These were the ultimate outcome of the fruitful experiments with the compasses which had prepossessed English designers for fifty years. At the south transept of Gloucester Abbey, we find in the years 1331–37 a juxtaposition of Curvilinear, Kentish, and Perpendicular forms. The side windows are still purely Curvilinear in their tracery; the great south window, perhaps designed slightly later, is superficially Perpendicular, but the tracery lights which seem straight-sided at a distance are really incurved; they also contain split cusping (**125**). It is evident that the new work at Gloucester depends directly on what was happening in London, where in 1332 William Ramsey, who had worked under Thomas of Canterbury at St. Stephen's, began a new chapter house and cloister for St. Paul's Cathedral. The remains of this work, and the views of it by Hollar, show that its character was distinctively Perpendicular, and extremely close to the refacing of the choir at Gloucester from 1337 to 1350.

William Ramsey, probably son of the John Ramsey who had worked at Norwich early in the century, continued the Norwich cloister, perhaps had a hand in the works of Ely Cathedral, became King's Master Mason in 1336, was appointed advisory master to Lichfield Cathedral in the following year, and died in 1349. Before the Black Death he had co-ordinated all the main elements of the Perpendicular style, of which he may fairly be termed the inventor. The new invention was taken up by the Court school who succeeded him, and particularly by Henry Yevele, King's Mason from 1360 to 1400, and William Wynford, mason at Windsor Castle from 1360 and later associated through his whole career with the works of William of Wykeham. By 1400 these two masters and a number of disciples had carried the style to Exeter and Worcester in the south and west, to Chester, York and Durham in the north-west and north (33). The greatest achievements of this first mature Perpendicular are immensely impressive, combining sturdy detail with admirable composition, and mostly of exquisite workmanship. The greatest works include the naves and west fronts of Westminster Abbey and Canterbury Cathedral by Yevele, the rebuilt great hall at Westminster with walls and front to his design, and roof of sixty-nine feet span by Hugh Herland, the King's Carpenter; and New College, Oxford, and Winchester College built by Wynford for Wykeham. Wynford also began the transformation of the nave of Winchester Cathedral, while John Clyve, another mason who had worked at Windsor, completed the nave of Worcester Cathedral and built its fine central tower.

After the usurpation of the English throne by Henry IV in 1399, artistic inspiration slackened. Under Henry VI there was a temporary revival, when the great educational buildings of Eton College and King's College, Cambridge, were designed, by Robert Westerley and Reginald Ely respectively. Splendid church towers were built, notably that of St. Michael's, Coventry, possibly by Robert Skillington, and that of the chapel of Merton College, Oxford (1448–50), by Robert Janyns, senior. Tower building became almost a cult, and for a century parish vied with parish in obtaining elaborated and improved designs. To give one example of many, the tower of Walberswick, Suffolk, is dated to 1426 by the surviving contract with the masons Richard Russell of Dunwich and Adam Powle of Blythburgh; the work was to be modelled on the towers of Tunstall and Halesworth (82). No mention is made of the tower at Kessingland, which resembles Walberswick far more closely, though it is distinctly larger and has more costly enrichments. It is evident that Kessingland was not begun until after 1426, while it was ready for the bells by 1454. The design can be attributed to Russell, a leading citizen, several times Bailiff of Dunwich and M.P. in 1427; but changes in detail show that the upper part of the tower was completed by another master (83).

Lines of artistic descent can be traced linking many of the prominent architects of the fifteenth century, and proving the direct handing down of tradition until, under Edward IV and the Tudors, English Gothic flared up into its magnificent swan-song. Towers, as at Canterbury Cathedral, and collegiate chapels such as St. George's, Windsor, and King's College, Cambridge, were built or completed. The greatest architects were John Wastell, the designer of the Canterbury central tower, of the vaults and completion of King's College Chapel, and of the eastern chapels of Peterborough Abbey; members of the Janyns family; and the brothers Robert and William Vertue. Robert was trained at Westminster Abbey, and with William, designed the new Abbey Church at Bath, and Henry VII's

Chapel at Westminster. Robert dying in 1506, William continued his work and later collaborated with Henry Redman, son of the Abbey architect and descended from a family of Ramsey, Huntingdonshire. Redman was the chief architect of Cardinal Wolsey's grandiose schemes at York Place, Westminster, Hampton Court, and Cardinal College (now Christ Church), Oxford.

After the Wars of the Roses English sculpture, painting and poetry were at a low ebb. Flemish and German sculptors and painters, glaziers and minor craftsmen began to enter the country in numbers, and introduced Flamboyant and

126 Ireland: only places mentioned in the text are shown. For England see **33**; for Scotland see **136**.

Sondergotik motives and feeling. This did not affect architecture to a notable degree, except that the florid and over-enriched early Tudor buildings to some extent reflected continental fashion. But towards the end of the age a new spirit of simplicity was at work and is very marked in the buildings of Redman. Even after the onset of the classical Renaissance, the Gothic tradition of civic building remained strongly entrenched, and yielded the great Halls of the Inns of Court in London, country houses transformed from monastic houses, such as Thomas Bertie's Titchfield Place, Hampshire; Leez Priory, Essex; and Lacock Abbey, Wiltshire. In collegiate and church building the tradition lasted even longer, and produced such belated works as Wadham College, Oxford (1610–13), and the Chapel at Lincoln's Inn, said to have been designed by Inigo Jones in 1618, and carried out by John Clarke, freemason.

In Ireland, style followed that of England, but by 1400 only the area close to Dublin, Drogheda and Trim still remained in English hands. Beyond the Pale was a great resurgence of Irish art, in the hands of Irish and relapsed Anglo-Irish craftsmen, working for Irish princes and religious houses. This art was by no means neo-Celtic, but essentially Gothic. Its course was from the fourteenth century onwards distinct from English style, and developed a rich version of Curvilinear which became a form of Flamboyant. Within the Pale, the chief work to survive is the tower of St. Patrick's Cathedral, Dublin, begun about 1363. This may have been designed by John More, a mason who was keeper of the King's Works in Ireland (i.e. the Pale) by 1372, worked in Carlow Castle in 1381, and in 1386 was to rebuild the Old Bridge of Dublin.

127 Sligo Abbey, 1416.

The typical Irish buildings of the later Middle Ages are the friaries, commonly called abbeys. They normally consist of a long, narrow unaisled church, of chancel and nave, with central tower, added south transept, and claustral buildings on the north side. The transepts are generally of great and disproportionate length, and the towers are square and taper markedly to the top. An early and dated example is the tower of the Franciscan Friary, Kilkenny, begun 1348. Of the same period is the south transept of the Black Abbey in Kilkenny, with its large five-light window (**132**). Soon after 1405 was built a great part of Holycross Abbey, with fine piscina and sedilia, and cloister arcades, all of a simplified early Perpendicular type (**129**). Rather later are Kilconnell Abbey (c. 1414) and Sligo Abbey (1416) (**127**). At Sligo the High Altar remains, a good example of the canopy-work in flat, low relief so typical of the period in Ireland. Also at Sligo is the splendid O'Craian tomb of 1506, which approaches the Flamboyant. A still finer example is the great wall tomb in Galway Church, believed to date from 1484 or soon after (**130**). Even within the English Pale, as at Newcastle Lyons, Flamboyant forms might be found (**128**).

The flat relief carvings, and the flat appearance of the many small mouldings give Irish work a character very different from either English Decorated or Perpendicular, even when the design of doors, piers or windows is not unlike. Quin Abbey (1433–), the Dominican Friary at Cashel (1450–82) and the Franciscan Friary at Adare (1464–) are characteristic of the Irish religious revival under the native princes (**131**). At Clonmacnois Cathedral is a fine inserted north doorway of about 1460, rather late Decorated in feeling, but within a square surround, a feature much used even where no other trace of the Perpendicular spirit appears. An Irish feature very rare in England, but not uncommon in late Gothic work on the Continent, is the use of spirally twisted columns, found as early as c. 1360–70 in the sedilia of Limerick Cathedral, and after 1400 on a tomb in Holycross Abbey. Magnificent vaulted monuments to the Kings of Thomond existed at Ennis Abbey, dating from c. 1470 and c. 1500, and have been reconstructed from the fragments by Mr. Conor O'Brien. By the sixteenth century there was a flourishing school of native tomb-sculptors, who executed such works as the Grace and Purcell tombs in St. Canice's, Kilkenny in 1552, signed by Rory and William O'Tunny; and the Fitzgerald tomb and effigy in St. Brigid's, Kildare, dated 1575, and signed by Walter Brennagh (Walsh). These are entirely Gothic in form, as is the grand tomb-slab of Bishop Walter Wellesley of Kildare (died 1539) at Conall Abbey. The Irish tower, with

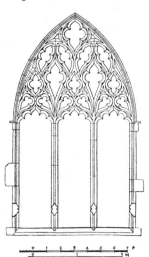

128 Newcastle Lyons: east window.

131 (*top*) ADARE ABBEY, 1464–.
132 KILKENNY: Black Abbey. South transept, *c.* 1350; tower, 1507.

IRELAND

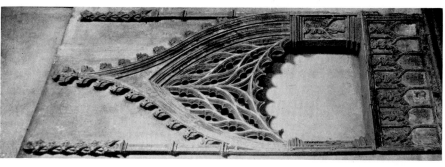

130 GALWAY: Church of St. Nicholas. Joyce tomb, *c.* 1484.

129 HOLYCROSS ABBEY: sedilia, *c.* 1405–10.

133 ABERDEEN: King's College
Chapel, 1500–06.   Designer
probably *Thomas   Franche*.

134 LADYKIRK: "Kirk of Steil",
1500–12.   Designer *Nicholas
Jackson*. Cupola a late addition.

135   STIRLING CASTLE: The Palace, 1539–.   Designer *Nicholas Roy*.

SCOTLAND

square clasping buttresses and corner turrets with crow-stepped battlements, belongs to the later Middle Ages, that at St. Patrick's, Dublin, being an early specimen. There is often little difference between the towers of churches and those of castles; both were used defensively. St. Michan's Church in Dublin has a good example of the fifteenth century, while that of the Black Abbey, Kilkenny, is of 1507 (**132**). Trim, with its castle and remains of churches, is one of the most

136   Scotland. The Orkney Islands
remained part of Norway until 1468.
For England see **33**; for Norway see **200**.

impressive relics of mediaeval Ireland. Gothic art long survived in Ireland as the ruling style, and at Londonderry Cathedral the excellent Gothic nave of simple design was not finished until 1633. Even later, rebuilding was done to religious houses, still occupied in districts remote from official control.

In Scotland, though the course of events was somewhat similar, the results were different. Scottish as well as Irish Gothic had been derived from England, though from another region. While the Somerset and west of England style had been transported to Ireland, Scotland before the end of the thirteenth century had formed a part of the northern artistic province whose centre was at York and whose simple and austere character stemmed from the great Cistercian abbeys. With very few exceptions, this stern simplicity is a marked characteristic of the later Scottish Gothic also. This applied not only to decorative elements, but to structure. Many of the Scottish churches of the fifteenth and sixteenth centuries retained pointed barrel vaults with cross-ribs of the type found at Autun early in the twelfth century, and spread throughout Europe by the Cistercians. As in Ireland, long and narrow churches without aisles were common, but the cruciform plan, with and without aisles, was also retained. Apses also, due to direct French influence, were common. French influence in the fifteenth and early sixteenth centuries was also the cause of the Scottish adoption of Flamboyant rather than Perpendicular tracery. Perpendicular work is mostly close to the Border, or can be traced to the few years of friendly intercourse following the marriage of James IV to Margaret Tudor in 1503.

During this short period alabaster was bought from "John Gelis Inglisman" for Stirling Palace, an English portrait painter named "Mynour" spent over a year at the Scottish Court, and in 1506 Aberdeen University contracted with John Burwell, the Serjeant Plumber to Henry VII, to roof the collegiate church, founded in 1494. To this period also belongs the markedly Perpendicular work of the presbytery and south nave chapels of Melrose Abbey, known to have been in progress in 1505. The south transept at Melrose is some fifty years earlier, and as pronouncedly French as the later work is English. This lends colour to the theory that the master, John Morow, whose epitaph states that he was born in Paris, was a Frenchman, Jean Moreau. Even if he had been one of the many Scots associated with the French Court towards the end of the Hundred Years' War, he would have learned the French Flamboyant tradition and brought it with him on his return to Scotland.

Much earlier than this French influence had entered Scotland. The tomb of Robert the Bruce was made of marble in Paris in 1329 and brought to Dunfermline Abbey. There is nothing to show whether the Robert who was master mason to the Bruce, and who at the King's personal directions undertook the building of Tarbert Castle in 1326, was Scots or French. In 1368 Queen Margaret had alabaster tombs for herself and for her husband David II brought from London, but in 1379 the tomb of Robert II was home-made by Master Nicholas the mason, with Andrew the painter, who was also keeper of the Mint at Edinburgh. At this period there were native masons of competence, for part of St. Giles, Edinburgh, was let to contract in 1387 to three men with the Scottish names John Prymros, John of Scone and John Skuyer. Most of the church was rebuilt between 1385 and 1416. Other great church works were the choir of St. John the Baptist, Perth (c. 1401–48), the nave of Stirling, begun in 1413, that of St. Machar's Cathedral, Aberdeen (1424–42), and the Church of Linlithgow, started in 1425.

Colleges of private foundation were also being built, as in England at the same time. Notable among them is Lincluden (c. 1429–40), with the splendid wall monument of Margaret, Countess of Douglas; and even more famous is that of Roslin, begun 1447. At Roslin are high vaults of pointed barrel type, but the astonishing feature is the profuse enrichment, suggestive of a Portuguese origin. But the comparison with Belem is not tenable, as the Portuguese monastery was not founded until fifty years later. Flemish influence is more probable; in 1441 Melrose Abbey had ordered their new stallwork from Cornelius de Aeltre of Bruges. The later stalls of Dunblane Cathedral, which survive, are in an extremely rich, Flemish style. Native craftsmen, Michael Waghorn at Glasgow Cathedral, and John Ferdour at St. Nicholas, Aberdeen, were making stalls and other timberwork between 1490 and 1510, and the fine ceiling of the nave of Aberdeen Cathedral, made c. 1520–30, was by James Winter of Angus. Castles of chiefly military purpose were probably designed and built by natives, as was Inverness

(1411–15) by John of Soulis, and the forework of Rothesay in the Isle of Bute begun by John and Hugh Cowper in 1512 "efter the Kingis devise", that is, to the instructions of James IV.

King James IV was a great builder and encourager of the arts, and he employed many master masons, some native and others French or probably French. Works had begun in Stirling Castle in his father's time (1469), when the master was Robert Jackson. This work probably included the Parliament Hall. James IV undertook further building in the castle, which he put in the hands of Walter Merlioun, a mason who had also built at Dunbar Castle and the nave of Perth Church (c. 1489–1500). Merlioun, who is thought to have been of French extraction, also built the original palace of Holyroodhouse by Edinburgh in 1499–1503. Another mason of great distinction was Thomas Franche, again probably of French origin, though his father, John Franch, was buried in Linlithgow Church in 1489. Master Thomas built the Bridge of Dee at Aberdeen and completed the works of St. Machar's Cathedral there (c. 1518–32). He was also master in charge of the Tay Bridge at Perth, and became King's Master Mason to James V in 1535. For the King he worked at Linlithgow and at Holyrood, and the chapel of King's College at Aberdeen, founded by Bishop William Elphinston and built in 1500–06, may well be his work (133). Contemporary with the college at Aberdeen is the Kirk of Steil, identified with the votive Church of Ladykirk, built 1500–12 (134). This was in charge of Nicholas Jackson, who also worked at Linlithgow, and perhaps a descendant of the Robert Jackson whom we have already met. Ladykirk is all the same typical of the French influence in Scottish churches. It has polygonal apses to choir and transepts, and the nave windows have three-centred heads. But it follows the local tradition in being aisleless, and in employing pointed barrel vaults with cross ribs. Another native mason was William Thom, who built much of Falkland Palace by taskwork in 1508–12.

The last Gothic buildings of Scotland were again built under direct French influence. Many French masters were brought in by James V: Moyse Martin from Orléans, Nicholas Roy, appointed a chief mason in 1539, and Martin's son of the same name. Roy worked at Stirling Palace (135) and at Falkland, where a series of statues was carved by "Peter Flemisman". Through the sixteenth century the French influence was maintained by the chief mason John Roytell, who though a Frenchman became a burgess of Edinburgh in 1550, and was King's Mason from 1557 to 1582 or later. Only at the end of the sixteenth century did the native Gothic reappear before giving place to the Renaissance, in the buildings of the famous Master of Work, William Schaw, including the noble north-western tower and spire of Dunfermline Abbey, rebuilt by him in 1594.

From Francophil Scotland it is fitting to return to France itself. The Gothic of northern France had, when we left it at the close of the thirteenth century, penetrated to all parts of western Christendom. It still had great possibilities of development, and in fact French architecture was changing rapidly at the outbreak of the great war with England. Much work on a grand scale was in progress. At Tours, where the cathedral choir had been finished about 1270, the transept was in progress in the early fourteenth century under André Frèredoux, master and sculptor; Orléans Cathedral had been started in 1287; Bayonne, begun with the chevet chapels in 1258, only carried out the main works of the high choir, transept and nave from 1310 (140). At Bayonne, under English rule, the nave shows influences related to the earliest Perpendicular works. But these influences were becoming common property, and are found also in the choir of Nevers Cathedral, built between 1300 and 1332. At the Benedictine Abbey of the Trinity at Vendôme work began on a church of very advanced design in 1306, though the nave was not built until the next century. A similar fate befell St.-Ouen at

Rouen (**139**), where the choir and crossing were completed in the twenty years 1319–39, but the central tower of Alexandre de Berneval was not proceeded with until *c.* 1430. Even so, its last stage was not built until the beginning of the sixteenth century, and the west front remained unfinished until it was pulled down in 1845.

Work went on also at cathedrals in the remoter provinces such as Brittany, where the choir of Quimper was built, and Tréguier begun in 1339. Later on, after 1375, the remarkable chapel of the Kreisker was founded at St.-Pol-de-Leon, though this again was not completed until the fifteenth century. The northern French works of the earlier fourteenth century were inspired by the verticalism and luminosity which had been developed by Pierre de Montreuil and his successors, but they were slow to adapt details such as window tracery to the new spirit. The use of the ogee curve was practically unknown before the last quarter of the century, and by that time the centre of interest had moved from great churches to great palaces and mansions. Royal, noble and private houses were the leading architecture of the reigns of Charles V and Charles VI. The minor arts were falling into the hands of the Flemings, and even the sculptors and painters, men such as

137 Caudebec Church, 1426.

André Beauneveu of Valenciennes and Jacquemart de Hesdin, came from the northern borders. By 1400 the plastic arts of France were governed by men in no sense French: Claus Sluter, Jan Maelweel (Malouel) and his nephews, the three brothers Limbourg. But for a generation or more the architects were still native born.

Chief of these court architects was Raymond du Temple, who began the old Louvre in 1362 and in 1364 was working on its great staircase, one of the marvels of the mediaeval world. In 1370 he had charge of the work of Notre-Dame and of the Collège de Beauvais. From 1367 he was working on the Church of the Célestins, from 1379 was building the Château de Vincennes, between 1389 and 1400 completed the Hôtel of the Duke of Orléans. When he died in 1404 he left two sons, Charles and Jean, who continued his work. Among his assistants were two members of the famous architectural family of Dampmartin, Drouet and Guy, both of whom were at work on the Louvre in 1365. Drouet de Dampmartin in 1383 became the master-general of the works in Burgundy, and designed the Chartreuse de Champmol by Dijon. Guy, or possibly his son (Guyot), became chief master to the Duke of Berry (**21**) and was architect of the Tour Maubergeon at Poitiers, as well as the famous fireplace in the great hall there, and the Ste.-Chapelle of Riom. It was an age of grandiose building largely for lay patrons, and Maître Raymond du Temple and the Dampmartins were the French counterparts of the English Yevele and Wynford. In the fourteenth century even a functional structure such as the fortified bridge at Cahors (**4**) was a specimen of calculated aesthetic design.

English, Flemish and German ideas in vaulting and enrichment began to be accepted in France, and were naturalized by French masons. Much ingenuity was displayed in planning and design, and the classic monotony of the thirteenth-century cathedrals was abandoned. Every work has marked individuality, and it is only possible to enumerate a number of outstanding buildings and their designers. The church at Caudebec (**137**, **138**) (1426–1520) by Guillaume Le Tellier has a single column behind the altar, a daring innovation* probably derived from Pamplona Cathedral (1397–1427), designed for Charles III of Navarre, possibly by the French mason-sculptor Jacques Pérut. This singularity was copied by Pierre Robin in his exquisite St.-Maclou at Rouen (1434–70). A more conservative design, with high blind triforium walls, was that of Pierre Chauvin and Pierre

* Also found in the hall-choir added to Dorpat Cathedral, Estonia.

139 ROUEN: Abbey Church of St. Ouen, looking east. Choir 1319–39, perhaps by *Jean Camelin*; nave 1459–1536.

138 CAUDEBEC: interior of church, 1426–1520. Designer *Guillaume Le Tellier*.

FRANCE

140 BAYONNE CATHEDRAL: nave and
west towers, 1310–.

141 (*below right*) COUTANCES CATHE-
DRAL: west front, *c.* 1220–50.

142 BORDEAUX CATHEDRAL AND
TOUR PEY-BERLAND, 1440–66.
Designer *Colin Tranchant*.

Lepage at Cléry (c. 1440–82); while at Eu the choir of the collegiate church was begun in 1455 as a traditional scheme with Flamboyant detail. Other great works of this period are the choir of Mont-St.-Michel, begun in 1448; the collegiate choir of Moulins (1468–1500), attributed to the canon Guillaume Foissier; and the Abbey Church of St.-Riquier, rebuilt after a fire from 1488 by Nicolas Lesveillé, with tierceron vaults. Here the stallwork was by Alexandre Huet who had worked on the famous stalls of Amiens Cathedral (1508–19) under Jean Turpin (**96**).

The last of the great cathedrals was begun at Auch in 1489 by Jean Chesneau, but was not completed until the reign of Louis XIV. Of the same period are the great churches of St.-Ouen at Pont Audemer (1488–1525) by Michel Gohier; St.-Wulfran of Abbeville* (1488–1539) (**31**); and Simon Moyset's lierne-vaulted St.-Nicolas-du-Port in Lorraine (1494–1530). Here are elements introduced from the hall-church: three parallel apses, and main arcades abutted by panelled cross walls above the arches in the aisles. Here and at Abbeville much was made of the entrance fronts, and much ingenuity was expended in designing Flamboyant portals and façades. The greatest master of this special form of work was Martin Chambiges of Paris, who designed the transept fronts of Sens (1494) (**32**), of Beauvais (1499), and the west front of Troyes (1502–31). He died at Beauvais in 1532, leaving a family who carried on his traditions of richly Flamboyant design. Rivalling the work of Chambiges is the magnificent central frontispiece of Rouen Cathedral (1509–14) by Roulland Le Roux. Le Roux was continuing the tradition begun by Jean Davy on the transept fronts about 1280 (**24**), and furthered by his predecessor Guillaume Pontifs, architect of the mighty Tour de Beurre (1485–1507).

Tower design, not in earlier periods a marked feature of French Gothic outside Normandy, was now cultivated. Jean Texier "de Beauce" designed the northern steeple at Chartres (1507–13); Jean de Felin, a disciple of Chambiges, that of St.-Jacques-de-la-Boucherie in Paris (1509–23) (**255**); and Antoine Salvan that of Rodez Cathedral (1513–26) (**243**). At Bordeaux, in addition to the four transeptal towers of the cathedral, an isolated bell-tower was built (1440–66) by Colin Tranchant for Bishop Pey-Berland, whose name it bears (**142**). The Church of St.-Michel also has a free-standing belfry with a tall spire, by Jean Lebas, a mason brought from Saintes. The tower was in progress from 1472 to 1486, and the spire was completed in 1492. The architecture of display was not limited to churches: it occurs equally in the great Hôtel of Jacques Cœur (**20**) at Bourges (1443–51) and even in the hospital at Beaune, designed like a great mansion by Jean Rateau for the Chancellor Nicolas Rolin (1443–49). As a final example of the secular buildings of northern France let us cite the Palais de Justice at Rouen, built between 1499 and 1526 to the designs of Roger Ango and Roulland Le Roux (**5**). But the last and most daring enterprise of French Gothic, an enterprise doomed to failure, was to crown the greatest of French churches. To the foolhardy Cathedral of Beauvais ambition was to add an incredible steeple, perched above the already overstrained piers of the crossing, and reaching a height of 502 feet, all but the last 100 of stone. The architect was Jean Vast, son of an elder Jean Vast who had been assistant to Chambiges and had died in 1524. The younger Vast, like his predecessor the younger Montreuil, must have been seized by a strange frenzy: he would complete the greatest of all buildings on the earth. As far as the steeple was concerned, he did complete it, in 1569, but it lasted only four years. Vast was not dismissed with ignomiry; on the contrary, he directed the necessary repairs which took five years, and only died in 1581, aged 72. His was the last as it was the wildest faith in the upward surging power of Gothic art.

The art of the South attempted no such fantastic heights. We have seen that

---

* At least one of the Abbeville masters, Jacques Cretel, came from Tours, where the cathedral was building its magnificent Flamboyant front.

its message of space and movement spread not merely into the Mediterranean lands but farther afield into Germany, Scandinavia and central Europe. But in France itself, after the victory of the North in the political field, its course was less spectacular. Among the cathedrals this southern art has left only one supreme monument, that of Albi (**241**). Begun in 1282 and complete in its main structure a century later, it stands as the type of the cellular church of one span, with side chapels between the counterforts buttressing the vault. The fact that Albi is built of a rose-red brick greatly adds to the beauty of the exterior, but the vast space of the interior is rendered tawdry by the Italian wall-paintings of the early sixteenth century. The structural additions on the contrary are well worthy of their setting: the portal of *c.* 1400, the Baldaquin or south porch of *c.* 1520–35, and the magnificent carved jubé and choir-screens of *c.* 1500.

Albi, though the type, is by no means the earliest church of its class. As we have seen, the cellular nave has distant roots, and among Gothic churches the Lamourguier at Narbonne must be considered a generation at least earlier than

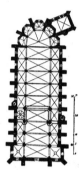

143 La Chaise-Dieu Abbey, 1342–75, by Hugues Morel.

Albi Cathedral. Later is St.-Bertrand-de-Comminges (1304–49), and the type is widespread through the region of the central South. The hall-church, with side-aisles as high or nearly as high as the central nave, received some development on French soil in the later mediaeval period, notably at Uzeste (*c.* 1295–1313) built for Pope Clement V. The architect is unknown, but the Pope's monument within the church was carved by the sculptor Jean de Bonneval, prosecuted for his slow progress in 1321. At Uzeste is seen that arrangement of hexagonal chevet chapels derived from Soissons Cathedral, which was to be adopted a century later at Pamplona Cathedral, and during the fifteenth century at churches covering a wide area: Caudebec, Rouen St.-Maclou, Troyes Ste.-Madeleine (1508–19) by Martin de Vaux, and Notre-Dame-de-l'Épine (1509–24), designed by Regny Gouveau and built by Antoine Guichart of Reims. In the opposite direction this plan passed through Tournai and Bruges to Lübeck and other Hanseatic churches, as far as St. Peter's in Riga.

The Abbey of La Chaise-Dieu was built for Pope Clement VI by Pierre de Cébazat from Clermont-Ferrand, to plans provided by Hugues Morel (**143, 242**). The chevet and six bays were built between 1342 and 1350, and the last three bays and the front were completed about 1375. The vault is relatively low, and the work of the greatest simplicity, with plain octagonal piers and little enrichment. La Chaise-Dieu is entirely southern in inspiration, but two other important churches of the South combine northern and southern motives. These are St.-Antoine-de-Viennois and St.-Maximin. Begun in the last years of the thirteenth century, each has three aisles, with lateral chapels beyond the outer aisles, and a central apse without ambulatory. St.-Maximin has in addition lateral apses set obliquely. Its nave chapels were added between 1327 and the middle of the fifteenth century, and the nave vaults were not finished until after 1512. At St.-Antoine the first work lasted from *c.* 1298 to 1342, after which the side chapels were added until 1384, and the last bay and the front were built *c.* 1450 by Jean Roberti, master of the works of King René's castle of Tarascon.

The greatest work of southern architecture in France is the Palace of the Popes at Avignon. The work includes two main sections. The first or Old Palace, built for the Cistercian Pope Benedict XII, is simple and austere, by Guillaume de Cucuron and, more especially, Pierre Poisson from Mirepoix, where Benedict XII had been bishop. This work began in 1334 and really ended at Poisson's death in 1341. Benedict died in the following year, and his Benedictine successor,

Clement VI, began the New Palace, to the south of the Old, and in a far more magnificent and ostentatious manner. The principal front and Pontifical Chapel were begun in 1344 and completed soon after 1352 (**6, 7**). The architect was Jean de Loubières, a mason who is thought to have come of a Tarasconese family. Of great interest are the contacts between artists of different nationalities, for which the papal works formed a clearing house. The chief masons were Frenchmen, but among the lesser masters were at least two Englishmen, Hugh Wilfred who built the Chapel of the Angels in the Cathedral of Notre-Dame des Doms,

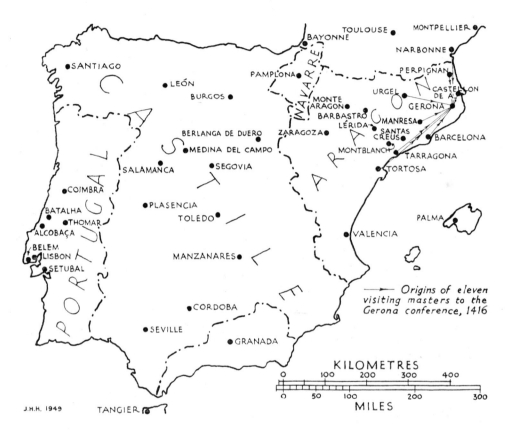

—▶ Origins of eleven
visiting masters to the
Gerona conference, 1416

J.H.H. 1949

144   Spain and Portugal, before the expulsion of the Moors and union of the Spanish kingdoms.

beside the Palace, in 1321–22; and Master John the Englishman (*Englicus, Anglicus*) who between 1336 and 1341 was among those building some of the northern parts of the Old Palace. An English painter, Master Thomas,* is also mentioned, in 1333, but the surviving paintings, deservedly famous, are mostly the work of the Italian, Matteo Giovinetti of Viterbo, who was working on the exquisite decorations of the Garderobe tower from 1343 to 1347. Simone Martini of Siena reached Avignon in 1336. Contact with the Italian painters or their work at Avignon is almost certainly a major factor in the great advances made by English painting between 1350 and 1400, under Master Hugh of St. Albans and his successors.

    The style of the French Midi was, even in the fourteenth century, still closely related to that of Catalonia and the kingdom of Aragon. We have already traced

---

* Possibly the great Master Thomas, son of Walter. Thomas worked at Westminster under his father from 1290; later, as chief painter was probably responsible for the abbey sedilia of *c.* 1307.

the earlier movements of Catalonian style, but there is a number of late buildings which constitute almost a national style, distinct at any rate from that of Castile. Immense artistic riches of sculpture, painting and the minor arts are still centred in Barcelona, and it is there that the finest series of Gothic buildings are to be seen. At the cathedral, the cloisters were begun in 1365 by Bernat Roca with the north walk, and finished on the opposite side by Andreu Escuder in 1448. At the north-east angle stands the lavatory beneath an enriched vault whose key-stone of St. George and the Dragon is a masterpiece of the sculptor Joan Claperós. The western nave of the cathedral, with the great lantern and details reminiscent of contemporary English work, was in progress under Bartomeu Gual in 1418–22 (**150**). Valencia Cathedral also boasts a fine lantern, built about 1404 by Juan Franck, but much more famous is the octagonal belfry or Miguelete. This was founded in 1381, but its architectural features are due to Pedro Balaguer, who in 1414 visited Lérida, Narbonne and other towns to examine towers with a view to the design (**244**). The Miguelete was completed in 1424 by a mason-contractor Martin Llobet.

Civil architecture in Catalonia is especially noteworthy. At Barcelona the Lonja or Exchange retains its great hall of 1380–92, of three aisles separated by arcades of three semicircular arches on very slender clustered piers. At the Ayuntamiento is the Hall of the Hundred, begun in 1373, and a fine main front of 1399–1402 by Arnau Bargués. This hall is a smaller version of the great Tinell in the Royal Palace, built by Maestro Guillem Carbonell between 1359 and 1370, with a wooden roof supported on stone semicircular arches (**8**). The span of the Tinell is fifty-six feet. Another great public building is the Palace of the Diputación General de Cataluña, begun by Marc Safont in 1416. On its main front is a magnificent carved panel in high relief of St. George and the Dragon (1418) by the sculptor Pere Johan (**160**). St. George was the national patron of Aragon, as he was of England. Finally two more of the great mercantile exchanges must be mentioned, those of Palma in Majorca and of Valencia. That of Palma (**147**) was designed by Guillermo Sagrera, who was master of Perpignan Cathedral in 1416. He superintended the works from 1426 to 1448, then quarrelled with his employers and went to Naples, where from 1450 he was in charge of rebuilding the Castel Nuovo.* Sagrera was one of the last great architects of Catalonia, and the Palma Lonja is of charming delicacy, with slender pillars surrounded by spiral mouldings. The design was adapted by Pedro Compte for the Lonja of Valencia, begun in 1482 and finished in 1498 (**239**). At the very end of the Gothic age, when the kingdoms of Aragon and Castile became united, the true hall-church began to spread in Aragon. Most of the examples are in Renaissance style, but there is Gothic work at the old Cathedral of Zaragoza and at Barbastro Cathedral (1500–33), while the last word of southern Gothic was spoken in the Collegiate Church of Berlanga de Duero, built in 1526–30 by Juan Rasinas, with circular columns and stellar vaulting.

The national Gothic of Castile was far more ecclesiastical than that of Aragon. There are few important civil buildings but many castles, some of them splendid examples of deliberately impressive design. One of the very finest is La Mota at Medina del Campo, built in brick from 1440 to the designs of Fernando de Carreño (**237**). Architecture on the largest scale was in progress at the Cathedrals of Toledo and Seville. Seville, the greatest Gothic cathedral in Europe, was begun in 1402 at the west end. Its architect was probably Alfonso Martínez; a century later it was still in progress, and its then architect, Alfonso Rodríguez,† was to design the first cathedral in the New World, at Santo Domingo in Hispaniola

* It is of this work that the story is told of the King of Aragon, Alfonso the Magnanimous, consulting a copy of Vitruvius for practical advice.

† Though it has now been shown that Rodríguez did not visit America, it seems premature to discard the tradition of his authorship.

(1521–) (**153**). Toledo Cathedral began its western front in 1418, under Alvar Martínez, and in 1425 the tower was begun. After completion of the square tower the octagon and spire were added in 1448–52 by Hanequin of Brussels, who continued master of the cathedral works until his death about 1471. Hanequin introduced the Flamboyant style from Flanders, and from his time Flemish and German influences played a leading part in Castile.

At Burgos the upper part of the west front with the openwork stone spires was due to Master Hans of Cologne (1442–56), who also provided the star-vaulting of the Chapel of the Visitation. His son Simon of Cologne and others built the Chapel of the Constable (1482–1532), while the central lantern with its curious mixture of Flamboyant and Renaissance elements, is the work of Felipe Biguery from Burgundy. This was not finished until 1568. The last great building begun before the union of the crowns of Castile and Aragon was the Church of San Juan de los Reyes at Toledo (1476), by Juan Guas (**66**). Guas had been the servant of Hanequin of Brussels in 1453, and in 1480 designed the castle of Manzanares. The work of Guas is of the richest Flamboyant, but just escapes decadence by its vitality. After the union of Spain and the conquest of Granada, there was a last burst of energy in cathedral building, in the hands of a small group of important masters. Juan de Alava began the Cathedral of Plasencia in 1498, also built the Church of San Esteban in Salamanca, and in 1531 became master of the works of Salamanca New Cathedral.

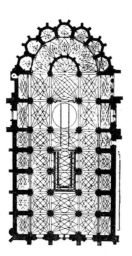

145 Segovia Cathedral, 1522–, by Juan Gil de Hontañón.

Started in 1512 by Juan Gil de Hontañón and Juan Campero, this was nearing completion at the death in 1577 of Rodrigo Gil de Hontañón, son of the first master. At Segovia work began under Juan Gil in 1522 and after his death in 1531 was continued by Rodrigo. The chevet was not begun until 1563, and the ambulatory completed in 1591 (**145**). The cloisters were begun in 1524 by Juan Campero, Juan Gil's partner. Segovia and Salamanca are splendid productions of a mature intelligence. Juan Gil de Hontañón had undoubtedly a wide knowledge of Gothic art and attempted, on the whole successfully, to combine the particular virtues of the greater schools. His great clustered piers and subordination of aisles recall Bourges; his stellar vaulting with curved ribs is derived from Germany. Only a certain tendency to disintegration of detail and to undue horizontality betrays the onset of the Renaissance. The contemporary work at Córdoba, on the other hand, by Fernán Ruiz, is a degenerate Plateresque, sadly unworthy of the immense mosque on which it intruded. The story of Spanish Gothic was not however quite finished. From the founding of Santo Domingo Cathedral in 1521 there was a new Gothic art in America.

Santo Domingo, designed by a Spanish master mason of high standing, and largely complete by 1527, was naturally a genuine European cathedral transplanted overseas (**153**). The original parts of the beautiful Dominican church (now San José) at San Juan, Puerto Rico, in course of construction in 1528, are also pure Gothic in style. But as the Spaniards extended their conquests to Mexico and Peru, several influences intervened to prevent the development of a great American Gothic art. Few if any craftsmen of importance actually reached America; the design of most of the early churches and civil buildings fell to amateurs, members of the clergy and nobility. This assisted the spread of Renaissance elements at the expense of Gothic. Besides this, the need to find a body of building craftsmen led to the employment of Indians, who introduced many native American conceptions into their work. The rarity of existing Gothic remains is also due to destruction, rebuilding, and damage from fires and earthquakes. In spite of this there remain important churches of Gothic plan and construction in Mexico, and Gothic vaults of stellar and reticulated patterns lasted for a century or more. Notable examples are the churches at Oaxtepec, Huejotzingo (*c.* 1530–70) and Tepeaca, while many others preserve Gothic features to a greater or less extent (**154–157**). In Peru, where also there were Gothic works, accident has served them less kindly, and little remains but fragments of the Dominican church at Lima, built in 1547 by Maestro Jeronimo Delgado; the ruins of the Church of San Agustin at Saña (1584–) and the Church of Guadalupe* with its star vaulting (**151, 152**). Complicated lierne vaults cover the great Renaissance cathedrals of Lima and Cuzco.

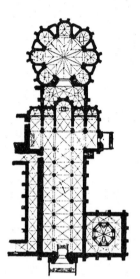

146 Batalha, 1387–, by Affonso Domingues

The art of Portugal has always remained unexpectedly distinct from that of Spain. There is no natural barrier, and the Portuguese people are perhaps rather closer than are the Catalans to the Spaniards of Castile. But by historical accident Portugal attained a highly individual status. Comparatively little of importance survives from the early Gothic period, apart from the great Cistercian Abbey Church of Alcobaça, begun in 1158 and finished by 1223. The nave and transept form a hall-church of unusual type, with immensely heavy and obstructive piers. The work was presumably carried out at least in part under French supervision. But by 1310, when the cloister was started, it was in charge of a native master, Domingo Domingues. Lisbon Cathedral was given a new choir of French design about 1350, but this was destroyed in the earthquake of 1755.

The first great national building, appropriately commemorating the victory of Aljubarrota which secured Portuguese independence, is the Abbey of Batalha. Founded in 1387, its chief architect was Affonso Domingues, perhaps a descendant of the master of the Alcobaça cloister. In spite of very strong English influences, shown in the long nave, square west front, and centrally planned chapter-house, Founder's Chapel, and eastern octagon, Domingues showed his genius in absorbing these factors into a whole greater than the sum of its parts (**17, 146**). His own work includes most of the church and the layout of the cloisters; he died in 1402. His successor Huguet brought the church to completion in 1415, then built the Founder's Chapel until 1434 (**159**), and during the next four years set out and began the octagonal series of chapels beyond the east end. The Founder's Chapel is certainly derived from the octagonal chapter-house within a small square cloister built at Old St. Paul's by William Ramsey; and the eastern chapels from the Ely octagon. Again, the nave of Batalha has been compared to that of Canterbury with some justification (**149**). Watson's objection that Prior Chillenden's work on the Canterbury nave was posterior to Batalha is unjustified, for the plan of Canterbury had been settled in 1377 and the aisle walls built by 1381. But the details at Batalha, though in some ways suggestive of English work, are not Perpendicular, but rather late Decorated in feeling. These curious contradictions are perhaps best explained by supposing a number of small-scale drawings to have been sent from England, drawn by a master of the Court, Henry Yevele or one of his staff; and the work detailed on the spot by a native master.

---

* It is uncertain whether this church was rebuilt after an earthquake of 1619, or if it is substantially the work begun in 1563.

147 PALMA: vaulting of the Lonja, 1426–48. Designer *Guillermo Sagrera*.

148 BELEM: Convent of Jeronimos, vaulting, 1500–22. Designers *Boutaca* and *João de Castilho*.

149 BATALHA: interior of church looking east, 1387–1415, by *Affonso Domingues*.

150 BARCELONA CATHEDRAL: western lantern, 1418–22, by *Bartomeu Gual*.

IBERIAN GOTHIC

151 SAÑA: ruins of the Church of San Agustin, 1584–.

152 CUADALUPE: detail of vault, 1563 or 1620?

153 SANTO DOMINGO CATHEDRAL: Interior looking east, 1521–27. Designer *Alfonso Rodriguez*.

PERU AND HISPANIOLA

154 HUEJOTZINGO: Friary Church,
c. 1530–70.

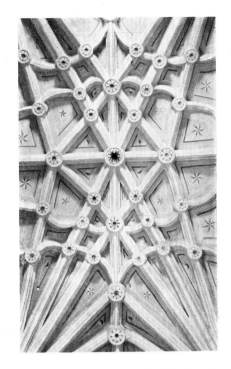

155 HUAQUECHULA: detail of vault.

156 TEPEACA: Friary Church.

157 OAXTEPEC: Friary Church.

MEXICO

158 THOMAR: south portal of convent, 1492–1513. Designer *João de Castilho*.

159 BATALHA: interior of Founder's Chapel, 1415–34, by *Huguet*.

160 BARCELONA: Diputación General, St. George, 1418. Sculptor *Pere Johan*.

161 BATALHA: portal of the Capellas Imperfeitas, *c.* 1503–09. Designer *Matheus Fernandes*.

Though the most important single building in Portugal, Batalha did not form a school. The southern hall-church was introduced in the College of Jesus at Setubal, founded in 1487 and designed by one Boutaca. He again was the first architect of the famous Convent of the Jeronimos at Belem, begun in 1500 by him, continued from 1511 to 1517 by Lourenço Fernandes, and completed after 1517 by the great João de Castilho (**148**). At Belem from 1524 a French sculptor, Maître Nicolas, was at work, and to him is due the mixture of Renaissance detail. Castilho in his earlier career was a convinced Gothicist, and though he died *c.* 1552 as a Renaissance designer, we must here remember his work on the convent of Thomar (1492–1513), including the noble south doorway (**158**). Apart from the actual door, surrounded by bands of Renaissance detail, this is late Gothic of Spanish type, as might be expected from an architect with such a surname. But the crowning glory of this period, the reign of King Manoel (1495–1521), was the incorporation into Gothic art of motives and enrichment derived from the Indies.* The results are often of astonishing beauty, and reach their finest expression in the work of Matheus Fernandes at Batalha. This was the unsuccessful attempt to complete the eastern octagon, since known as the Capellas Imperfeitas. The great doorway connecting the chapels to the church is an inspired masterpiece of the first class (**161**). This Manoeline Gothic is an architecture made up of carving, sculpture which has become the building itself. It was the worthy outcome of the Peninsula's century-long intercourse with the carvers and painters of Flanders, missionaries of achieved portrayal of nature. And to their work was wedded the imagination that had discovered the sea route to the Indies, and the new world of America.

We must now cross Europe to Flanders itself, which in the fourteenth century had succeeded Paris as the artistic centre of the Continent. The period of political union between the French and Imperial sections of the Low Countries really began in 1383, though it was not complete until 1430. At first under the protection, and later in the hands of the great dukes of Burgundy, Brussels attracted artists from the whole of the Netherlands. The classic instance of this, as M. Duverger has shown, was Claus Sluter or de Slutere, who came from Haarlem to Brussels where he was enrolled as a stone-worker, and thence passed on to the Court of Dijon. While France was being torn to pieces by prolonged war, Burgundy was consolidating its position into that of a great Middle Kingdom. On the Imperial side of the frontier, Holland, Guelders, Brabant, Limburg, Hainault and Luxemburg; and on the French side Flanders, Artois, Ponthieu and most of Picardy were added to the duchy and county of Burgundy. The dukes were enormously rich, and spent lavishly upon every aspect of art and cultural life. Their taste was hardly as pure as had been, for instance, that of Charles V of France or Richard II of England. Hence Flemish art covered itself with a profusion of surface decoration. Yet even this is excusable where the scale of the whole work was monumental.

We have seen that during the thirteenth and fourteenth centuries the Netherlands had become a province of the cathedral Gothic of North France, though retaining certain peculiarities: a love for western towers, and the use of triplet windows. As time went on, differentiation became more marked. The psychology of the great bourgeois patrons and mercantile corporations of the Netherlands was utterly different from that of the clerics and courtiers of France. The emphasis in these great manufacturing towns and river ports, even more than in the sea-ports of Catalonia, came to be placed on trade and civic pomp. Town halls, municipal belfries, gabled warehouses were almost as dominant as the greatest churches. The churches themselves were treated as the property of the burghers

---

* Portugal was the first European nation with possessions in other continents: Ceuta (1415), whose citadel is of the fifteenth century; and Tangier (1471). There are also fragments of Gothic work at Goa in Portuguese India.

and of the craft gilds and companies. Here, and in the Rhineland and along the North Sea and Baltic coasts, was the empire of mercantilism.

The churches of the later fourteenth and fifteenth centuries in Belgium were masterly works of eclecticism. The designers were well acquainted with what had

162 Greater Flanders. For France see **44**; for Germany see **9, 18, 200**; for England see **33**.

been going on in the surrounding lands, France, England and Germany, and produced a compound style of stateliness and splendour. The slender verticalism of St.-Ouen, Rouen; the spaciousness of the Wiesenkirche, Soest; and the panelled unity of Gloucester Cathedral choir are combined in works such as Antwerp Cathedral, begun in 1352 by Jean Amel (Appelmans) of Boulogne (**163, 164, 167**).

The choir was ended in 1411 under Pierre Appelmans, son of Jean Amel, the building of the nave followed, the west front was erected between 1422 and 1474, and the enormous north tower by Rombaut Keldermans and Dominique de Waghemakere was finished in 1518. The first architect's coming from Boulogne explains the close relations with both French and English cathedral art, and similar causes must lie behind the even more marked English characteristics in Notre-Dame (formerly St. Martin) at Hal (1341–1409). The statue of the Virgin and Child in the south porch at Hal (26) also comes very close indeed to the contemporary Madonna of the Outer Gate at Winchester College, though the Belgian work is slightly stiffer.

Fourteenth-century churches by known masters are Aerschot, begun in 1337 by Jan Prickart, and St. John at Diest, in progress in the second half of the century under Hendrik van Thienen. Another van Thienen, Master Jakob, was the chief mason of St.-Gudule in Brussels in 1388, and Jan van Thienen was

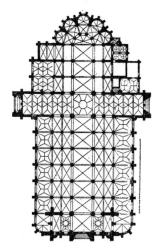

163 Antwerp Cathedral, 1352–, by Jean Amel.

164 Antwerp Cathedral: sections, 1352–1411, by Jean Amel and his son Pierre.

responsible for the nave there (1425–75). Again at St. Gudule there seems to be a close connexion with contemporary English work, in the likeness of its west front to that designed by Henry Yevele for Westminster Abbey. The main tradition of Belgian churches is continued by St. Sulpice at Diest by Sulpice van Vorst (choir 1417–37; completed after 1455 by Mathieu de Layens); St.-Gommaire at Lierre, largely by Jan II Keldermans and Jan Waghemans (nave 1425–43, tower 1460–75, choir 1471–1515); Louvain St.-Pierre (1425–97) by Sulpice van Vorst, continued by Jan II Keldermans, Mathieu de Layens and Alard van Hameel; Ghent St.-Michel (1440–80); and Mons St. Waudru (1450–82) by Mathieu de Layens. These great buildings were excelled by St.-Bavon at Ghent, whose nave and tower were built between 1461 and 1533, and by St. Rombaut at Malines (254). This had been begun in 1341 by a master from Picardy, Jean d'Osy, but its most striking feature is the vast tower, started in 1452 by Andries Keldermans and continued by his son Antoon I. These two members of the family and others built the town hall of Middelburg in Holland and its tower, from 1455 onwards. The Keldermans were from the end of the fourteenth century the greatest architectural clan in the Low Countries, and built not only churches but a large number of civic buildings in Belgium and Holland. Like earlier mason-architects, they were sculptors as well.

The Flemings travelled widely: Janin Lomme of Tournai made tombs at Pamplona in 1411–16; Hanequin of Brussels carried Flamboyant to Toledo. A later Brussels architect, Louis van Boghem, designed the Church of Brou (1513–32), and its rich carvings were the work of other Flemings, notably Conrad Meyt (**166**). At Troyes the magnificent jubé in the Church of Ste.-Madeleine was made in 1508–17 by Jean Gahilde, another Fleming. These are a few instances out of many, stretching from the fourteenth century to the sixteenth. On the other hand, foreign influences continued to enter Flanders, and at Liège is the fifteenth-century hall-church of Ste.-Croix. Renaissance elements began to reach the Netherlands fairly early, and are notable for instance in the remarkable work of Aert van Mulcken at Liège: the Church of St. Jacques (1513–38) (**170**) and the Palace of the Prince-Bishops, begun in 1526.

The civic buildings of the country are very numerous, in spite of losses due to war. The immense Cloth Hall of Ypres went back to the thirteenth century (1202–1304). At Bruges is the famous Belfry of the late thirteenth century, and the town hall begun in 1376; the Brussels town hall was started in 1402 by Jakob van Thienen, and its tower of 1449 was added by Jan van Ruysbroeck. The Louvain town hall (1448–63), a particularly fine work by Mathieu Layens; that of Ghent, begun in 1517 by Rombaut Keldermans and Hermann de Waghemakere; and that of Oudenarde (1525–29) by Henri van Pede belong to the same class. All are imposing buildings of several storeys with enrichments and statuary, steeply pitched roofs and ornamental turrets. Normally they are intended to be seen broadside, in contrast to the Baltic German type of town hall, with its end façade, a towering showfront.

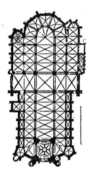

165 Breda: Church of Our Lady, *c.* 1380–.

The area of modern Holland was debatable ground between the Franco-Flemish and the north German spheres of influence. Towards the end of the Middle Ages it became more definitely linked to Flanders, and as we have seen there were considerable interchanges of craftsmen. Probably the greatest single influence was the building lodge of Utrecht Cathedral. Certainly the great tower (1321–82) by Master Jan van Henegouwen (i.e. Hainault) was the exemplar for a whole series of noble versions. Apart from the towers, which are sometimes quite rich, as at Our Lady's Church in Breda (1468–1509) (**165**), the Dutch churches are much simpler and less extravagant than those of Belgium. This effect has often been exaggerated by post-mediaeval whitewashing in Holland, but is deeply rooted in the architecture itself. A noteworthy example of this extreme simplicity is St.-Bavon at Haarlem, whose nave was begun about 1400 and finished in 1445 by Godevaert de Boscher and Steven van Afflighem (**251**). The choir followed and was complete in 1483. The simple style is perhaps surprising in view of the southern origin of the architects, from the borders of Belgium. The name de Boscher refers to sHertogenbosch (Bois-le-Duc), where the Cathedral of St. Jan forms the one outstanding exception to the rule of Dutch austerity (**168, 171, 249**). sHertogenbosch is extremely rich in treatment, Flemish rather than Dutch, and with a striking combination of French and English characteristics: the full chevet and plain quadripartite vaults of France, and the wiry vertical emphasis and quasi-Perpendicular panelling of England. The choir was built in 1419–39 by Willem van Kessel, on the foundation of the older chevet begun in 1280 by Marcilius de Colonia. Much of the nave and external sculptures was carried out between 1478 and 1529, largely by the famous Alard van Hameel.

Other important churches are the Hooglandsekerk at Leiden, begun in 1377 but not finished until the sixteenth century (**250**); and the Nieuwe Kerk of Delft

166   BROU: interior of Church, 1513–32, by *Louis van Boghem*.

FLEMISH GOTHIC IN FRANCE

167 ANTWERP CATHEDRAL: interior looking east, 1352–1422, by *Jean Amel.*

168 SHERTOGENBOSCH CATHEDRAL: choir 1419–39, by *Willem van Kessel.*

169 HUY: Church of Notre-Dame, 1311–.

170 LIÈGE: Church of St. Jacques, 1513–38, by *Aert van Mulcken.*

THE LOW COUNTRIES

(1383–1496), with its choir of 1465–74 by Jakob van der Borch, the then master of the works of Utrecht Cathedral. The Chapel of the Sacrament at Meersen of the mid-fifteenth century is a work of unusual delicacy, with finely cut mouldings and transomed windows and panellings of almost English appearance. The Tabernacle itself is, however, thoroughly Flemish (**264**). Of the towers, some of the finest after those of Utrecht and Breda are at St. Jan, Maastricht (*c.* 1450); Zierikzee St. Lievenskerk, begun in 1454 by Andries Keldermans from Malines; and that of the Martinikerk at Groningen (1468–82).

Civil buildings of importance are relatively rare, apart from a number of picturesque castles, for example the early thirteenth-century moated quadrangle at Muiden (**3**). At the Hague the mediaeval hall of the palace, known as the Ridderzaal, was designed about 1275 by Gerard van Leyden; it belongs wholly to the North German type of brick hall with show-front, of which it is a fine and early example (**212**). The timber roof, now a modern restoration, is important structurally for its single arched span, and artistically for its unadorned simplicity. There are some fine town gates, particularly the Amsterdamsche Poort of Haarlem, built about 1488. This forms an impressive turreted pile, with low forework and tall main gateway behind. The last days of Dutch Gothic, before the coming of the Renaissance, were strongly influenced by the work of Flemings such as the Keldermans, who produced the town hall of Middelburg and other civic buildings, as well as some church work. Dutch thrift was giving way before Flemish opulence.

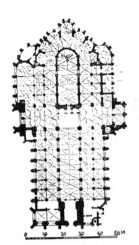

171 sHertogenbosch Cathedral, 1419–, by Willem van Kessel.

Holland and eastern Belgium had been within the nominal area of the Empire, but the special conditions of the region had drawn them into artistic union with provinces of France. From the fourteenth century the Low Countries had reached almost national status, and the Flemish style in architecture, sculpture and painting ranks in the fifteenth and early sixteenth centuries with that of England, and takes the place previously occupied by Paris. In contrast to this tendency of diverse groups to coalesce was the super-national organization of art in central Europe. The Empire was far from being national, although at its core lay a body of German vernacular sentiment. This became widely dispersed outside the strictly German territories through the colonies of German merchants planted in various parts of Hungary, Poland and the Baltic. Neither the Magyars nor the Slavs were makers of urban settlements, and their princes welcomed the aptitude of the Germans for trade and their skill as craftsmen. The history of Gothic art, largely urban as it is, is therefore in these countries the story of groups of alien settlers. Apart from the Gothic work of these settlers, and of individual artists from France, Italy or England, there was a lively current of folk-art in each country. So far as there may be said to be a national Gothic in each of the countries of central Europe, it is the outcome of this current of folk-art taking counter-effect upon the German and other settlers and visitors. But this effect was minimized in two ways: the German lodge-masons responsible for the greater buildings were subject to remote control from Strassburg; and the great art-patrons commissioned works from masters of international repute whose homes might be in Flanders or Italy.

The German Gothic sphere in the stricter sense can be divided into two main regions: the area of stone building covering the central Empire (exclusive of the Netherlands), Switzerland and the Austrian provinces; and the northern realm of brick building from Friesland across the North German plain and up to the head of the Baltic. The first was dominated by the Strassburg Lodge and its subordinates at Cologne, Bern and Vienna, and corresponded to the region of the High German language. The second was the area of the Hanseatic League, and of "Dutch". Outside the Empire, Hungary was under the control of the Vienna Lodge; most of Poland as well as the Baltic belonged to the Hanseatic sphere of brick. Within the Empire, the Slavonic nationalism of Bohemia gave it a special character, which was reinforced by the direct introduction of French masters. Discussion of the whole area must, simply as a matter of convenience, be divided under several heads: central Germany, with Switzerland and Austria; Bohemia and Moravia; Hungary with Transylvania and Croatia; northern Germany with Poland and the Baltic.

We left the development of German Gothic at the point where the new hall-church had come to stay, and when Master Erwin had at Strassburg united the elements of a new style. This style, the first native to Germany, bears the same relation to later work as Rayonnant does to Flamboyant, or Decorated to Perpendicular. It soon produced results across the Rhine, and the dominance of

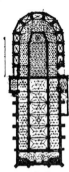

172 Schwä-bisch-Gmünd: Kreuzkirche, 1330–, by Heinrich Parler.

Strassburg can be traced at Cologne, at Oppenheim in the nave of the Katharinenkirche (c. 1320–40), and in the octagon of the tower of Freiburg in the Breisgau (c. 1310–50) (**252**). At Freiburg there seems already an awareness of what was happening in England, the move towards Perpendicular panelling; and similar details occur thereafter. Without accepting the Perpendicular style, German architects were profoundly affected by it, and motives derived from it occur everywhere after 1350, but more particularly in northern Germany. Transomed windows of English inspiration are combined with the Ste.-Chapelle motive in the choir of Aix-la-Chapelle (1355–), and the panelling motive and suppression of the triforium at Halberstadt Cathedral choir (1354–1402). At Halberstadt the English plan of a lower Lady Chapel on the main axis was also adopted, in 1362. That the English influences came by way of Cologne is a natural supposition, and its probability is heightened by the fact that it was from Cologne that the family of Parler derived. It was Heinrich Parler from Cologne, at the Holy Cross Church of Schwäbisch-Gmünd (nave from 1330, choir begun in 1351) (**172**), and his son

Peter at Prague and elsewhere in Bohemia, who more than any other architects initiated Sondergotik. The choir at Gmünd is derived from that of the Cistercian Abbey at Zwettl (1343–48); the sweeping outer wall enclosing ambulatory chapels was a very old Cistercian plan; what was new was the raising of the ambulatory itself to hall-church height.

The buildings of the new art of the Parlers were dominated by the idea of unity, even when they were traditional in their main outlines. Hans or Johann, brother of Peter, went from Gmünd to Freiburg to begin the new choir in 1354, and in 1357 he was at Basel. Master Michael of Cologne, who was starting the cathedral nave in the years between 1350 and 1395, was a connexion by marriage. Also to the Parlers belongs the Frauenkirche at Nuremberg, founded in 1355 by the Emperor Charles IV, Peter's patron. In 1399 Wenzel, Peter's son, went from Prague to Vienna to give his advice on the great tower of St. Stephen's, and the tower and its spire were completed in 1433 by Hans von Prachatitz, who had been a pupil of Peter (**270**). Other members of the family were masters of the Cathedrals of Ulm and Milan during the last twenty years of the fourteenth century.

The great clan of Parler led the way, but there was no lack of followers. At Ulm from 1392 to 1471 the mastership passed from father to son through the three Ensingers, Ulrich, Matthäus and Moritz. The choir had been built in 1377–83 under Heinrich and Michael Parler; the Ensinger family completed the nave and the lowest stage of the great tower; finally the rest of the tower, with the design for the spire only built in the nineteenth century, was the contribution of Matthaeus Böblinger (1474–92). The west porch, built before Ulrich's death in 1419, was provided with statues carved by Meister Hartmann (**257**). The Ulm choir-stalls of 1469–74, by Jörg Syrlin the elder, are one of the finest examples of German joinery and wood-carving (**97**). Regensburg Cathedral (**2**) also was built under the Parler influence, for Wenzel Roritzer, master until 1414, had been their pupil, and the work remained in charge of his sons and close relatives until 1519, when all was finished except the spires. Konrad, son of Wenzel Roritzer, provided the designs for the choir of St. Lawrence in Nuremberg, and it was built in 1445–72 under his direction and that of his son Matthaeus, the author of the famous treatise (**175**).

The churches of the largest scale, such as Vienna, Ulm, Regensburg and Cologne, inevitably took so long to build that their designs were subject to extensive modification. Some buildings of more modest size show to better advantage the genius for design possessed by a number of the masters of the late fourteenth and fifteenth centuries. The greatest of these masters apart from the Parlers, was Hans Stethaimer of Burghausen, about thirty miles north of Salzburg. He was in very close touch with the Parler circle of Prague and its offshoot at Vienna, and designed a series of large churches of magnificent spatial content and movement. The chief of these are St. Martin at Landshut (*c.* 1390–1432), with immensely tall and slender octagonal piers; and the Church of the Franciscans at Salzburg, begun in 1408, with a "surprise" effect of a hall-choir, brilliantly lit, seen through an archway beyond a darker nave (**176**). The same idea appeared in the contemporary Black Church of Brassó (Kronstadt) in the extreme south-eastern corner of Transylvania (choir *c.* 1390–1447; nave *c.* 1435–65), 600 miles away; in spite of the distance involved there seems little doubt that Stethaimer must have provided the original designs. The completion of the work at Brassó was in local hands, which provided a west doorway that owes nothing to German precedent (**193**).

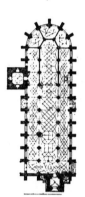

173 Dinkelsbühl: St. Georg, 1448–92, by Nicolaus Eseler.

Two other architects who deserve mention are Nicolaus Eseler the elder, and Aberlin Jörg (Albrecht Georg) (**18**). Eseler had an extensive practice in northern Swabia, and was even employed as far away as Mainz by the Archbishop. He built most of the church of St. Georg in Nördlingen, and several others in the region, but his greatest work is St. Georg in Dinkelsbühl (1448–92), a well-nigh perfect hall-church design (**173**, **177**). Jörg, an almost exact contemporary of Eseler (he died in 1494), was born in Stuttgart, and became architect to the Counts of Württemberg, as well as to the great collegiate church of their capital, his own home town. He was brought into close contact with the work of the Parlers at Gmünd, where he built some of the nave vaults of the Holy Cross Church, and in the course of his extensive work carried out a "Parler-Renaissance", as Herr Kletzl has termed it. This has the greater significance, in that the important fragments of Prague and other Parler drawings studied by Kletzl were found at Stuttgart.

The splendid Frauenkirche at Munich was built in brick by Jörg Ganghofer in 1468–88 (**174**, **253**). His home was near Landshut, and he follows closely the Parler tradition as interpreted by Stethaimer; his designs were approved by a committee of which a leading member was Konrad Roritzer of Regensburg. An interesting point of design in Ganghofer's work, found also in that of Roritzer at St. Lorenz, Nuremberg, is the high pitch of the vaults, taken from that used much earlier at Strassburg and Metz (**13**), and elsewhere in the debatable ground between France and the Empire. Peter Parler at Prague and many of his followers had been content with the rounded effect of a relatively low-pitched vault, emphasizing the spatial unity of their art. The reintroduction of sharper arches and vaults restored the aspiring quality of northern Gothic, which had been endangered though never extinguished in the German hall-churches. The northern tradition in vaulting seems to have been preserved in the exquisite mid-fourteenth century churches of Breslau in Silesia, the Sandkirche and Dorotheenkirche. Both were in progress during the early years of the union of Silesia with Bohemia, and the Dorotheen-kirche was actually founded by the Emperor Charles IV in 1351.

The design of lierne, stellar and net vaults became in Germany, as in England, an absorbing occupation. Germany never adopted the true fan-vault, but after exhausting the possibilities of lierne ribs began to explore the forms produced by interlacing curves. Such a vault spans the hall-church of Annaberg in Saxony (1499–1520), begun by Peter Ulrich von Pirna and completed by Jakob Heilmann von Schweinfurt. A rich harvest of such forms was reaped by Bohemia when, late in the fifteenth century, the disturbed period of the Hussite Wars came to an end. There and in Poland an even more daring experiment was made, of eliminating vault-ribs entirely, and reverting to groin-lines which marked out stellar patterns of honeycombed cells. Alternatively, net-patterns of lozenges in ribbed vaults remained in use until the very end of the Gothic period. A fine example covers the Liebfrauenkirche of Halle-an-der-Saale, begun in 1529; it greatly resembles that of the Franciscan Church at Szeged in Hungary, founded 1503. A similar vault covers the early Renaissance north porch (1513) of Gyulafehérvár Cathedral in Transylvania (**197**). Halle is noteworthy for its use of tall columns of concave hexagonal section, similar to those found in England at Chipping Campden and Northleach.

A few remaining works in central Germany deserve mention. At Erfurt Cathedral the nave was converted into a hall-church, retaining its thirteenth-century piers with attached shafting, and a great central tower erected, by Hans von Strassburg after 1452. At Meissen in Saxony the cathedral was provided with a tall rectangular showfront, begun in 1479 by Master Arnold of Westphalia (**273**). Arnold had come to Meissen to build the palatial castle known as the Albrechts-burg (1471–85), one of the most outstanding of German monuments, with a spiral staircase based on that of Raymond du Temple in the old Louvre at Paris. Another Westphalian master, Erhard Küng, went to Switzerland to build the west front of Bern Cathedral (1483–1506); the upper section of the tower was added by Peter Pfister, and the octagon leading to the spire by Peter Kleinmann, who died in 1545 (**271**). At Basel (**269**), the west front was designed (1414) by Ulrich von Ensingen. The northern spire was complete by 1429; the southern tower built by Vincenz Ensinger (1470–75), and the spire added (1488–1500) by Hans von Nussdorf. Another important spire, based on that of Freiburg in the Breisgau, was that of Freiburg, Switzerland (1470–92) by Georg Jordil from Geneva. The statues of the fine western porch were carved in 1474 by Gylian Aetterli (**272**). The Swiss masters, under the chief master at Bern, and later at Zürich, formed part of the German lodge organization until after the end of the Middle Ages, and their work has no separate national characteristics. An attractive example of it is the church of St. Oswald at Zug, built in 1478–83 by Hans Felder of Oettingen in Bavaria (**260**).

German civil architecture is of considerable importance; until the recent war Germany's ancient cities had remained less altered than any in Europe. Not only ordinary houses of all types, but every form of specialized building was well represented. The enriched fountains, for instance, were often works by the great

174 MUNICH: Frauenkirche, interior looking east, 1468–88.
Designer *Jörg Ganghofer*.

THE GERMAN NEW ART

175 NUREMBERG: Church of
St. Lorenz, choir 1445–72.
Designer *Konrad Roritzer*.

176 SALZBURG: Franciscan
Church, choir, 1408–.
Designer *Hans Stethaimer*.

177 DINKELSBÜHL: Church of St. Georg,
1448–92. Designer *Nicolaus Eseler the elder*.

178 LANDSHUT: Church
of St. Martin, *c.* 1390–
1432, by *Hans Stethaimer*.

GERMAN HALL-CHURCHES

masters: that at Nuremberg known as the Schöne Brunnen (1385–96) was probably by Heinrich Parler. Among the town halls of stone perhaps the finest was the Altes Rathaus at Brunswick (1393–1468) (**215**), while the mediaeval hall of dancing and entertainment at Cologne, called the Gürzenich (1441–47), is of admirably simple design. It was by Johann von Bueren, the city architect, who may well have known English work of similar treatment. Other types of building may be represented by the Parsonage of St. Sebaldus at Nuremberg (**213**), and the sturdy Osthoventor (1523–26) at Soest, a noble town-gate designed by Meister Porphyrius from Neukirchen in Hesse.

Between the Gothic art of Germany proper and that of Bohemia there is a subtle difference. In spite of the settlement of the Bohemian towns by Germans,

179 Bohemia and Moravia. For Germany see **9**, **18**, **200**; for Hungary see **182**.

their interpenetration by Slavs and the political history of the country combined to create a separate artistic entity. Alone among the divisions of the mediaeval Empire, Bohemia had a connected history as an organized national state. This gave its architecture a high degree of internal cohesion, and made it possible to assimilate conflicting elements from France and from various parts of Germany. Throughout Bohemian Gothic art there is a common fondness for sharp, clear outlines, high-pitched roofs and vaults, lancet windows, well-defined mouldings and crisp carving. There was not the same quantity of heavy Romanesque work in being, as in Germany, and Bohemia seems always to have been more ready for innovation. Even in the second half of the thirteenth century the country accepted French work of a very pure style, such as the Chapel of St. Barbara in the Convent of St. Agnes at Prague (*c.* 1250–) and the chapels of Zvíkov (Klingenberg) Castle (*c.* 1270–) and Bezděz (Bösig) Castle (*c.* 1285). By about 1300 Bohemia possessed great monastic churches like that of the Cistercians of Sedlec by Kutná Hora (Kuttenberg), with fully developed chevet of seven chapels and simple lancet windows. Even in Moravia, then a borderland, the church of Třebíč (Trebitsch), begun in the mid-thirteenth century, possessed extremely advanced Gothic ribbed vaults of striking design.

Paradoxically, national art in Bohemia was the child of an inspired inter-nationalism. We have already seen that it was the Emperor Charles IV of the House of Luxemburg who caused Prague to become an archbishopric, and its cathedral to be the greatest in central Europe. His first architect was a northern Frenchman, brought from southern France; his second master a Rhinelander who had been educated in Swabia, and was fully aware of the new currents from Strassburg and from England. The outcome of Peter Parler's work in Prague from 1353 to his death in 1399 was a new and complete style: the Sondergotik. That this style became essentially German rather than Czech was in some measure due to the outbreak of the Hussite Wars in 1419. Bohemian art is cut in two by this politico-religious upheaval; there is the rich harvest of the Parlers before it, and quite separately a late-Gothic flowering for about a century from 1480. So it was that the main lines of development from the Parlerian revolution of necessity grew outside Bohemia.

Within Bohemia there had been a predominance of French influence even before the arrival of Matthias of Arras. Another master from the same source, William of Avignon, had been called in to build the bridge of Roud-nice (Raudnitz) in 1333. Even in the Old-New Synagogue of Prague, rebuilt after the burning of the Jewish quarter in 1338, the octagonal piers with simple vaults supported on carved corbels instead of a single capital, have kinship with the vaulted halls of the Midi. Of the simpler churches of the period St. James in Kutná Hora is outstanding: a hall-church with tall moulded piers and no capitals, and simple quadri-partite vaults. On both sides of the nave piers are statues on pedestals, following the tradition of the Ste.-Chapelle. There is an aisleless chancel and twin western towers: a scheme often to be repeated through central Europe; here it dates entirely from 1340 to 1420. At Hradec Králové (König-grätz), the Church of the Holy Ghost has a tall aisleless presbytery between slender towers, and a nave with raised central aisle but side-lit from the outer aisle windows. The Dean's Church at Dvůr Králové (Königinhof) has a true hall-nave with acute vaults on tall round columns with heavy capping (c. 1400); and a more graceful form of the same design appears in the nave of the Holy Trinity at Kutná Hora, completed by 1420. Dvůr Králové resembles St.-Serge at Angers, while the Kutná Hora church approaches the attenuation of the fifteenth-century work in the Abbey of St.-Germain at Auxerre. The French two-aisled scheme of friars' church occurs in the Augus-tinian Convent at Třebon (Wittingau) (c. 1369–80) (**180**), and the influence of south-western France may also be seen in the slightly domical lierne vaults (mid-fourteenth century) of the Conventual Church of the Minorites at Hradec Jindřichův (Neuhaus).

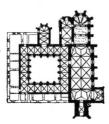

180   Třebon:
Augustinian Friary,
c. 1369–80.

The remaining Bohemian buildings of the later fourteenth and early fifteenth cen-turies belong mainly to Peter Parler and his sons, Wenzel and Johann, and brother Michael. The completion of the choir of Prague Cathedral is the masterwork of the family, and combines English with French and German elements. The glazed triforium with its transparency of screens recalls St.-Denis nave and Troyes Cathedral; the slender attached vaulting shafts seem based on Gloucester, as is the transomed quasi-Perpendicular panelling of the exterior (**186, 266**). The work of the great south front began in 1396, three years before Peter's death, and was con-tinued by his sons until 1420. Master Peter was directly responsible for the choir of St. Bartholomew, Kolín (1360–78), and for the Tower on the Charles Bridge at Prague (1376–78), as well as for the bridge itself, begun in 1357. He must also have made designs for the tall presbytery of the Týn Church in Prague, begun about 1380, and for the choir of St. Barbara at Kutná Hora, only started after his death. The great polygonal vault of the Karlov Church in Prague, though in its present state dating from 1575, also owes its plan to him. At the abbey of Zlatá Koruna (Goldenkron) the west front with a four-light window of rather English design (c. 1359–) is by Michael Parler; and to Peter's son Johann are attributed St. Jiljí at Milevsko (Mühlhausen) (c. 1407) and St. Vít at Český Krumlov (Krumau) (1407–39) with fine star-vaulted presbyteries and hall-naves. Also to the Parler school belongs the presbytery of the Dean's Church at Klatovy (Klattau). The great imperial castle of Karlštejn (Karlstein) (1348–67), with its important paintings by Master Theodoric in the Chapel of the Holy Cross (1357–67), was the grandest domestic building of its age, but has suffered greatly from alterations. The sculpture of the period includes the portraits in Prague Cathedral and such exquisite works as the Pilsen Madonna (**22, 27**).

A gap of some three-quarters of a century intervenes between the age of the Parler and the late Gothic architecture of Bohemia, owing to the Hussite revolution. This is partly filled by some buildings in Moravia, less affected by the wars, and of these St. Maurice's Church at Olomouc (Olmütz) is the chief (**181**). Begun in 1412, and mainly built between 1453 and 1491, it is a fine example of the hall-church with three parallel apses; the piers are of moulded section, and have no capitals. A further and most beautiful development is at St. James's in Brno (Brünn), with a hall-choir on moulded piers without capitals (**185, 263**). This was a long time in construction, from 1480 to 1552, but much of the work was in the hands of the famous Master Anton Pilgram, from 1495 to his death twenty years later. He was also the architect of the "Jews' Tower" (1508) and of the magnificent pinnacled portal of the town hall of Brno (1511). At St. James's, Pilgram was succeeded by Mert Hübel, who designed the church at Doubravník, not carried out until 1535–57. An earlier Moravian architect who worked in the extreme south, around Znojmo (Znaim), was Niklas von Edelspitz (Mikuláš ze Sedlešovic), who flourished from 1440 to 1498, completed the choir of the Premonstratensian Church of Bruck by Znojmo, in 1445–48 built the town-hall tower there, and between 1480 and 1496 began the Church of St. Wolfgang at Gnaderlsdorf.

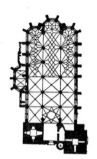

181 Olomouc: St. Maurice, 1412–91.

Several important churches in the south of Bohemia took up the thread of design: Dolní Dvořiště (–1488), a hall-church with slender panelled pillars and a net-vault; the Dean's Church at Chvalšiny (1487–1507) with curious vault-ribs like broken-off twigs; and the cloisters of the Dominican Friary at České Budějovice (Budweis), with simple vaults and elaborate traceried windows. A little farther north, the Franciscan Church at Bechyně (1491– c. 1520) exemplified a further daring advance in vaulting: the adoption of the cellular vault with groining of stellar patterns, but no ribs (**190**). On the other hand, in the Chapel of Křivoklát (Pürglitz) Castle (1493–1522), the vault-ribs are greatly emphasized, and there is an elaborate skeleton pendant (**261**), analogous to that in Alcock's chantry chapel at Ely. Various local masters produced important Gothic churches in the sixteenth century, such as the Dean's Church at Pardubice (Pardubitz) by Vilém z Pernštejna (1507–); the Sternberg Chapel of the Archdeacon's Church at Pilsen (1510–); Master Staněk's broad hall-church at Tábor (1512–) with simple octagonal piers; and more notable, the Dean's Church of Most (Brüx). This was built 1517–48 after plans by Jakob Heilmann von Schweinfurt, of Annaberg in Saxony. This has tall octagonal piers with hollow faces, no capitals, curving vault-ribs, and skeleton pendants. Heilmann, who may have been a pupil of Benedikt Ried, completed Peter Ulrich's Annakirche at Annaberg (1515–25), built the

Wenzelskirche at Naumburg (1517–) and the Zwickau Marienkirche (1521–23). His predecessor Ulrich, also known as Peter von Pirna, built the town Church of Pirna, began the important Church of Annaberg, and seems to have worked at Dresden and elsewhere.

The last great Gothic masters who worked in Bohemia were Matthias Rejsek and Benedikt Ried (Rejt). Rejsek completed the Prague Powder Tower, begun by Master Wenzel in 1475; worked on the Týn Church from 1493; completed the presbytery of St. Barbara in Kutná Hora (*c.* 1499); and carried out domestic work in Prague and elsewhere. Rejsek's style is an enriched version of that of Peter Parler, strong and virile. He probably designed the fine fountain at Kutná Hora (1493–95) (**274**). Benedikt Ried, though another great artist, showed signs of the decadence of Gothic, notably in his vaults of meandering and indecisive curves in

182   Hungary.   For Bohemia see **179**; for Germany see **9**, **18**, **200**.

the Vladislav Hall of the Castle at Prague (1493–1503) (**187**), and the naves of St. Barbara at Kutná Hora (*c.* 1540) (**188**), and Louny (Laun) (*c.* 1520–30). But in spite of a certain weakness, his buildings have a noble spaciousness and are filled with movement.

The full story of Gothic art in Hungary can never be known, for its most important monuments were ruthlessly destroyed by the Turks during their rule of a hundred and fifty years. Only in the remote principality of Transylvania, among the mountains of Slovakia, and in a few isolated remains, can its development be traced with certainty and in detail. The loss is the greater, in that the remains and documentary record make it clear that Hungarian Gothic was one of the most important national flowerings of art outside France and England. The isolation of the country within great mountain ranges, and its early political organization, gave it a curious likeness to England. Its isolation was relatively much less, however, and during the later Middle Ages it depended largely upon the German and Bohemian masters who worked within the Empire. In the reign of Matthias Corvinus (1458–90) there was much intercourse with Italy, resulting in the very early importation to Hungary of Renaissance forms. Long before this

183 PRAGUE: St. George, 1373, by *Martin* and *George of Kolozsvár*.

184 HUSUM: St. George, *c.* 1520, by *Hans Brüggemann*. (Now in National Museum, Copenhagen).

GOTHIC ST. GEORGE

185 BRNO: Church of
St. James, 1480–, by *Anton
Pilgram* and others.

186 PRAGUE CATHEDRAL: choir
looking east, 1344–85, by *Matthias
of Arras* and *Peter Parler*.

187 PRAGUE: Vladislav Hall, 1493–1503,
by *Benedikt Ried*.

188 KUTNÁ HORA: Church of
St. Barbara. Choir *c.* 1400,
by *Peter Parler*; nave *c.* 1540,
by *Benedikt Ried*.

BOHEMIA

189 CRACOW: cloister of Jagellonian Library, 1492–97.

190 BECHYNÈ: Franciscan Church,
1491–1520.

191 KASSA: Church of St. Elizabeth, interior
looking west, 1380–1480; tabernacle (*right*),
1472, by *Stefan Crom*.

192 KOLOZSVÁR: Church of St.
Michael, looking west, *c.* 1430–44.

CENTRAL EUROPE

193 BRASSÓ: the Black Church, *c.* 1390–
1447. Designer possibly *Hans Stethaimer*.

194 KASSA: Church of St. Elizabeth.
West front, *c.* 1440–80, by *Stefan
Crom*; upper north tower, *c.* 1496–
1506, by *Nicolaus Crompholz*.

195, 196 GYULAFEHÉRVÁR CATHEDRAL: choir and west portal,
c. 1287, by *John son of Tyno*.

HUNGARY

there had been importations of Italian artists, owing to dynastic links, and to Hungary's position as suzerain of Croatia.

The earliest Gothic churches were mostly those of the Cistercian and Premonstratensian abbeys. They were evidently designed by masters imported from France, Villard de Honnecourt among them, but carried out in part by natives who did not fully understand the intention of the details. Thus at Iák (*c.* 1225–56) the nave arcade piers have shafts with diagonal capitals that support no vault-ribs and are unrelated to the arched orders. During the second half of the thirteenth century there was a wave of building and rebuilding after the destructive Tartar invasion of 1241–42. At Gyulafehérvár (Karlsburg, Alba Iulia) Cathedral in Transylvania, the master stonemason John son of Tyno of Saint-Dié (?*de civitate Sancti a Deo dati*) was engaged in 1287, and he was responsible for the western porch and doorway, and probably also for the enlarged chancel in French style (**195–197**).

But the national period of Hungarian architecture was under German influences; soon after 1300 a hall-church was built at St. James's, Lőcse (Leutschau,

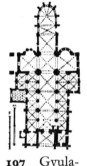

197 Gyula-fehérvár Cathedral.

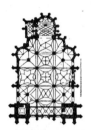

198 Kassa: St. Elizabeth, 1380–.

Levoča) (**265**), and during the century following 1325 the Germans of Nagyszeben (Hermannstadt, Sibiu), erected their great church with its many chapels. A large proportion of the town-dwellers throughout Hungary, especially in Transylvania and upper Slovakia, were in fact purely German, and have retained their language and individuality to the present day. It is consequently difficult to be sure how far the remaining buildings typify Hungarian art, for survivals are mostly in the more mountainous and remote districts settled by Germans.

What is certain is that by the second half of the fourteenth century there was a flourishing Gothic art on the very highest level. Chief witness of this is the splendid equestrian statue of St. George (1373) by the brothers Martin and George of Kolozsvár (Klausenburg, Cluj), now at Prague (**183**). It is one of the supreme masterworks of the whole age, and worthily stands beside the sculptures of Claus Sluter, the illumination of Pol de Limbourg, and the Wilton Diptych. This brilliant piece of stylized realism was executed nearly a generation before any of these north-western works. Among the influences responsible was the presence in Hungary of the Sienese goldsmith Pietro di Simone, who held an appointment at the court of King Charles Robert of Hungary (1308–42).

Remains of fourteenth-century work exist in the south porch of the Coronation Church at Budapest (*c.* 1370), and in the Black Church at Brassó (Kronstadt, Braşov), begun about 1390 and unfinished in 1447 (**193**). The Brassó work, as already mentioned, belongs to Hans Stethaimer or his associates. The greatest Gothic church of old Hungary is St. Elizabeth's at Kassa (Kaschau, Kořice), where work started in 1380 (**191, 193, 194, 198, 267**). Master Nicholas the carver, who was to go from Kassa to King Sigismund at Viségrad in 1411, may possibly have been the designer, but several architects were employed. Much of the west front, and the south porch and chapels, were built under Stefan Crom or Krumau, who had worked at St. Stephen's, Vienna, in 1429, and was in charge at Kassa from about 1440 to 1480. He made the great carved tabernacle, completed in 1472, and that for the Church of St. Giles at Bártfa (Bartfeld, Bardejov) (1464), where he also built the vaults. He also worked for King Matthias at Buda and Diósgyor; and probably designed the Zápolya Chapel at Csütörtökhely. At Kassa the upper part of the north tower and certain other works were done by Nicolaus Crompholz (c. 1496–1506). The vaults and details by Crom are distinctively in the Parler tradition.

The contemporary Church of St. Michael at Kolozsvár has an unaisled choir with tall three-light windows (c. 1350–75), and a hall-nave (c. 1430–44) of very great beauty (**192**). The slightly domical tierceron vaults spring direct from the

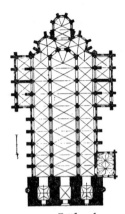

199 Lübeck: St. Mary, 1251–.

moulded piers, and there is fine calculation in the nicely managed heights of nave and aisles and in the pitch of the vaults. Masons' marks have been identified as belonging to the Vienna "school". Kolozsvár was the official residence of John Hunyadi as voivode of Transylvania, and birthplace of his son Matthias. John, though famous as a general in the field, an illiterate until late in life, must have acquired in the Transylvanian capital a taste for art. To him are due the most notable features of the castle at Vajda-Hunyad (Eisenmarkt, Hunedoara), the chapel of c. 1446, and the great hall begun in 1452, with its gallery of oriel windows supported on massive buttresses.

Towards the end of the fifteenth century there was a final wave of enriched Gothic, owing much to followers of the Parler tradition such as Stefan Crom. The very tall narrow chapels of the Zápolya family at Csütörtökhely (1479–) and Szepeshely (1488–93) are noteworthy works in Slovakia, and in Sopron (Ödenburg) by the Austrian border work was carried out on St. John's Church (c. 1480–84), and on the tower of St. Michael's Church (1482). In Transylvania work went on later than in Hungary proper, as it was less directly affected by the Turkish invasions. Everywhere in the principality are fortified churches, always remarkable as defensive works, but often containing buildings of great artistic value. The "Bergkirche" at Segesvár (Schässburg, Sighişoara) (c. 1480–90) (**259**), and the large fortified church of Berethalom (Birthälm, Biertan), whose nave was rebuilt as late as 1520–22, are outstanding examples, both containing fine furniture. The friaries are represented by the Minorite (now Reformed) Church in the Farkasstrasse, Kolozsvár, with its elaborate west doorway of intersecting mouldings; and the German town churches by that of Besztercze (Bistritz, Bistriţa), built between 1525 and 1563.

With few exceptions, we have up to now been concerned with the architecture of stone. Only in England have we found an important competitor in timber. The essentially distinct character of the buildings of the whole Baltic region is due to the almost universal use of brick. From Holland to the head of the Gulf of Finland, and on both sides of the sea, is a great region with an art of its own. For the sake of convenience, this region will be considered in two parts; first the North German plain, with Poland, Lithuania, Latvia and Estonia; second, the Scandinavian countries and Finland. There is too a real justification for this division. The first area, that on the southern coasts, was in the later Middle Ages under the commercial control of the Hanseatic League, and politically dominated by the

200 Poland, the Baltic, and Scandinavia. For Germany, see also **9**, **18**; for Bohemia, see **179**; for Hungary, see **182**. Refer also to endpaper.

16

Teutonic Order. Of the Hansa towns, Lübeck was always in fact if not in name the chief, and it is appropriate that the model for the great brick town churches of the whole area should be that of St. Mary there (**199, 219**). The choir and ambulatory with hexagonal radiating chapels on a plan derived from France (Soissons) by way of Belgium, were built between 1251 and 1291, and the western towers were begun in 1304 and 1310.

Throughout the whole of the region of brick architecture, one thousand miles long by up to three hundred in width (from Danzig to Cracow), the style is surprisingly uniform. The nature of the material enforced simplicity of massing and large expanses of plain wall surface. Piers normally took simple forms without elaborate shafts or mouldings, and vault-ribs were of shallow projection and purely decorative significance. Polychrome patterning is a common method of avoiding monotony of surface, but from the thirteenth century onwards it was usual to panel the fronts with blind recesses of varying shape. Gradually the vertical element came to be accentuated in this panelling, and the effect was strengthened by the provision of turrets and turret-shaped buttresses. In course of time the treatment of windows and of panelling became more elaborate, as complicated brick tracery was developed. This elaborated tracery, and the vault forms, reflected the new trends in design of the Parlerian revolution to Sondergotik; the enriched brick tracery is a translation from stone, and exists side by side in the same building with the plain forms natural to the material. Another symptom of artificiality is the enormous development of the showfront: a gable or screen-wall having little or no structural purpose, but devoted entirely to display. This is rarely found outside the region of brick; exceptionally, a similar treatment in stone of the west front of Meissen Cathedral is due to a Westphalian architect, working, moreover, in a border district.

Though never national in a political sense, but given a semi-independent status through the activities of the Hansa, this brick architecture can only be considered a national style. Towards the end of the Middle Ages it even passed over to England, having a marked effect on early Tudor development, and we shall see that it was a main component of the style of southern Scandinavia. The typical formulae were already in existence early in the fourteenth century. The Cistercian Monastic Church at Chorin has the extremely tall windows of the Soest-Lichfield type, and a west front of marked verticality, with a show-gable (1273–1334). At Thorn (Torun) the Jacobikirche, begun in 1309, has an east front with traceried panelling and emphasized, turreted buttresses. At Pelplin the west front of the Cistercian Church (cathedral) has great octagonal turrets and a five-light traceried window above the west door, while the main gable and side aisles are surmounted by show-pieces (**204**). Work was going on in all parts: far in the south at Cracow, where the Wawel Cathedral was built (1320–46); in the centre, at Prenzlau, whose Marienkirche (c. 1325) has an enormous false east front of traceried work, square on plan (**220**); in the east, where Frauenburg Cathedral (1329–88) (**277**) was built with vaults rather resembling those of Bristol Cathedral;* and in the north-west, at Wismar. The Marienkirche there (c. 1339–53) has the traditional French chevet, but eliminates the triforium; the master mason was Johann Grote. Against these churches of the basilican type must be set others like the Marienkirche at Greifswald, built as a hall-church in the second half of the thirteenth century.

Perhaps because of its dependence upon the Hanseatic traders, this architecture is hardly differentiated into civil and ecclesiastical. The same forms serve all purposes, and there is little to choose between the front of Dorpat Cathedral in Estonia (**278**), and the castle of Rheden in Prussia (c. 1290–1300) (**279**), or between Heinrich Brunsberg's Fronleichnamskapelle in the Church of St. Catherine at

---

* Very similar vaults occur near by at Braunsberg and elsewhere in East Prussia.

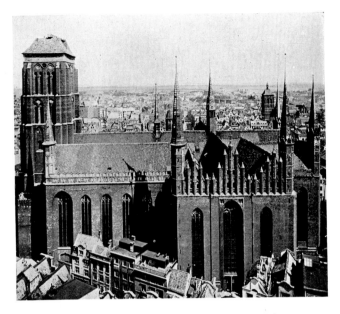

201 VILNA: Church of St. Anne, 1516.

202 DANZIG: Church of St. Mary from the south. Begun 1343; transept *c.* 1400–46, by *Meister Steffens*; completed 1502.

203 VILNA: Church of St. Anne from the south-east.

204 PELPLIN: Cistercian Church, *c.* 1300–50.

GREATER POLAND

205 CRACOW: Church of St. Mary, *c.* 1360–, by *Master Peter*; altarpiece, 1477–81, by *Veit Stoss.*

206 DANZIG: Church of St. Mary, choir, 1343–80; vaulting, 1379–, by *Hinrich Burmeister.*

Brandenburg-an-dem-Havel (1401–37) and his contemporary Rathaus at Tangermünde (**209, 210**). Again at Neubrandenburg the Stargard gate and the double Treptow gates are provided with frontals which might be those of churches or of town halls. If there is something ecclesiastical about the traceried fronts of gildhalls and gates, there is civic pomp in such enormous churches as the Marienkirche of Danzig, whose construction went on from 1343 to 1502 (**206, 207**). It is the chief example of the influence of the British square plan upon Baltic art, and its complex vaults are reminiscent of Gloucester; that of the choir (1379–) is by Hinrich Burmeister; the transepts (*c.* 1400–46) are by Meister Steffens, and the later vaults, completed in 1502, by Heinrich Hetzel.

The Church of St. Mary at Cracow, by Master Peter, is a beautiful example of Polish architecture of the fourteenth and fifteenth centuries (*c.* 1360–), and contains the magnificent altarpiece (1477–81) by Veit Stoss (**205**). Here, as in the contemporary churches of Breslau, the somewhat heavy character of northern German art has been replaced by a refinement which seems characteristic of Slavonic Gothic. As elsewhere, the first Gothic was introduced to Poland by the Cistercians, who founded several monasteries between 1210 and 1232, including those of Jędrzejów and Sulejów. Soon afterwards the Dominicans brought their own technique from Toulouse, and built the first brick church at Sandomierz (1226–50); the Franciscans also built in brick, single-naved churches of very simple type. By the second half of the thirteenth century the hall-church had appeared, according to M. Żarnecki, with the Church of Benedictine nuns at Staniątki near Cracow.

In the fourteenth century a national type of church was foreshadowed by Cracow Cathedral, begun *c.* 1322; its brick walls with stone dressings and internal pier-buttresses were the model for Gniezno Cathedral and later churches throughout the country. During the reign of Casimir the Great (1333–70) work proceeded on Cracow Cathedral and upon the Churches of St. Mary and St. Catherine, as well as upon royal foundations such as Wiślica, of double-naved type with vaulting of

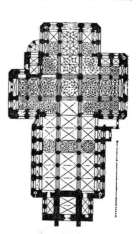

207 Danzig: St. Mary, 1343–, choir by Hinrich Burmeister.

the Parler "school". As in Bohemia, Gothic detail was used in synagogues at Cracow and Szydłów. Outside the area of the Teutonic Order a Polish Gothic developed, of which later examples are the belfry of the Church of the Virgin at Warsaw (1479), and the Cathedrals of Lwów (1479–94) and Tarnów in the extreme South. In the north-east at Vilna, the capital of ancient Lithuania, the Church of St. Anne (1516) is the outstanding specimen of Polish Flamboyant (**201, 203**). This style, with strangely twisted intersecting mouldings used as surface decoration, appears also in the fifteenth-century house at Kaunas (Kovno) known as the "Temple of Perkunas", and is found in the canopy of the tomb of King Casimir Jagellon (*d.* 1492) at Cracow, made by Jorg Hubert of Passau over the effigy carved by his master Veit Stoss.

The Polish towns had received many German settlers after the Tartar invasions of 1241, and these communities became linked with the Hanseatic League. In spite of strong French influences, architecture was largely dominated by German masters, and their influence was paramount through the whole of the Baltic region. Surviving records prove extensive travel. The Church of St. Nikolai at Wismar was first built (*c.* 1380–1403) by Heinrich von Bremen, who completed the choir. The nave (*c.* 1440–59) was designed by Hermann von Münster, who also worked on the Georgenkirche (1442–49); and the clock story of the tower was added

(–1487) by Hans Martens, who vaulted the nave of St. Georg. Other travellers were the sculptors and painters, notably Bernt Notke of Lübeck who carved the great St. George in the Church of St. Nicholas, Stockholm; Marquard Hesse who left Lübeck to work in Reval (Tallinn) (c. 1426–59) and made the new burgomaster's bench for the town hall there; and above all the Sittow family. Clawes Sittow, born in Wismar, settled in Reval in 1452 and died there thirty years later, after doing much work as a sculptor. His son Michael, both carver and painter, was born in 1469, left Reval in 1482, and was studying in Bruges under Memling in 1484. He became court painter to Isabella of Spain, moved back to the Netherlands, revisited Reval; then again travelled to Denmark, worked for the courts of Burgundy and Spain, and finally returned home, to die in Reval in 1525.

Architectural motives tell the same story of distant intercourse. The Marienkirche at Stralsund (1382–) and St. Mary's (the Protestant cathedral) in Riga (c. 1254–1300; upper tower rebuilt by Master Bartholomäus, 1586–) (**281**) have western transepts with medial towers, clearly inspired by Ely; and there are commonly isolated pieces of Perpendicular detail in the brick traceries, notably at Prenzlau. English influence doubtless came for the most part from trading contacts, but also perhaps from such expeditions as those of Henry IV as Earl of Derby to Lithuania in 1390 and 1391. Partly as an outcome of these "crusades", Lithuania became Christian, and new churches were built, such as that of Vytautas in Kaunas (Kovno) (1400–). Other churches in the farther north were St. Olai at Reval (Tallinn) (**217**), whose hall-choir has domical tierceron vaults on octagonal piers (c. 1400), and St. Peter at Riga (choir 1406–9 by Johann Rumeschottel of Rostock; nave 1456–; tower 1466–91). Noteworthy also are Stendal Cathedral (1429–50), a grand brick hall-church with circular piers, attached moulded shafts, and simple quadripartite vaults; and St. Catherine's at Danzig, with star vaults of c. 1500, and a large series of show gables.

Some civic building have already been mentioned. The town halls and guildhalls include both gable-front and side-front types, the former well exemplified by Tangermünde (**210**) and the House of the Black Heads (c. 1330–) at Riga; the latter by the town hall at Stralsund, built in the late fourteenth century (**216**). There are also simpler pieces of unpretentious architecture such as the town hall of Reval (1330–) and the Hall of the Great Guild there (**280**). The Rechtstädtisches Rathaus at Danzig (1379–82) by Heinrich Ungeradin is a simple building of grand scale provided with a later steeple; while the town hall of Thorn (Torun) with its severe vertical panelling (1393–) surrounds an earlier tower (**208**). Later Polish buildings which deserve mention are the brick barbican of Cracow (1488–98), the largest known (**276**); and the Jagellonian Library (1492–97) whose cloistered courtyard has cellular vaults like those at Bechyně in Bohemia (**189**). Similar vaults occur in Lithuania, as in the sacristy of the church of the Bernardines in Vilna.

The castles, particularly those of the Teutonic Order, are too numerous and form too specialized a study to find a place here. But in the cases of Marienburg and Marienwerder the castles are actually palaces and enclose great churches as well. At Marienwerder the castle dates from c. 1300–36, and the cathedral from a little later (c. 1343–84) (**214**). It seems to follow Johann Grote's Marienkirche at Wismar, but has elaborate stellar vaulting. Marienburg, which equals the Palace of the Popes at Avignon in architectural importance, is especially noteworthy artistically for its great halls ("Remter") built in 1380–98 by the Rhenish master, Nikolaus Fellenstein. They fixed a type of vaulted hall widely followed, as for instance at Vajda-Hunyad. The buildings are of brick, with massive walls of great simplicity, but the apse of the church and some of the other ranges are surmounted with show-gables of the usual type. A certain number of details is of inserted stone.

208   THORN: Town Hall. Tower, *c.* 1250; outer walls, 1393–.

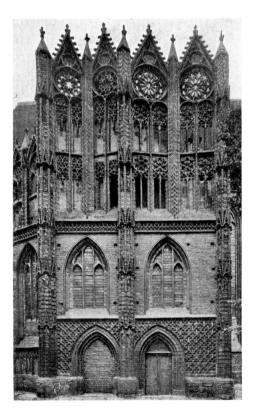

209   BRANDENBURG-AN-DEM-HAVEL: St.
Catherine's Church, chapel by *Heinrich
Brunsberg*, 1401–37.

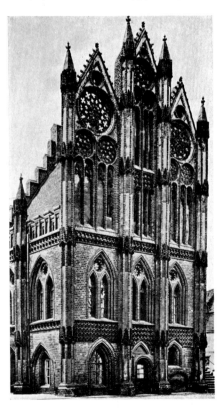

210   TANGERMÜNDE: Rathaus,
c. 1420. Designer probably
Heinrich Brunsberg.

GOTHIC IN BRICK

211 (*above*) YSTAD: Convent Church, fourteenth century.

212 THE HAGUE: the Ridderzaal, *c.* 1275. Designer *Gerard van Leyden*.

213 NUREMBERG: Parsonage of St. Sebaldus, *c.* 1370.

214 MARIENWERDER: Castle and Cathedral, *c.* 1300–84.

215 BRUNSWICK: Altes Rathaus, 1393–1468.

216 STRALSUND: Town Hall front, late fourteenth century.

217　REVAL: the Town and Church of St. Olai, *c.* 1400.

218　ROSKILDE CATHEDRAL from the south-east, *c.* 1215–1300.

219　LÜBECK: Church of St. Mary.
Choir 1251–91; towers 1304–.

220　PRENZLAU: Church of St. Mary,
east front, *c.* 1325.

AROUND THE BALTIC

The mixture of brick and stone also occurs, though on a small scale, in southern Scandinavia, and with elaboration at Uppsala Cathedral. There are in fact at least three main zones across Scandinavia, each with its own Gothic. In the north, covering Norway and the Isles, English influence is so strong that much of the stone building is practically a transplantation. But here the wooden mast-churches preserve an older native tradition which had some effect on masonry buildings in transferring to them a spiky sharpness of outline. In the south, across Denmark, Scania (the southern tip of present Sweden which belonged to Denmark), up the eastern side of Sweden, and in Finland, there ruled during the later Middle Ages the Baltic brick Gothic; sometimes directly transplanted by German architects, in other cases native. Between the two extremes was an area of mixed currents from England, France and Germany, gradually tending towards a national Swedish art.

The great Danish Cathedral of Roskilde, begun about 1215, seems to have been based upon Belgian models (**218**). It adopts the old plan of apse with ambulatory, though its brick construction gives a new tone. At Aarhus the cathedral is apsidal,

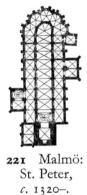

221 Malmö:
St. Peter,
c. 1320–.

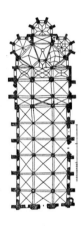

222 Linköping
Cathedral, *c.* 1250–;
choir 1400–12 by
Gerlach of Cologne.

but became a hall-church, and has tierceron vaults and formerly had a number of crow-step gables in the simpler Baltic tradition (**227**). There is again a conflict of sources at St. Knud's Church, Odense (–1301), basilican with a single western tower, triforium and vaults based on those of Lincoln nave, and with brick crow-stepped gables (**283, 286**). At St. Peter's, Malmö (*c.* 1320–80) the ambulatory plan with radiating chapels is combined with a long-panel clerestory, though the quadripartite vaults remain completely old-fashioned (**16, 221**). Much more definitely in the Baltic tradition, with vertical brick-featured showfronts, is the fourteenth-century Convent Church of Ystad, also in Scania (**211**). At Ribe Cathedral there is a good simple brick tower, and a fine piece of straightforward brick design in St. Katrine's Monastery. The Baltic showfront appears on St. Mary's at Elsinore (Helsingör) in the fifteenth century, and in simplified form on the mansion of Glimmingehus near Simrishamn in Scania, built by Adam von Düren in 1499. Here the influence of a German master is directly provable, as it is in the case of the magnificent St. George carved by Hans Brüggemann (*c.* 1520) for the Church of Husum in Sleswig (**184**).

In Sweden proper the earlier Gothic was definitely French in origin and stone-built. A sturdy instance of the thirteenth-century monastic style is Varnhem Abbey (*c.* 1234–66), heavily basilican in character. On the other hand, later in the century the hall-church had reached Linköping Cathedral, a building which has passed through many major alterations. The transept is of *c.* 1250, while the late choir (*c.* 1400–12) is by Meister Gerlach of Cologne (**222, 226**). Uppsala, with its adaptation of a French cathedral, largely built by French craftsmen between 1270 and 1315, has already been mentioned (**63, 73**). Skara Cathedral (*c.* 1300) is another somewhat archaic church of French basilican type (**287**). A more definitely Swedish style is found in the hall-churches built from the fourteenth century. The Convent Church of Vadstena is a particularly fine example in stone, with simple octagonal piers and broad-spreading tierceron vaults (**284**). The fifteenth century built more in brick, notably at Västerås (1443–66) (**231**), Strängnäs (1448–62) (**225**) and Växiö Cathedrals, and the great Church of Stockholm (*c.* 1470) with a raised central aisle and lierne vaults (**19**).

The one great Gothic monument of Finland is Åbo (Turku) Cathedral, built in a mixture of stone and brick. Beginning as a rectangular hall-church (*c.* 1300), a new polygonal choir was added (*c.* 1338–66), and early in the fifteenth century a sacristy with a tierceron vault (**282, 285**). The present vaults of the raised central nave date from about 1466, and were built by Master Petrus from Kimito. Finland was considerably influenced by work in Gotland (**28**), and probably much of the portable sculpture derived from the island and from Sweden. The country churches are important for their excellently preserved schemes of painted decoration (**224**).

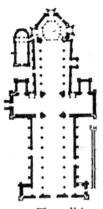

223 Trondhjem Cathedral, *c.* 1160–; octagon 1186–; nave 1232–48.

Norway, separated from Sweden by almost impassable ranges of mountains, and in the Middle Ages depending upon sea transport from fiord to fiord, naturally derived its art from its nearest maritime neighbours in Britain. The square east end of churches is almost universal, not only in village and smaller town churches such as the Mariakirken of Bergen, but also in the cathedrals. At Hamar, now in ruins, a square choir was added towards the end of the thirteenth century, and that at Stavanger (1285–) still exists. This is an excellent example of Anglo-Norwegian work, with sharp mouldings, carvings of high quality, and a high-pitched vault without ridge-ribs (**230**). The alternate side windows have hexagons instead of circles above paired lancets, apparently a precocious sign of the coming Perpendicular. The twin towers flanking the east front are a curious feature of the plan. At Bergen the cathedral is the former Franciscan church, with a single western tower and a polygonal apse, probably due to direct French influence from the friars; the church was begun about 1248 and altered in the fourteenth century. Also at Bergen is the much restored Håkonshallen, the most important Gothic civil building in the country.

Quite outweighing all other Norwegian buildings in importance is the Cathedral of Trondhjem (**223, 229**). The plan of the original church, with central tower, transepts with square projecting eastern chapels, and clasping buttresses resembles that of St. Magnus in Orkney (**228**) and other cathedrals within the sphere of Norse influence: Iona and Cashel. But in its later developments it became almost wholly English and highly eclectic, choosing plan and details from the best and most recent sources. The west front with towers outside the aisles, and the octagon east of the choir, give the plan close similarity to Wells, while details and shafting are derived from the work of Master Alexander at Lincoln. There is probably also direct influence from St. Albans, brought by Matthew Paris; his visit (1248) coincided with a period of energetic work, and he was particularly concerned with the church affairs of Trondhjem. But the most interesting of the English features are those of the fourteenth century, introduced in the repairs after a fire of 1328. These include screens and triforium in the octagon, and the great screen at its entrance from the choir (**88**). The detail is so definitely of the Canterbury "school", with rich Kentish cusping, that it seems clear that large-scale drawings

224 TAIVASSALO: Painted
church, *c.* 1470–80, probably
by *Petrus Henriksson*.

225 STRÄNGNÄS CATHEDRAL: interior
looking east, 1448–62.

226 LINKÖPING CATHEDRAL:
nave, *c.* 1260–.

227 AARHUS CATHEDRAL:
interior looking east.

228 KIRKWALL CATHEDRAL from the south-east, *c.* 1250.

229 TRONDHJEM CATHEDRAL: west front, *c.* 1232–.

230 STAVANGER CATHEDRAL: choir, *c.* 1285–.

231 VÄSTERÅS CATHEDRAL: side aisle, 1443–66.

NORWAY AND SWEDEN

must have been sent out from Westminster, where Thomas of Canterbury was just beginning his work on St. Stephen's Chapel. The spandrels above the main arch are almost identical with part of the tracery design of the window of 1336 inserted in St. Anselm's Chapel in Canterbury Cathedral, while the shafted columns with their caps and bases are almost those of Archbishop Meopham's monument. Francis Bond pointed out that the whole scheme of the central arch with its sub-divisions is reproduced on a small scale at Stebbing in Essex. At Trondhjem we have evidence of immense value of the state of art at the English court immediately before the coming of Perpendicular.

We have now followed all the greater Gothic styles which took on a national or distinctively regional form. They cover the greater part of northern and western Europe. Outside this area there were sporadic local outbursts of Gothic art which never attained complete development. The chief of these were in Italy, where diverse political interests and a geographical position exposed to outside influences from all directions prevented unity. During the later Middle Ages Gothic work belongs to three main regions: that of the northern city-states; Venice; and Sicily. So far as there was a national style of Italian Gothic, it was in the first of these areas, and the prime example is Siena Cathedral. The body of the church is in Romanesque tradition, with remarkable use of polychrome masonry. But the distinctively Gothic feature is the west front, which is thought to have been designed by Niccolo Pisano who died in 1278. It was certainly built under the supervision of his son Giovanni between 1284 and 1300.

232 Perugia Cathedral, section.

The art of the Pisanos shows the classic influences of round arch and Corinthian column fighting, for the time, a losing battle against the leaping spirit of Gothic. The upward tendency of gables, crockets and pinnacles was welcomed for a little space. The richly carved pulpits tell the same tale; those of Siena and Pisa are bound by the rounded outlines and classically static sculptured scenes; that of Giovanni Pisano at Pistoia, in spite of its awkwardness, has adopted the Gothic poignancy of feeling as well as some of its details. In the following generation, Lorenzo Maitani of Siena carried on the work of the Pisanos, and in his design for the front of Orvieto Cathedral (1290–1330) achieved a specifically Italian solution of Gothic, marred only by the central round-headed portal. Lorenzo's original drawing survives.

The greatest architectural centre was Florence. Three important churches were in progress together at the end of the thirteenth century: S. Maria Novella (1278–*c.* 1300) by the Dominican friars Fra Sisto and Fra Ristoro* (**235**); S. Croce 1294–), and the Cathedral of S. Maria del Fiore (1298–), both by Arnolfo del Cambio. The Church of S. Maria Novella is strictly Gothic, but emphasizes the spatial content with the very wide arches of its arcades and the simple ribbed vaults. At S. Croce the design is more definitely basilican, but there are wooden roofs instead of vaults. The immense cathedral, progressively enlarged from the first designs, again adopts very wide bays, and almost from the beginning was invaded by a completely non-Gothic spirit. The tall campanile designed by the painter Giotto di Bondone and begun by him in 1334, is on the contrary one of the noblest examples of the Italian tradition in design and materials allied to the soaring verticality of Gothic. Furthermore, it was intended to be crowned with a spire.

The hall-church from southern France appeared early in the fourteenth century in Umbria, at Perugia Cathedral (**232**) and the Church of S. Fortunato at Todi.

* They also designed S. Maria sopra Minerva in Rome.

S. Fortunato, with its cellular nave whose chapels simulate additional aisles, might almost be a work of Languedoc, and its shafted piers are in the tradition of Poitiers and Bourges. Only the extreme width of the arches is Italian. The last of the greater Italian churches of the north to have a predominantly Gothic spirit is S. Petronio at Bologna, designed by Antonio di Vincenzo and built in 1390–1430. The Gothic effect is much purer than in the cathedral at Florence, and only the intended dome, which was never built, interrupted the unity of the design. Milan Cathedral, founded in 1387, hardly belongs to the story of Italian Gothic (233, 234). Its design was the subject of dispute between German, French and native architects, chief among them Heinrich Parler of Gmünd, and it had no artistic progeny beyond the first portion of the nave of the Certosa at Pavia, begun in 1396 for the same patron, Giovanni Galeazzo Visconti, first Duke of Milan. The civic architecture of Italy covers an enormous field, but is seldom Gothic in spirit; buildings such as the Foro dei Mercanti at Bologna belong to the Mediterranean Gothic tradition of space, but their detail is in part of Classic derivation. The fish-tail battlements here, and on fortifications, are typical.

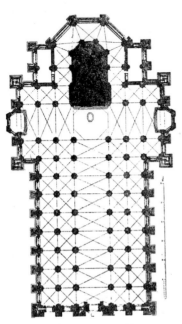

233 Milan Cathedral, 1387–, by Heinrich Parler and others.

Leaving Venice and its colonies until later, we jump to Sicily, where a flourishing late Gothic was introduced by the Kings of Aragon. It was due to the Aragonese connexion that Sicily shared with Spain rather than with the mainland of Italy in attachment to Gothic and avoidance of Renaissance features. But the Sicilian style took root in the earlier Norman-Saracenic tradition of the island, and produced a rich Flamboyant in the fifteenth century. At Palermo the south porch of the cathedral has affinities to the Lonjas of Catalonia (236), and the Church of S. Maria della Catena is in good Gothic with columns of sub-classic type. Later in the century are S. Maria del Gesù, with Flamboyant tracery in the head of its main portal, and the splendid Flamboyant windows of the Archbishop's Palace. The Palazzo Abatelli and Palazzo Marchesi have late tracery verging on the Perpendicular and intersecting mouldings. Similar work existed at Messina Cathedral, and there is a fine portal at S. Maria del Gesù, Modica. Finally, interesting in comparison with the St. George sculptures of Barcelona, is the tympanum of the patron saint beneath an ogee hoodmould at the Church of S. Giorgio in Ragusa Inferiore.

Throughout the Middle Ages Venice lived to itself, and for its Adriatic and eastern trade routes. Its relations with Italy were comparatively slight. Consequently the Venetian Gothic, in the city and in the Venetian colonies such as Dalmatia and parts of Greece, almost became a national style. Characteristic are round columns, rather heavy richly foliated capitals, ogee arches, and ogee reticulations not unlike those of English Curvilinear, but on a much larger scale. Marble and brick are both commonly used, as elsewhere in northern Italy. The two important Gothic churches are those of the great orders of Friars: S. Maria Gloriosa dei Frari of the Franciscans, and SS. Giovanni e Paolo of the Dominicans (102). Both were begun about 1250, from designs by Niccolo Pisano or an architect in close touch with his ideas, and were not completed for more than a century.

234 MILAN CATHEDRAL: interior looking east, 1387–, by *Heinrich Parler* and others.

235 FLORENCE: Church of S. Maria Novella, 1278–1300, by *Fra Sisto* and *Fra Ristoro*.

236 PALERMO CATHEDRAL: south porch, fifteenth century, set in work of the late twelfth century.

ITALY AND SICILY

237   MEDINA DEL CAMPO: Castle of la Mota, 1440–. Designer *Fernando de Carreño.*

238 (*right*) RHODES: Street of the Knights. Auberge de France, 1492–1503.

239   VALENCIA: the Lonja or Exchange, 1482–98, by *Pedro Compte.*

SOUTHERN WALLS

The golden age of Venetian native style was from 1350 to 1450. In 1343 the water front of the Doge's Palace was begun by Pietro Baseggio, and finished in 1404 (**290**). The front on the Piazzetta was begun in 1424 by Giovanni Bon and his son Bartolommeo, who also built the Porta della Carta (1440–43) at the northern end of the palace (**289**). The Bons also built the famous palace known as the Ca' d'Oro (1430). A simpler building in the same style is the Palazzo Franchetti or Cavalli (**288**). Outside the city itself, the Venetian Messer Antonio, son of Pietro Paolo, was architect in 1430–41 of the lower storey of nave and aisles at Sebenico Cathedral in Dalmatia. Other Gothic works are the tower of Trau Cathedral (1422–1598); Curzola Cathedral (1438–65); and stalls in the cathedrals at Rab (1445) and Zara (**292, 293**). Venetian Gothic also reached Crete. Independently of Venice the Republic of Ragusa in 1435 began a palace for its rectors, under the supervision of a Neapolitan master, Onofrio Giordani di la Cava (**291**).

In Greece there was Gothic on a small scale after the Frankish occupation of 1204, and to this early period belong the remains of the church at Isova, which had been completed before it was burnt in 1264. This was an aisleless church with polygonal apse of pure French type, with apse windows subsequent to the design of those of Reims Cathedral. In parts of the Peloponnesus, under Angevin rule until 1375, and still Italian in the fifteenth century, there are slight remains of later work, recorded by Professor Ramsay Traquair at Andravida and Gastouni (late thirteenth century), and at Blachernai (c. 1350). But the most important piece of Gothic work is at S. Paraskeve in Chalkis on the island of Euboea, a Venetian possession. The church is Byzantine in plan, but has pointed arches, and a late thirteenth-century south-eastern chapel with a ribbed vault and very fine foliated bosses of pure Gothic workmanship (**240**).

In the eastern Mediterranean the Christian kingdoms did not last long enough to produce any national styles, though the great Crusader fortresses of Palestine and Syria, such as the Krak des Chevaliers (**294**) and Tripoli, works of the early thirteenth century, had a great effect upon the design of the Gothic castles of Europe. The later history of this military architecture is preserved on the island of Rhodes, occupied from 1309 to 1522 by the Knights Hospitallers of St. John of Jerusalem. In the city of Rhodes, protected by grand gateways resembling that of Villeneuve-les-Avignon (**295**), are the Hospitallers' quarters in the Street of the Knights (**238**), the Great Hospice, and the Castellania. The buildings of the late fourteenth and fifteenth centuries are diverse in character, owing to the national divisions within the Order. There is however an interesting tendency to adopt square-headed windows and square label-moulds, together with sharply cut mouldings and cable ornament. The dominant impression belongs to southern France and Catalonia.

We have already seen that in Cyprus, whither the Crusader Kingdom of Jerusalem was transferred after the loss of Palestine, the Church of S. Sophia in Nicosia (**36, 39**) begun c. 1209–28, was continued by Eudes de Montreuil. It is a pure French church in the manner of the Ile-de-France. The other great church of the island, St. Nicholas at Famagusta, was in progress in 1311, when the chevet had been completed (**38**). The work is derived from Champagne, and details are especially close to St.-Urbain at Troyes. Though relatively small in scale, it is a worthy representative of transplanted French architecture of the first class. At the Abbey of Bellapais, on the other hand, the cloister and vaulted refectory of c. 1324–39 are definitely southern in style, and the refectory much resembles the work of Jean de Loubières at Avignon (**37**). Architecture in Cyprus, until the conquest of Famagusta by the Genoese in 1376, was unusually closely linked to that of France; but at the end of the Middle Ages the style was in a state of decadence, its glory had departed.

IX

The Gothic Age

IT is time to stand upon the great parting between Gothic and modern times, and indulge in retrospect. We have followed the course of architecture from its first pushing against the dead weight of Romanesque, through trunk and great branches into the manifold twigs of separate development. And standing at a distance, the whole tree can be seen in its outline and mass, no longer a collection of disparate fragments, but an organic unity. At the end as at the beginning there are living links binding together the separate parts: Eudes de Montreuil working beside St. Louis on the walls of Jaffa; Michael Sittow sailing from end to end of the known world and back again, reaching the Court of Ferdinand and Isabella at the moment that Columbus was leaving it to discover a new world. The division of Gothic into national styles had not diminished but enhanced its value; their individual discoveries were becoming a common heritage.

We have seen Gothic grow up as a natural and almost inevitable expression of a certain inward spirit, an unresolved tension caused by the firing of an eastern spark within the northern soul. It adapted itself to variations in climate and in psychology, all the time producing an outward shell, a coral, whose form was dictated by the dwellers within. It is in this sense that Gothic art, like Chinese or Egyptian or Greek art, differs essentially from the art of modern times: that is, from the art of Europe in the seventeenth to the nineteenth centuries. The Renaissance, even in Italy, was a foredoomed attempt to resurrect a *status quo ante*; outside the Mediterranean area it was a tasteless strutting in borrowed clothes. The revolutionary instead of evolutionary form taken by both Renaissance and Reformation betrayed an inner uncertainty, a sudden poverty of inspiration.

Perhaps this exhaustion was a token that the men of the North had worn themselves out with much doing in five hundred years. And truly, their productions were most astonishing in quantity as well as in quality. Architecture was the framework into which the other arts were fitted, each in its appropriate place. We have seen a few samples of the immense output of sculpture which formed an integral part of the architecture, and indeed came from the same brains and hands. In one or two cases we have noticed contemporary links with painting. But beyond these major plastic arts there was a vivid world of craftsmen engaged in the production of illumination and enamel work, ivory-carving or embroidery. Still others were poets and composers of music: authors of a new series of vernacular literatures and a new system of harmony. All were manifestations of a single over-ruling spirit. In spite of the inconsistencies between churches and commerce, between pagan and Christian outlooks, there was a single spirit that informed the whole. It was a spirit of activity and uplift, of dynamic energy consecrated to a higher Cause. Besides the pointed arch, the Gothic Age had borrowed something else from Islam, the throbbing call of the muezzin: Up to Prayer! Up to Salvation! Prayer is better than Sleep!

It was this vital urge that led students from all parts of Europe to come together at Paris and to form the first universities. Like Dr. Johnson's young waterman, they were ready to give all that they had for knowledge: in the first place knowledge of the Creator and First Cause; secondly, of the world of nature. This great movement was to culminate in the early thirteenth century in the life and work of St. Francis of Assisi. The exploration of nature, including human nature, was of the essence of the Gothic age; the scientific research and wide travel of Adelard of Bath and his contemporaries were taking place even before such a thing as Gothic art existed. The new natural science and the new artistic techniques went hand in hand. It was inevitable that in Paris, the centre of teaching and of disputation, great scholars should seek to bring together in one completed whole the mass of observed facts which were steadily being brought to light. To the century of discovery and adventure, the twelfth, succeeded the thirteenth, occupied by the labours of encyclopaedists.

Early in this book I remarked on the close relation between the organization of scholars in the universities, and of craftsmen in the guilds. Both adopted variants of the same system; more than this, to a certain degree they adopted similar methods. For about a century, the increasing skill of the lay craftsman, based on trial and error, was matched by a corresponding empiricism in philosophy. In fact, it was the explorations of the philosophical scientists that in part at least, made Gothic technique possible. But by the middle of the thirteenth century the scholars, having perfected their system, became reluctant to make the progressive alterations demanded by fresh inquiry. Their rediscovery of Aristotle's immense knowledge damped original research: they began to chew the cud which had been cropped, and erected a barrier against the external world. The universal encyclopaedism of Vincent of Beauvais, and the closed-circle philosophy of Thomas Aquinas were the result.

It was this all-embracing but deadening scholasticism that descended upon Paris, and indirectly stopped the flow of northern French art. Belief in a perfected system of thought and knowledge led to the acceptance of the then state of religious art as final. Hence it is that at the very moment when France was leading Europe into a new art, the leadership passed from her to Germany and to England. For it is significant that the two great experimental thinkers of the age were a German, Albertus Magnus, and an Englishman, Roger Bacon. Neither Albert nor Bacon was able entirely to break open the self-satisfaction of official circles; but they bequeathed their methods to the lay craftsmen. Free from the authority of universities and the Church, so long as they obeyed the official system of iconography, the lay artists could experiment to their hearts' content. They did so.

From that point onwards the real history of Europe was to be made less in the schools than in the lodges. The men who counted more and more were those who could design vaults or roofs for even greater spans; economize in masonry to lavish glass; make a ship to round Africa or cross the Atlantic. By refusing to seek further, the clerical order had abdicated. Human nature demands that there shall always be new territories to explore, fresh worlds to conquer. And this is more evident in some communities than in others; it was for many centuries particularly true of the English. So it came about that in England a particular set of circumstances produced a highly individual result: the Perpendicular or English national style. After 1300 the spirit of the Sondergotik, the ideas of space and movement joined to a new development of verticality, became generalized throughout Europe outside of France. But nowhere to the same extent as in England did they achieve, together with the host of lesser arts, a completely integrated national unity. This was due to natural isolation; to the centralizing policy of the English Kings, from William the Conqueror's Oath at Salisbury onwards; and, paradox as it may seem, to the rugged individuality of the mediaeval Englishman.

This national style was constantly undergoing adaptation; late in the fifteenth century it was changing itself into Tudor, whose practically unlimited possibilities never found full expression. It was precisely this protean adaptability that to the precious followers of sixteenth-century and later classicism seemed barbaric. The national style had reached a position where mastery of form could be achieved without the sterilization of that form. Latin and Greek architecture, like the languages, were dead because they had ceased to adapt themselves to a changing environment. Even their revival could only be made feasible by the introduction of change, in Mannerism, Baroque and Rococo. These may be well enough, but the destruction of the Gothic tradition in architecture can only be regarded as a calamity.

It may be that there are lessons still to be learned from the dead hand of the old Mediterranean world, which had its own high standard, albeit a static one. But by its nature this ancient art was bound to earth, hardly capable of enthusiasm, of soaring in unfettered imagination. The ability to soar is the keynote of the Gothic achievement: a capacity which could make of a household utensil a thing of exquisite beauty; and which in building a gateway of defence or a house of prayer could rise above the cold commands of human perfection towards the Spirit that moves in the empyrean.

240 Chalkis: Church of S. Paraskeve, detail of
south-east chapel, *c.* 1300.

241 ALBI CATHEDRAL from the east. Begun 1282; portal c. 1400; south porch c. 1520–35.

242 LA CHAISE-DIEU: Abbey Church from cloisters, 1342–75. Designer *Hugues Morel.*

243 RODEZ CATHEDRAL: west front, c. 1500, by *Bernard Anthony*; tower, 1513–26, by *Antoine Salvan*

244 VALENCIA CATHEDRAL: Miguelete, 1381–1424, by *Pedro Balaguer.*

SOUTHERN GOTHIC

245 MARBURG: Church of St. Elizabeth, looking east, 1257–83.

246 Erfurt: Severikirche, *c.* 1270.

247 KOLÍN: Church of St.
Bartholomew, choir, 1360–78.
Designer *Peter Parler.*

248 SOEST: Wiesenkirche, 1331–76.
Designer *Johann Schendeler.*

GERMANIC HALL CHURCHES

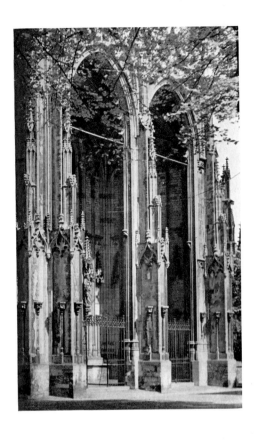

249 *(above left)* SHERTO-GENBOSCH CATHEDRAL: south porch, *c.* 1470–90, by *Alard van Hameel.*

250 LEIDEN: Hooglandse-kerk, 1377–*c.* 1500.

251 HAARLEM: St. Bavo, looking east, 1400–83. Designers *Godevaert de Boscher* and *Steven van Afflighem.*

HOLLAND

252 FREIBURG-IM-BREISGAU: the Minster. Tower octagon, *c.* 1310–50; choir, 1354–60, by *Hans Parler*; completed 1510–13.

253 MUNICH: Frauenkirche, west front, 1468–88, by *Jörg Ganghofer*. The bulbous cupolas existed in 1530, and may be original.

SOUTH GERMANY

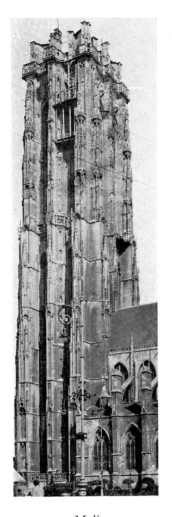

254 Malines.   255   Paris, St.-Jacques.   256   Breda.

MALINES: the tower of St.-Rombaut, 1452–.
Designer *Andries Keldermans*.

PARIS: tower of St.-Jacques-de-la-Boucherie,
1509–21, by *Jean de Felin*.

BREDA: tower of Church of Our Lady,
1468–1509.

257   ULM CATHEDRAL: the west front, before
completion of the tower. Nave and porch,
1392–1419, by *Ulrich von Ensingen*; second stage
of tower, 1420–34; upper tower, 1474–92, by
Matthaeus Böblinger.

GOTHIC TOWERS

258 SZEPESSZOMBAT: interior
of church.

259 SEGESVÁR: interior of
Bergkirche, *c.* 1480–90.

260 ZUG: Church of St. Oswald, north
aisle, 1478–83. Designer *Hans Felder*.

261 KŘIVOKLAT: Castle Chapel,
1493–1522.

262 VIENNA: St. Stephen's Cathedral, vault in Chapel of St. Barbara, 1492–1501.

263 BRNO: choir aisle of Church of St. James, c. 1495–1515, by *Anton Pilgram*.

264 MEERSEN: Bartholomeuskerk, Chapel of the Sacrament, c. 1430.

265 LŐCSE: Church of St. James, c. 1310–50. Altarpiece by *Master Paul*, 1508.

266 PRAGUE CATHEDRAL from
the east, 1344–85. Designers
Matthias of Arras and *Peter Parler*.

267 KASSA: Church of St. Elizabeth
from the south-east, 1380–.

268 AIX-LA-CHAPELLE CATHEDRAL:
choir, 1355–.

269 BASEL CATHEDRAL:
north tower, 1414–29, by
Ulrich von Ensingen; south
tower, 1470–75, by *Vincenz Ensinger*; spire added
1488–1500.

270 VIENNA: St. Stephen's Cathedral.
Nave, 1399–1446, by *Wenzel Parler*; tower,
c. 1407–33, by *Peter and Hans von Prachatitz*.

271 BERN CATHE-
DRAL: square tower,
1506–, by *Peter
Pfister*; octagon, by
Peter Kleinmann;
spire, modern.

272 FREIBURG (SWITZERLAND)
CATHEDRAL: west porch, 1470–75.
Designer *Georg Jordil*;
sculptor *Gylian Aetterli*.

273 MEISSEN: west front of cathedral,
1479–, and staircase of Albrechtsburg,
1471–85, by *Arnold of Westphalia*.

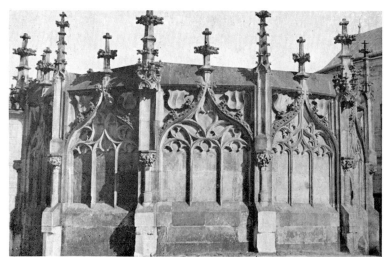

274 (*above*) KUTNÁ HORA: Fountain, 1493–95, probably by *Matthias Rejsek*.

275 (*right*) VISBY: the north walls and towers, thirteenth and fourteenth centuries.

276 CRACOW: the Barbican, 1488–98.

277 FRAUENBURG CATHEDRAL, from the south-west, 1329–88.

278 DORPAT CATHEDRAL: west front, thirteenth century.

279 RHEDEN: Castle of the Teutonic Order, c. 1290–1300.

TEUTONIC GOTHIC

280 REVAL: Town Hall, 1330–.

281 RIGA: St. Mary's Cathedral, *c.* 1254–1300; upper tower by *Master Bartholomäus*, 1586–.

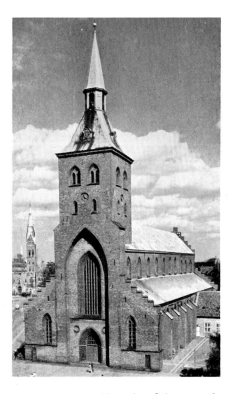

282 ÅBO CATHEDRAL: west front and tower, *c.* 1300.

283 ODENSE: Church of St. Knud, *c.* 1300.

284 VADSTENA: Convent Church, 1303–73.

285 ÅBO CATHEDRAL: interior looking east, *c.* 1338–66. Vaults, *c.* 1466, by *Petrus of Kimito.*

286 ODENSE: Church of St. Knud, *c.* 1300.

287 SKARA CATHEDRAL: nave, *c.* 1300.

288   VENICE: Palazzo Franchetti, *c.* 1430.

289   VENICE: Porta della
Carta, 1440–43, by *Giovanni
and Bartolommeo Bon.*

290   VENICE: angle of the Doge's Palace,
1343–1404. Designer *Pietro Baseggio.*

291   RAGUSA: the Rectors' Palace, 1435–, by *Onofrio Giordani di la Cava*;
loggia altered 1464.

292   CURZOLA CATHEDRAL: portal, 1438–65.

293 TRAU CATHEDRAL: tower,
c. 1410–22, by *Matteo Goycovich*.

DALMATIA

294 LE KRAK DES CHEVALIERS, early thirteenth century.

295 VILLENEUVE-LES-AVIGNON:
Fort St.-André, *c.* 1364–68.

GOTHIC DEFENCE

A Short Bibliography

This is confined to a selection of the most important titles for further reading, with particular attention to works in English; to well-illustrated works; and to those on the more obscure regions. Reference should be made to the detailed Bibliography in the *Cambridge Medieval History*, VIII, 1936.

GENERAL

Bunt, C. G. E.: *Gothic Painting*, London, 1947.
Clasen, K. H.: *Die gotische Baukunst*, Potsdam, 1930.
Dehio, G. and G. v. Bezold: *Die kirchliche Baukunst des Abendlandes*, Stuttgart, 1901.
Focillon, H.: *Art d'Occident*, 2nd ed., Paris, 1947.
[Sturgis, R. and] Frothingham, A. L.: *A History of Architecture*, vols. III, IV, New York, 1915.
    The best general account in English of international Gothic.
Gall, E.: *Die gotische Baukunst in Frankreich und Deutschland*, Leipzig, 1925.
Jackson, Sir T. G.: *Gothic Architecture in France, England and Italy*, Cambridge, 1915.
Karlinger, H.: *Die Kunst der Gotik*, 2nd ed., Berlin, 1934.
    Probably the most useful collection of illustrations of Gothic.
Lethaby, W. R.: *Mediaeval Art*, 1904, etc.; 3rd ed. by D. Talbot Rice, 1949.
    A masterpiece by the greatest English writer on the subject. Caution: some fresh mistakes appear in the new edition.
Michel, A. ed.: *Histoire de l'Art*, vols. I–III, Paris, 1905ff.
Morey, C. R.: *Mediaeval Art*, New York, 1942.
Pevsner, N.: *An Outline of European Architecture*, 1943, etc.
Réau, L.: *Histoire de l'expansion de l'art français*, Paris, 1928–33.
Wanscher, V.: *Architekturens Historie*, vol. II, Copenhagen, 1929.
    Valuable for bold sketches to scale, showing proportion.

AMERICA

Angulo Iñiguez, D.: *Historia del Arte hispano-americano*, Barcelona, 1945.
    —: *El Gótico y el Renacimiento en las Antillas*, Seville, 1948.
Benavides Rodriguez, A.: *La Arquitectura en el Virreinato del Perú y en la Capitanía General de Chile*, Santiago de Chile, 1941.
Kubler, G.: *Mexican Architecture in the Sixteenth Century* (Yale Historical Publications: History of Art, V), New Haven, 1948.

AUSTRIA—see Germany.

BALTIC—see also Germany, Scandinavia.

Clasen, K. H.: *Die mittelalterliche Kunst im Gebiet des Deutschordensstaates Preussen*, Königsberg, 1927.
Danilowicz, C. de: *La Lituanie artistique*, Lausanne, 1919.
Grautoff, O.: *Die Baltischen Provinzen*, Bd. 3 (Bauten und Bilder), Berlin, 1916.
Karling, S.: *Medeltida Träskulptur i Estland* (Kungl. Vitterhets Historie och Antikvitets Akademien, Mono. 33), Stockholm, 1946.
    —: *Narva* (ibid., Mono. 25), Stockholm, 1936.
Neumann, W.: *Grundriss einer Geschichte der bildenden Kunst in Liv-, Est- und Kurland*, Reval and Leipzig, 1887.
    —: *Das mittelalterliche Riga*, Berlin, 1892.
Stiehl, O.: *Backsteinbauten in Norddeutschland und Dänemark*, Stuttgart, 1923.

BELGIUM

Altena, J. de B. d': *Œuvres de nos Imagiers Romans et Gothiques . . .* 1025–1550, Brussels, 1944.
Fierens, P.: *L'Art en Belgique*, Brussels, 1938.
—: *L'Art Flamand*, Paris, 1945.
Fierens-Gevaert, H.: *Histoire de la Peinture Flamande*, Brussels, 1927–29.
Friedländer, M. J.: *Die Altniederländische Malerei*, Berlin, 1924–37.
Laurent, M.: *L'Architecture et la Sculpture en Belgique*, Paris and Brussels, 1928.
Puyvelde, L. van: *Les Primitifs Flamands*, Paris, 1941.

BOHEMIA—see also Germany.

Kutal, A., Líbal, D. and Matêjček A.: *České Umení Gotické*, I, Prague, 1949.
    Includes summary in English.
Líbal, D.: *Gotická Architektura v Čechách a na Moravě*, Prague, n.d.
Neuwirth, J.: *Geschichte der christlichen Kunst in Böhmen*, Prague, 1888.
—: *Geschichte der bildenden Kunst in Böhmen*, Prague, 1893.

CYPRUS

Enlart, C.: *L'art gothique et la Renaissance en Chypre*, Paris, 1899.
Jeffery, G. H. E.: *Historic Monuments of Cyprus*, Nicosia, 1918.

DENMARK—see Scandinavia.

ENGLAND

    For a select classified bibliography of English Gothic Art, see Harvey: *Gothic England.*
Bond, F.: *Gothic Architecture in England*, 1906.
—: *An Introduction to English Church Architecture*, Oxford, 1913.
Borenius, T. and Tristram, E. W.: *English Medieval Painting*, Florence and Paris, 1927.
Evans, J.: *English Art*, 1307–1461 (Oxford History of English Art), Oxford, 1949.
Gardner, A.: *A Handbook of English Medieval Sculpture*, Cambridge, 1935.
Harvey, J. H.: *Gothic England*, 1300–1550, 2nd ed., 1948.
Oakeshott, W.: *The Sequence of English Medieval Art*, 1950.
Saunders, O. E.: *A History of English Art in the Middle Ages*, Oxford, 1932.
    Excludes architecture.
Victoria and Albert Museum: *Exhibition of English Mediaeval Art*, 1930.

ESTONIA—see Baltic.

FINLAND—see Scandinavia.

FRANCE

    For a recent list of books on French mediaeval Art, see Evans: *Art in Mediaeval France.*
Aubert, M.: *French Sculpture at the Beginning of the Gothic Period*, Florence and Paris, 1929.
Enlart, C.: *Manuel d'Archéologie française*, 2nd ed., Paris, 1919–32.
Evans, J.: *Art in Mediaeval France*, 987–1498, Oxford, 1948.
Gardner, A.: *An Introduction to French Church Architecture*, Cambridge, 1938.
—: *Mediaeval Sculpture in France*, Cambridge, 1931.
Lasteyrie, R. de: *L'Architecture religieuse en France à l'époque gothique*, Paris, 1926.
Lefrançois-Pillion, L.: *Les sculpteurs français du XIIe siècle*, Paris, 1931.
—: *Les sculpteurs français du XIIIe siècle*, 2nd ed., Paris, 1931.
Lemoisne, P. A.: *Gothic Painting in France*, Florence and Paris, 1931.
Réau, L.: *French Painting in the XIVth, XVth and XVIth centuries*, London, Paris and New York, 1939.
Rey, R.: *L'Art gothique du Midi de la France*, Paris, 1934.
Ring, G.: *A Century of French Painting*, 1400–1500, Paris, 1949.
Sterling, C.: *Les Peintres du Moyen Age*, Paris, 1942.

GERMANY—see also Baltic.

There is no adequate book in English on German Gothic, but Frothingham (see General list) gives a good summary account.

Dehio, G.: *Geschichte der deutschen Kunst*, 2nd ed., Berlin, 1921–31.

—: *Handbuch der deutschen Kunstdenkmäler*, Berlin, 1914–28.

—: — revised ed., E. Gall, I., II., (only) Berlin, 1935–38.

Gerstenberg, K.: *Deutsche Sondergotik*, Munich, 1913.

Claser, C.: *Die altdeutsche Malerei*, Munich, 1924.

Panofsky, E.: *Die deutsche Plastik des XI. bis XIII. Jahrhunderts*, Munich, 1924.

Pinder, W.: *Deutsche Dome des Mittelalters*, Königstein-Leipzig.

—: *Die deutsche Plastik des XIV. und XV. Jahrhunderts*, Munich, 1925.

Schmitt, O. ed.: *Reallexikon zur deutschen Kunstgeschichte*, I, Stuttgart, 1937.

Contains the important article by D. Frey: *Architekturzeichnung*.

Stange, A.: *Deutsche Malerei der Gotik*, Berlin, 1934–38.

GREECE

Traquair, R.: *Frankish Architecture in Greece* (Byzantine Research Fund; reprint from *Journal* of Royal Institute of British Architects, 3 S., XXXI), 1923.

HOLLAND—see also Belgium

Vermeulen, F. A. J.: *Handboek tot de Geschiedenis der Nederlandsche Bouwkunst*, The Hague, 1922–29.

Vriend, J. J.: *De Bouwkunst van ons Land*, Amsterdam, 1942.

HUNGARY

Bierbauer, V.: *A Magyar Építészet Története*, Budapest, 1937.

Divald, K.: *Old Hungarian Art*, London, 1931.

Forster, G., ed.: *Magyarország Müemlékei*, Budapest, 1905–18.

Gál, L.: *L'architecture religieuse en Hongrie du XIe au XIIIe siècle*, Paris, 1929.

Hekler, A.: *Ungarische Kunstgeschichte*, Berlin, 1937.

Szönyi, O.: *Régi Magyar Templomok* (English summary), Budapest, n.d.

IRELAND

Champneys, A. C.: *Irish Ecclesiastical Architecture*, London and Dublin, 1910.

Leask, H. G.: *Irish Castles and Castellated Houses*, 3rd ed., Dundalk, 1946.

ITALY

No general bibliography of Italian mediaeval art can be given here; a good selection of photographs is included in the series Touring Club Italiano: *Attraverso Italia*.

NORWAY—see Scandinavia.

PALESTINE AND SYRIA

Deschamps, P.: *Le Crac des Chevaliers*, Paris, 1934.

Enlart, C.: *Les Monuments des Croisés dans le royaume de Jérusalem*, Paris, 1925–28.

Palestine Exploration Fund: *Survey of Western Palestine, Memoirs*, London, 1881–83.

POLAND—see also Baltic.

Kopera, F.: "Sztuka polska" in *Polska* (ed. S. Lam), I, Warsaw, 1937.

Osieczkowska, C. and others: *Art Polonais, Art Français* (Collection de l'Institut Français de Varsovie, VII), Paris, 1939.

Piotrowska, I.: *The Art of Poland*, New York, 1947.

Soltynski, R.: *Glimpses of Polish Architecture*, London, 1943.

Szyszko-Bohusz, A.: "Études sur la cathédrale de Wawel à Cracovie", in *Prace Komisji Historii Sztuki*, VIII, 1946.

Topass, J.: *L'Art et les artistes en Pologne au moyen age*, Paris, 1923.

Walicki, M. and J. Starzynski: *Dzieje Sztuki Polskiei*, Warsaw, 1936.

Żarnecki, J.: *Polish Art*, Birkenhead, 1945.

Zubrzycki, J. S.: *Skarb Architektury W Polsce* (*Trésor de l'Architecture en Pologne*), Cracow, 1907–10.

PORTUGAL

Correia, V.: *Pintores portugueses dos Sec. XV e XVI*, Coimbra, 1929.
Crumm-Watson, W.: *Portuguese Architecture*, London, 1908.
Santos, R. dos: *Arquitectura em Portugal*, Lisbon, 1929.
—: *A Escultura em Portugal*, I, Lisbon, 1948.

RHODES

Belabre, (Baron de): *Rhodes of the Knights*, Oxford, 1908.
Gabriel, A.: *La Cité de Rhodes*, 1310–1522, Paris, 1921–23.

SCANDINAVIA—see also Baltic.

Aars, H.: *Norsk Kunsthistorie*, Oslo, 1925.
Beckett, F.: *Danmarks kunst—II. Gotiken*, Copenhagen, 1926.
Curman, S. and J. Roosval: *Sveriges kyrkor*, Uppsala, 1912–32.
Dietrichson, L.: *Die Holzbaukunst Norwegens*, Dresden, 1893.
Engelstad, E. S.: *Senmiddelalderens kunst i Norge*, ca. 1400–1535, Oslo, 1936.
Fett, H.: *Norges kirker i Middelalderen*, Kristiania, 1909.
Hahr, A.: *Architecture in Sweden*, Stockholm, 1938.
Lindberg, C.: *Finlands kyrkor*, Helsingfors, 1935.
Lindblom, A.: *La Peinture Gothique en Suède et en Norvège* (Kungl. Vitterhets Historie och Antikvitets Akademien, Mono. 10), Stockholm, 1916.
Lundberg, E.: *Byggnads Konsten i Sverige*, 1000–1400, 1400–1650, Stockholm, 1940–8.
Mackeprang, A. and C. Jensen: *Danmarks kirker*, Copenhagen, 1933.
Okkonen, O.: *Die Finnische Kunst*, Berlin, 1943.
Rinne, J., and K. K. Meinander: *Monuments médiévaux de l'art finlandais*, Suomen Muinais-muisto-Yhtiö, Helsingfors, 1930.
Romdahl, A. L.: *Konsten i Sverige*, Stockholm, 1943.
— and J. Roosval: *Svensk konsthistoria*, Stockholm, 1913.
Roosval, J.: *Swedish Art*, Princeton, 1932.
— : *Den Baltiska Nordens Kyrkor* (Foreningen Urds Skrifter, II), Uppsala, 1924.
Strzygowski, J.: *Early Church Art of Northern Europe*, London, 1928.

SCOTLAND

MacGibbon, D. and T. Ross: *The Castellated and Domestic Architecture of Scotland*, Edinburgh, 1887–92.
— —: *Ecclesiastical Architecture of Scotland*, Edinburgh, 1896–7.

SPAIN

Bevan, B.: *History of Spanish Architecture*, 1938.
Lambert, E.: *L'Art gothique en Espagne aux XIIe et XIIIe siècles*, Paris, 1931.
Lampérez y Romea, V.: *Historia de la Arquitectura Cristiana Española en la Edad Media*, Barcelona and Madrid, 2nd ed., 1930.
Lavedan, P.: *L'architecture gothique religieuse en Catalogne, Valence et Baléares*, Paris, 1935.
Lozoya, J. de C. (Marques de): *Historia del Arte Hispánico*, II, Barcelona, 1934.
— : *El Arte gótico en España*, Barcelona, 1935.
Mayer, A. L.: *Gotik in Spanien*, Leipzig, 1928.
— : *Mittelalterliche Plastik in Spanien*, Munich, 1922.
— : *Geschichte der spanischen Malerei*, 2nd ed., Leipzig, 1922.
Post, C. R.: *History of Spanish Painting*, Cambridge, Mass., 1930.
Street, G. E.: *Some Account of Gothic Architecture in Spain*, 1865. Revised edition by G. C. King, 1914, but the original should be consulted for its larger and better printed illustrations.
Weise, G.: *Spanische Plastik*, Reutlingen, 1925–7.

SWEDEN—see Scandinavia.

SWITZERLAND—see also France, Germany.

Jenny, H.: *Kunstführer der Schweiz*, 4th ed. (1946).

Abbreviations used in the Notes

In general, a title has been abbreviated when it occurs more than once.

AJ   *Archaeological Journal* (Royal Archaeological Institute).

ALF P. S. and H. M. Allen edd.: *The Letters of Richard Fox*, 1929.

AMB F. B. Andrews: *The Mediaeval Builder*, 1925.

BAA *Journal* of the British Archaeological Association.

BAH M. S. Briggs: *The Architect in History*, 1927.

BAN J. Britton: *Architectural Antiquities*, 1807–26.

CAR G. G. Coulton: *Art and the Reformation*, 1928.

CAS Cambridge Antiquarian Society.

CCR *Calendar of Close Rolls*.

CGB K. H. Clasen: *Die gotische Baukunst*, Potsdam, 1930.

CLR *Calendar of Liberate Rolls*.

CPR *Calendar of Patent Rolls*.

CSE F. R. Chapman: *Sacrist Rolls of Ely*, 1907.

DCL R. C. Dudding ed.: *The First Churchwardens' Book of Louth*, 1500–24, 1941.

EETS Early English Text Society.

EMF C. Enlart: *Manuel d'Archéologie française*, 2nd ed., Paris, 1919–32.

FAO H. Focillon: *Art d'Occident*, 2nd ed., Paris, 1947.

HGE J. H. Harvey: *Gothic England*, 1300–1550, 2nd ed., 1948.

HHY J. H. Harvey: *Henry Yevele*, 2nd ed., 1946.

HMC Historical Manuscripts Commission.

HTA J. H. Harvey: *An Introduction to Tudor Architecture*, 1949.

HWC W. H. St. J. Hope: *Windsor Castle*, 1913.

JMG *Journal* of the British Society of Master Glass-Painters.

KJF D. Knoop and G. P. Jones: *An Introduction to Freemasonry*, Manchester, 1937.

KJH D. Knoop, G. P. Jones, and D. Hamer: *The Two Earliest Masonic MSS.*, Manchester, 1938.

KJM D. Knoop and G. P. Jones: *The Mediaeval Mason*, Manchester, 1933.

KPP O. Kletzl: *Plan-Fragmente aus der deutschen Dombauhütte von Prag* (Veröffentlichungen des Archivs des Stadt Stuttgart, Heft 3), Stuttgart, 1939.

LAF R. de Lasteyrie, ed. M. Aubert: *L'Architecture religieuse en France à l'époque gothique*, Paris, 1926.

LMT *Transactions* of the London and Middlesex Archaeological Society.

MDR V. Mortet and P. Deschamps: *Recueil de Textes relatifs à l'histoire de l'Architecture et à la condition des Architectes en France au Moyen Age* (Collection de Textes), Paris, 1911–29.

OAS Oxfordshire Archaeological Society.

OHS Oxford Historical Society.

PEA N. Pevsner: *An Outline of European Architecture*, 1943, etc.

PSD E. Panofsky: *Abbot Suger on the Abbey Church of St.-Denis*, Princeton, 1946.

RFY J. Raine: *Fabric Rolls of York Minster* (Surtees Society, XXXV), 1858.

RS   Rolls Series (Chronicles and Memorials of Great Britain and Ireland).

SAG H. Stein: *Les Architectes des Cathédrales gothiques*, Paris, n.d.

SAW J. T. Smith: *Antiquities of Westminster*, 1807.

WCC R. Willis and J. W. Clark: *The Architectural History of the University of Cambridge*, Cambridge, 1886

Notes to the Text

INTRODUCTION

p. 2.   —M. Aubert: *La France Glorieuse au Moyen Age*, Paris, 1947, p. 25.
      —PEA.
      The North—see HGE, 27; and compare E. Lundberg in *Rig*, 1939, pp. 197–204.
      —W. R. Lethaby in C. G. Crump and E. F. Jacob edd.: *The Legacy of the Middle Ages*, Oxford, 1926 etc., 89.

p. 3.   —PEA.

p. 5.   —Suger—PSD.
      Holy Sepulchre—carvings illustrated in W. Harvey: *Church of the Holy Sepulchre, Jerusalem*, Oxford, 1935, figs. 25–32, 40–43, 51.

p. 6.   *Opusculum de Pulchro*—in M. Dvorak: *Kunstgeschichte als Geistesgeschichte*, Munich, 1924, 67n. 1.

p. 7.   Montreuil—see below, pp. 46, 66 and notes.
      Bonneuil—MDR, II, 305–6.
      Painter—*Itinerarium Ricardi Regis*, (RS) I, 197; cf. J. F. Dimock ed.: *Metrical Life of St. Hugh*, Lincoln, 1860, lines 833–965.
      Walter of Henley—*Husbandry*, ed. E. Lamond, 1890, 18–19, 27.

p. 8.   Crucifix—G. G. Coulton: *Social Life in Britain*, 473–4, quoting *Register of Ralph Baldock, Bishop of London* (Canterbury and York Society, 1911), 19; and Lucae Tudensis *De Altera Vita*, 1612, 93 (lib. II, c. 9).
      Schoolmen—H. Finke: *Aus den Tagen Bonifaz VIII*, Münster, 1902, 163–5.
      Auxerre—MDR, II, 203, quoting Labbe: *Nova bibliotheca manuscripta*, I, Paris, 1657, 487 ff.
      Seville—R. Lloyd: *The Golden Middle Age*, 1939, 118.
      King's College Chapel—WCC, I, 370.
      Bath Abbey—J. Armitage Robinson in *Proceedings of the Somerset Archaeological etc. Society*, LX, 1914–15, ii, 1–10.

p. 9.   Abbot Litlyngton—J. A. Robinson: *The Abbot's House at Westminster*, 1911, 21–2.
      Cistercians—MDR, II, 34–5; and no. CIV, quoting *Hist. mon. Viconiensis continuatio* in Mon. Germ., XXIV, 307.
      John of Waverley—W. St. C. Baddeley: *A Cotteswold Shrine*, 1908, 27; CLR, 1226–40, 8, 258, 271, 276, 285, 298, 300, 301, 364; 1245–51, 350; CPR, 1232–47, 177; CCR, 1234–7, 425, 500; 1237–42, 12; 1247–51, 439.
      Formulary—MDR, II, 135–6.
      Neckam—*De Naturis rerum*, ed. T. Wright (R.S.,1863), 281.
      Divinity School—*Epistolae Academicae Oxon.* (O.H.S., 1898), 191.
      St. Albans—Abbot Whethamstede's Register quoted by J. D. Sedding in *St. Paul's Ecclesiological Society's Transactions*, I, 1881–5, 42.
      Simon Simeon—*Itinerarium Symonis Symeonis . . .* ed. J. Nasmith, 1778, 46.

p. 10.   Florio—T. Cox: *Jehan Foucquet*, 1931, 7.
      Mass-production—R. H. C. Davis in OAS, 84th Rep., 1938–9; and *Oxoniensia*, XI–XII, 1946–7, 82; E. A. G. Lamborn in *Notes and Queries* (22 Sep. 1945), CLXXXIX, 125–7.

p. 11.   Reinforcement—see below, p. 18.

CHAPTER I

p. 12.   English archives—see Professor V. H. Galbraith's *Studies in the Public Records*, 1948, for a lively account of this early development.
      Chartres, St.-Pierre-sur-Dives, Amiens—MDR, II, 63–7, 260.

p. 13.   Confraternities—R. Graham in BAA, 3 S., X, 1945–7, 73 ff.

p. 14.   Office of Works—see Harvey in BAA, 3 S., VI, 1941, 20 ff.
      Masons and Carpenters—e.g. the provision in the contract of employment (1359) of John of Evesham as master mason of Hereford Cathedral, that he should instruct the labourers in the arts of masonry and carpentry—W. W. Capes: *Charters and Records of Hereford Cathedral* (Cantilupe Society, IV), 1908, 230–1.

p. 15.   Prest Money—CLR, 1226–40, 224; Harvey in BAA, 3 S., VIII, 1943, 52.
      Foreign materials—Norwich Cathedral Obedientiars' rolls, No. 3; W. P. Blore in *Archaeologia Cantiana*, LVIII, 1946, 29.

p. 16.   Cranes—J. R. Bloxam: *Magdalen College Register*, 1892, II, 227 ff; Westminster Abbey Muniments, No. 23492.
      Setting-out—H. E. Butler: *The Autobiography of Giraldus Cambrensis*, 1937, 89, quoting *De Rebus a se gestis*, c. xii; KJM, 245; and Knoop and Jones in *Miscellanea Latomorum*, Sep. 1937; W. Harvey in *The Builder*, CXXI (19 Aug. 1921), 220–1.
      Oxford etc.—J. G. Milne and J. H. Harvey in *Oxoniensia*, VIII–IX, 1945, 139, 145; Harvey in BAA, 3 S., VIII, 53.

p. 17.　Toulouse—R. Rey: *La Cathédrale de Toulouse*, Paris, 1929, 10, quoting *Monumenta conventus tolosani ff. predicatorum*, 2ᵉ partie, 77.

p. 18.　Battersea Church—Westminster Abbey Muniments, No. 19358; Yevele's shop is referred to in his will, Commissary Court of London, 453 Courtney; and in P.R.O., E.101/473/1, 4.

　　　　Reinforcement—W. R. Lethaby: *Mediaeval Art*, 1904, 161; W. A. Forsyth in *Journal* of the Royal Institute of British Architects, LIII (Jan. 1946); and information kindly given by Col. N. H. Waller, architect to Gloucester Cathedral. Col. Waller submitted a section to Dr. Desch of the National Physical Laboratory, who found that its characteristics, varying from those of good bloomery iron to high-carbon steel, could only have been produced under a power hammer.

　　　　Glass-painting—C. Woodforde in JMG, VI, 1935; B. C. Halahan in *Surrey Archaeological Collections*, XXXIV, 1921, 24 ff.

p. 19.　Masters not members of their Company—especially true of the distinguished masons of Henry VIII's time, none of whom appear in the complete list of Freemasons in 1538, printed in T. Allen: *London*, 1828, II, 407 from P.R.O., Misc. Books Treasury of Receipt of Exchequer vol. 93; cf. *Middlesex and Herts. Notes and Queries*, III, 1897, 39; IV, 19–20. For the German lodge organization, see below p. 21.

p. 20.　Guild oligarchy—J. A. Knowles: *Essays in the History of the York School of Glass-Painting*, 1936.

　　　　Compagnonnages—D. Knoop and G. P. Jones: *The Genesis of Freemasonry*, 1947, 56–60.

　　　　Masons' Guild—D. Knoop and G. P. Jones in *Economic History*, Feb. 1939.

p. 21.　London Bye-Laws—those of 1189 and 1212 in full in T. H. Turner: *Domestic Architecture in England*, I, 1851, 275–83.

　　　　Coke—B. Marsh: *Records of the Worshipful Company of Carpenters*, II, 228.

　　　　Tournai—MDR, II, 298–9.

　　　　Germany—R. Wissell: *Des alten Handwerks Recht und Gewohnheit*, Berlin, 1929, II, 332–408, 685–722; J. Neuwirth: *Die Satzungen des Regensburger Steinmetzentages im Jahre 1459*, Vienna, 1888.

p. 22.　German drawings—KPP, 18; *Festschrift der Nationalbibliotek in Wien*, 1926, 667–92; for reproductions of many of the Vienna Cathedral series see H. Tietze: *Geschichte und Beschreibung des St. Stephansdomes in Wien* (Oesterreichische Kunsttopographie, XXIII), 1931.

　　　　Hontañon's treatise is known only through matter and drawings incorporated in a treatise of 1681—J. Camón in *Archivo Español de Arte*, 1941, No. 45, pp. 300–5.

　　　　Paris organization—R. de Lespinasse and F. Bonnardot edd.: *Le livre des Métiers d'Étienne Boileau*, 1879, 88–92.

　　　　English masons—KJH; *Statutes of the Realm*, 34 Edw. III, c. 9; 3 Hen. VI, c. 1.

　　　　Walter of Hereford—*The Record of Caernarvon* (Record Commission, 1838), 220; for his career see Knoop and Jones in *Miscellanea Latomorum*, Dec. 1939; A. J. Taylor in *Caernarvonshire Historical Society's Transactions*, 1948, 16 ff.

p. 24.　Marks—CAR, 242–64; R. H. C. Davis in OAS, 84th Rep., 1938–9, and authorities there quoted; British Archaeological Association: *Report of Proceedings at Canterbury in 1844*, 1845, 258n.

CHAPTER II

p. 25.　Vinsauf—*Poetria Nova*, quoted in E. Faral: *Les Arts Poétiques du XIIᵉ et du XIIIᵉ siècle*, 1924, 198.

　　　　Almighty with compasses—G. McN. Rushforth: *Medieval Christian Imagery . . .*, 1936, 150.

　　　　Vitruvius—*De Architecturâ*, ed. F. Granger, I (Loeb, 1931), xv, xix; T. D. Atkinson: *Architectural History of the Benedictine Monastery of St. Etheldreda at Ely*, 1933, 53; BAH, 110.

p. 26.　Milan—P. Frankl in *Art Bulletin*, XXVII, 1945.

　　　　Honnecourt—H. R. Hahnloser: *Villard de Honnecourt*, Vienna, 1935. Plan-copying—KPP, 2, 6, 10.

　　　　Westminster Abbey—R. P. Howgrave-Graham in BAA, 3 S., XI, 1948–9, 76.

p. 27.　Architect-masons—N. Pevsner in *Speculum*, XVII, 1942, 561.

　　　　De Biard—MDR, II, 290–1.

　　　　Matthew Paris—Lives of the two Offas, British Museum Cotton MS. Nero D.I., f. 23 v.; compare the similar drawing in Paris's Lives of SS. Alban and Amphibalus, Trinity College, Dublin MS., illustrated in Victoria and Albert Museum: *Exhibition of English Mediaeval Art*, 1930, Plate 27.

　　　　Valenciennes—MDR, II, 237.

　　　　Florence—C. Guasti: *Santa Maria del Fiore*, 1887, 166.

　　　　Rouen—SAG, 32.

　　　　Winchcombe—Knoop and Jones in *Misc. Latomorum*, Dec. 1939.

p. 28.　Alexander—J. H. Bloom: *Original Charters relating to the City of Worcester* (Worcs. Historica Society, 1909), 3, 5, 7, 119; cf. J. C. Russell in *English Historical Review*, XLVII, 1932, 263–5; Lincoln Record Society, XXXII, 97–8, 101, 107; see also p. 75 below.

　　　　Ely—CSE, II, 45; D. J. Stewart: *The Architectural History of Ely Cathedral*, 1868, 90.

　　　　Norwich—Chapter Muniments, Obedientiary rolls, Nos. 1042, 1043, 1136.

　　　　Lichfield—Bodleian MS. Ashmole 794, f. 57 v.

　　　　Salisbury—W. Dodsworth: *Historical Account of the See and Cathedral Church of Salisbury*, 1814, 151n.; *Victoria History of Berkshire*, II, 66, quoting Chapter Act Book "Hemingsley", f. 103.

　　　　Exeter—H. E. Bishop and E. K. Prideaux: *The Building of Exeter Cathedral*, 1922, 8, 15. That Lesyngham came from Gloucestershire can be deduced from the fact that in 1377 his deputy John Swolwe, a known Gloucestershire man, was sent *versus partes proprias* to fetch the master. D. H. Findlay: *The Fabric Rolls of Exeter Cathedral*, Ph.D. Thesis, Leeds University, May 1939; a reference which I owe to the kindness of Mr. Findlay.

　　　　Yevele—P.R.O., E.101/472/8, writ under Privy Seal of 20 August 1360 referring to "*Henry Yeuele deuisour de la maceonerie de noz oeueraignes*"; HHY, 39, 49.

　　　　Wynford—C. R. Cockerell in *Proc. Archaeological Institute at Winchester*, 1846, 10; Harvey in *Winchester Cathedral Record*, XVIII, 1949, 4–7.

　　　　Raymond du Temple—Christine de Pisan: *Faits et bonnes mœurs du sage roi Charles* (V).

Ensingen etc.—KPP, 5.

Bolzano—KPP, 12.

French masters—SAG, 40, 101; MDR, II, 189.

Lydgate—*Falls of Princes* (EETS), Bk. I, lines 1,198–1,201.

p. 29.   Dunster—AJ, XXXVIII, 217; cf. F. C. Eeles: *The Church of St. George, Dunster*, 15–16.

Andover—T. F. Kirby: *Annals of Winchester College*, 1892, 175 is a very inaccurate transcript. The original is in the College Muniments, Drawer And. III, Kirby's And. II. xii. 2.

St. Stephen's Chapel—SAW, 191, 210, 216.

York—J. A. Knowles in JMG, VI, 1935, 92.

Broderers—CPR, 1396–9, 40; 1399–1401, 400; 1441–6, 49.

Louth—DCL, 11.

Prynce—Harvey in *Burlington Magazine*, LXXXIX, 1947, 303–5.

Reims—Didron: *Annales Archéologiques*, V, 1846, 87 ff.; VI, 1847, 139; H. R. Hahnloser in *Résumés du 13ᵉ Congrès International d'Histoire de l'Art*, 1933, 260.

Strassburg—KPP, 11.

p. 30.   Tower of London—Harvey in LMT, IX. i, 1944, 21.

Queen Mary's Psalter—British Museum MS. Royal 2 B. VIII, f. 37v.

St. Stephen's Chapel—SAW, 181–2; R. Willis: *Architectural Nomenclature of the Middle Ages* (CAS) 1844, 22–3.

Tracing houses—HWC, I, 132–3; AMB, 81n.; P.R.O., E.101/473/1; Cambridge Univ. Lib. MS. Add. 2956; RFY, 17; Norwich Chapter Muniments, Obedientiary rolls Nos. 1082, 1095; CPR, 1446–52, 510; 1452–61, 286; 1547–8, 100; Westminster Abbey Muniments No. 23526.

Strassburg—KPP, 9.

p. 31.   Westminster Hall—CCR, 1392–6, 352.

Louth—DCL, 21.

Wells—AMB, 89.

Glasgow—BAH, 88.

Christchurch—P. T. Jones: *The Priory Church of Christchurch*, Gloucester and London, n.d., 24.

Dijon etc.—KPP, 15, 16.

Didron—*Annales Archéologiques*, VI, 1847, 139–44: an illustrated article by F. de Verneilh on geometrical setting-out on flat roof-slabs at Limoges, Clermont and Narbonne.

Canterbury MS.—this was pointed out to me by Mr. Francis Wormald.

p. 32.   Tools—Norwich, rolls Nos. 284, 1050–52; Westminster Abbey rolls Nos. 23535, 23557; RFY, 88; P.R.O., T.R. Misc. 251, f. 106.

Ely—Cambridge Univ. Lib. MS. Add. 2956.

Westminster—KJF, 27.

Proportion—KPP, 16, 17.

Suger—PSD, 100.

Leonardo of Pisa—MDR, II, 50–2.

Models—KPP, 13; M. S. Briggs in *Burlington Magazine*, LIV, 1929, 174 ff.; R. Maere: *Maquette des Tours de l'église de St.-Pierre à Louvain . . .*, Brussels, 1936.

Drawings—KPP, 8, 11, 12; Canterbury Cathedral, MS. Christ Church Letters, I, 142; C. E. Woodruff and W. Danks: *Memorials of Canterbury Cathedral*, 1912, 208; J. Ainaud, J. Gudiol Ricart and F. P. Verrié: *Catálogo Monumental de la Ciudad de Barcelona*, Madrid, 1947, II, figs. 596–7; Archives du Puy-de-Dôme, Arm. 18, Sac B, cote 29, partly reproduced in Ambr. Tardieu: *Histoire de Clermont-Ferrand*, Moulins, 1870–1, I, 222; BAH, 70.

p. 33.   Cambridge tower—reproduced in HGE, fig. 115.

King's College Chapel—reproduced in HTA, 72–3.

German references to drawings—KPP, 5, 6, 8, 10, 12.

p. 34.   English patterns—Harvey in BAA, 3 S., VI, 1941, 61, 82, 83; W. J. Williams in *Masonic Record*, XVI, 1936, 160, 205; WCC, II, 282.

Pattern-books—KPP, 7; *Festschrift der Nationalbibliotek in Wien*, 1926, 667–92.

English drawings—M. R. James in *Walpole Society*, XIII, 1925, 1–17, Plates 17b, 20b, 21; A. H. Thompson: *The Cathedral Churches of England*, 1925, 141; Norwich rolls Nos. 1044, 1050; P.R.O., E.101/469/8; Westminster Abbey rolls Nos. 23497, 23552, 23566; CPR, 1391–6, 707, 725.

Moulds—Harvey in BAA, 3 S., VIII, 52; CSE, II, 33; BAN, III, 51; R. Willis: *The Architectural History of Canterbury Cathedral*, 1845, 36; T. D. Atkinson in CAS *Proc.*, XL, 1945, 45.

Slabs—CAR, 178–9; C. O'Brien in *The Architectural and Topographical Record*, I, 1908, 78–9.

p. 35.   Portraitures—*New English Dictionary* quoting Capgrave: *Life of St. Katherine*, I, 387; CSE, II, 83; E. W. Brayley and J. Britton: *History of the Ancient Palace at Westminster*, 1836, 185; *Victoria History of Middlesex*, II, 372.

Inventions—L. Thorndike: *Science and Thought in the Fifteenth Century*, 1929, 19.

p. 36.   Calais—C. Monro: *Letters of Queen Margaret of Anjou etc.* (Camden Society, LXXXVI, 1863), 19–21.

Eton—WCC, I, 398, 415, 418.

Woodstock—OHS, LXXX, 1924, 241.

Henry VII—BAN, II, 16; WCC, I, 608.

Horman—*Vulgaria Puerorum* ed. M. R. James (Roxburghe Club, 1926), 346 ff.

Louth—DCL, xv., 55.

Banwell—*Somerset Archaeological etc. Soc. Proceedings*, LI, 1905–6, pt. ii, 74.

L'Épine—Luc-Benoist: *Notre-Dame de l'Épine*, Paris, 1933, 12, 21.

p. 37.   Honorius of Autun—*De gemma animae* in Migne: *Patrologia latina*, CLXXII, col. 586 ff.

Geometry—KJH, 75, quoting "Cooke MS" lines 125–137; KPP, 18; Chaucer: *Knight's Tale*, line 1,039 ff.

Painting etc.—C. G. E. Bunt: *Gothic Painting*, 1947, 5–6; M. Drake: *A History of English Glass-Painting*, 1912, 42; C. Woodforde in *Proc. British Academy*, XXV, 1939, 29 ff.; C. K. Jenkins in *Apollo*, XLIV, 1946, 34; D. D. Egbert: *The Tickhill Psalter and Related Manuscripts*, New York, 1940.

Masons—Yevele's will, Commissary Court of London, f. 453. Courtney, refers to "*omnia bona mea marmoria et de latoun*"; Hyndeley's will, Prerogative Court of York, Reg. 2, f. 49, mentions his tools pertaining to "*les gravyng in plaite*".

p. 38.   Portraiture—*Chronique du Religieux de St.-Denis*, ed. Bellaquet (Collection des documents inédits), quoted in Huizinga: *Waning of the Middle Ages* (English ed.), 1924, 225; HMC, Rep. XI, pt. i, 27; W. J. Williams in *Masonic Record*, XVI, 1936, 205; see also HGE, 20, 63, 67, 150.

CHAPTER III

p. 39.   Hugh of St. Victor—*Eruditio Didascalica* (Migne: *Patr. lat.*, CLXXVI, 760) quoted by Pevsner in *Speculum*, XVII, 558.

Prior—*The Cathedral Builders in England*, 1905, 21–2.

p. 40.   Horman—see above, p. 36 and note.

Fox—ALF, 19–21.

Coorland—MDR, I, 141; Canterbury—*Vita S. Augustini, Acta Sanctorum*, VI maii. 414; St. Albans—*Gesta Abbatum Mon. Sancti Albani* (R.S.), I, 63; Croyland—*Petri Blesensis Continuatio ad Historiam Ingulphi*, 118; trans. H. T. Riley, 1854, 250.

Ordericus—quoted in MDR, I, 276; Lincoln—*Magna Vita S. Hugonis*, 336; Durham—*Reginaldi Dunelm. Libellus de Admirandis* (Surtees Soc., I, 1835), 112; St. Albans—*Gesta Abbatum*, II, 124–5.

p. 41.   Evesham—Leland: *Collectanea*, ed. 1774, 249.

Raymond du Temple etc.—SAG, 32; Froissart: *Chronicles*, ed. and trans. T. Johnes, II, 460.

Paris—M. Aubert: *Notre-Dame de Paris*, 1929, 138; Elne—F. de Mély in *Revue Archéologique*, 5 S., XI, 1920, 341.

St. Stephen Walbrook—T. Milbourn in LMT, V, 1879, 330–1.

p. 42.   Masters on Missions of trust—H. E. Salter: *Mediaeval Archives of the University of Oxford*, II (OHS, LXXIII, 1919) 1921, 338–9; ALF, 89.

Instruments—KPP, 16.

Money values—G. G. Coulton: *The Meaning of Medieval Moneys* (Historical Association Leaflet No. 95, 1934); cf. KJM, 235–9. A valuable study of craftsmen's remuneration in Holland is included with the published building accounts of Utrecht Cathedral—N. B. Tenhaeff: *Bronnen tot de Bouwgeschiedenis van den Dom te Utrecht, IIde Deel, 1ste Stuk, Rekeningen 1395–1480*, The Hague, 1946. For a series of German building accounts from 1356, see S. Beissel: *Die Bauführung des Mittelalters, Studie über die Kirche des hl. Victor zu Xanten*, 2nd ed., Freiburg i/B., 1889.

p. 43.   Ailnoth received 7d. per day; Maurice 12d.—*Pipe Rolls* (Pipe Roll Society).

Robert of Beverley—6d. daily, later 12d.—CCR, CPR; St. George—3s. daily; Lenginour 12d. An important paper on "Master James of St. George" was read before the British Archaeological Association by Mr. A. J. Taylor on 10 June 1949, and is to appear in BAA.

Tichmarsh—6d. and 4d. daily—*Black Prince's Register*, III, 236, 311.

Wynford—12d. daily; £10 yearly pension; £1 clothing—KJF, 81.

Herland—two pensions of £18 5s., one of £6 13s. 4d., £1 clothing—CPR.

Janyns—£12 yearly, £1 clothing, £3 6s. 8d. reward—HWC.

Hereford—Knoop and Jones in *Misc. Latomorum*, Dec. 1939.

Hurley—£8—CSE; Joy—£2 yearly and 6d. per working day—HMC, *Wells*, I, 220, 222; Lewyn—£13 6s. 8d. yearly, and 13s. 4d. for a robe—*Hist. Dunelm. Scriptores Tres* (Surtees Soc.), 132n.; Wintringham—£20 yearly and a vesture—*John of Gaunt's Register*, 1372–76, Nos. 590, 854; Colchester—£5, later £10 yearly, and 15s. for a robe—Knoop and Jones in *Misc. Latomorum*, Nov. 1937; Winchcombe—£2, gown worth 13s. 4d., and 4s. weekly—H. Anstey: *Epistolae Academicæ Oxon.* (OHS), I, 46.

p. 44.   Spalding—A. H. Thompson in *Visitations of the Diocese of Lincoln, 1436–49*, pt. ii (Canterbury and York Soc., XXXIII), 1927.

In 1520 William Brownfleet, master carpenter of Ripon Minster, had a retainer of 6s. 8d., and 6d. daily pay—*Memorials of . . . Ripon*, III (Surtees Soc., LXXXI, 1886–8), 181, 201–4; Redman had £18 5s. yearly from Wolsey, and as much from his two Crown offices together, with £5 and a vesture worth 13s. 4d. from Westminster Abbey.

Yevele—£18 5s. and £1 for robes as King's Master Mason, £10 as Bridge Warden, £5 and 15s. for clothing from Westminster Abbey—for sources see KJF; his work at Calais in 1359 is referred to in P.R.O., C.47/24/11(10), a reference which I owe to the kindness of Dr. G. P. Cuttino. His contract at St. Paul's is mentioned in P.R.O., E.101/473/4; and the making of Richard II's tomb in E.101/473/10.

Roslin—BAN, III, 52.

p. 45.   France—BAH, 69 ff.; also Paris, Bibl. Nat. MS. fr. 4485, pp. 164–5.

Chaucer—*Prologue*, line 361 ff.; *Miller's Tale*, 1 ff. and 475 ff.; *Prologue*, 589 ff.

Oxford—*Antiquaries Journal*, XXVII, 1947, 56n.; OHS, LXXIII, 1921, pt. ii, 21.

Precedence—F. J. Furnivall: *The Babees Book etc.* (EETS, O.S. 32) 1868, 117 ff.; Chaucer Soc.: *Life Records of Chaucer*, pt. iii, 1886, 174.

p. 46.   Rameseye—St. Paul's Cathedral MS. A.6, No. 1.

Winchester—Cathedral Register I, ff. 8, 29v.; and see Harvey in *Winchester Cathedral Record*, XVIII, 1949, 4 ff.; HHY, ix, 46, 53.

Tombs—BAH, 121 ff.; J. Weever: *Ancient Funerall Monuments*, 1631, 582; N. Pevsner in *Speculum*, XVII.

Robes—CCR, 1254–6, 91, 239; A. Gardner: *Handbook of English Mediaeval Sculpture*, 1935, 13.

p. 47.   Literacy—J. W. Thompson: *The Literacy of the Laity in the Middle Ages* (University of California: Publications in Education, IX), Berkeley, Cal., 1939; G. G. Coulton in CAS *Publications*, XIX (*Medieval Studies*, No. 12), 1915; HWC, I, 46–64; CLR, 1245–51, 15; Westminster Abbey Muniments Nos. 16000 (f), (g); Bishop and Prideaux; *Building of Exeter Cathedral*, 7; Harvey in *Journal R.I.B.A.*, 3 S. LII, 1945. See also above, note to p. 36 (Calais).

Signatures—*Letters and Papers of Henry VIII*, X, p. 194; B. Marsh: *Records of Carpenters Company*, III, 21–2; W. H. Turner: *Records of the City of Oxford*, 1880, 64; *Archaeologia Cantiana*, XX (of Robert Lynsted).

Ghent—MDR, II, 164–5.

p. 48.   Apprentices—Westminster Abbey Muniments No. 19344; MDR, II, 315; Cambridge University Library, Add. MS. 6392, f. 396: "*Thomas Peyntour de Ely latamus . . . tractabit ac bene et fideliter meliori modo quo sciverit ac potuerit et formabit tres apprenticios*"; cf. Knoop and Jones in *Economic History Review*, April 1932.

Clerical artists—A. H. Thompson in *History*, N.S., X, 1925–6; CLR, 1226–40, 28, 219, 220, 273, 316; 1240–5, 26, 222; 1245–51, 172, 187, 255; CCR, 1237–42, 333; J. de B. d'Altena: *Œuvres de nos Imagiers Romans et Gothiques*, Brussels, 1944 (Shrine of St. Gertrude, Nivelles); SAG, 70; F. Devon: *Issues of the Exchequer*, 1837, 160, 185; A. H. Thompson: *Visitations in the Diocese of Lincoln* (Canterbury and York Soc., XXIV, XXXIII, 1919–27), pt. i, 61; pt. ii, 383n. 4.

p. 49.   Supervision—Fagniez: *Documents relatifs a l'Histoire de l'Industrie*, I, 325; Norwich Cathedral Obedientiary rolls No. 1058; Westminster Abbey Muniments Nos. 23460–4, 23467; P.R.O., E.101/479/23, 24; WCC, II, 450; J. T. Fowler: *Memorials of Ripon* (Surtees Soc., LXXXI), pt. iii, 181.

Individuality—G. G. Coulton: *Medieval Panorama*, 566; KPP, 11.

Conferences—BAH, 59; MDR, II, 268–9; F. de Mély in *Revue Archéologique*, 5 S., XI, 1920; V. Lusini: *Il duomo di Siena*, 1911; J. Bayley: *History of the Tower of London*, 1821, App. to pt. i, 273; C. Guasti: *Santa Maria del Fiore*, 1887, 167 ff.; P. Frankl in *Art Bulletin*, XXVII, 1945; G. E. Street: *Gothic Architecture in Spain*, ed. King, 1914, II, 319 ff.; Westminster Abbey Muniments No. 23552; H. du Ranquet: *La Cathédrale de Clermont-Ferrand*, 1928, 25.

p. 50.   Travel—H. Read: *English Stained Glass*, 35n. 2; MDR, II, 129–31; *Dictionary of Architecture* (A.P.S.), *s.v.* "William of England"; W. H. St. J. Hope and H. Brakspear in AJ, LXIII, 1906, 136, quoting Close Rolls; CLR, 1240–5, 81; CPR, 1266–72, 147; F. de Mély in *Revue Archéologique*, 1920; W. R. Lethaby: *Mediaeval Art*, 251–3; MDR, II, 296; Norwich Obedientiary rolls No. 3; MDR, II, 305–6; BAH, 111; P.R.O., D.L. 42/11; Westminster Abbey Muniments No. 23455; H. W. Garrod: *Ancient Painted Glass in Merton College, Oxford*, 1931, 48n. 1; Devon: *Issues of the Exchequer*, 189; EMF, I. ii, 740–50; KPP, 2, 6.

CHAPTER IV

p. 54.   Jerusalem—see Bibliography, Palestine—Enlart: *Monuments des Croisés*, II, 140.

CHAPTER V

p. 59.   In general, dates for work in France have been taken from LAF; EMF; and FAO. Names are from SAG; F. de Mély in *Revue Archéologique*, 5 S., XI, 1920, 290 ff.; XIII, 1921, 77 ff.; C. Bauchal: *Nouveau Dictionnaire biographique et critique des Architectes français*, Abbeville, 1885; supplemented from the volumes of the *Congrès Archéologiques*. Cluny—K. J. Conant: *Early Mediaeval Church Architecture*, 1942.

p. 64.   Paris —M. Aubert: *Notre-Dame de Paris, sa place dans l'histoire de l'architecture . . .*, 2nd ed., 1929.

p. 65.   Reims—I adhere to the generally accepted order of masters; the precise dates are uncertain. V. Wanscher: *Architekturens Historie*, II, 1929, 441; CGB, 55; and FAO, 172n., give slightly varying solutions. The choir was certainly begun in 1211 and completed thirty years later, and the west front was finished before 1299.

Perpendicular—Professor Geoffrey Webb in a lecture to the Royal Archaeological Institute on 26th January 1949 stressed the importance of these panelled internal "fronts" in the development of rectilinearity.

p. 66.   Le Mans—C. M. Girdlestone in AJ, CII, 1945–7, 111 ff.

Reyns—The English character of the work at Westminster Abbey is so pronounced, in spite of the French scheme of the church, that it seems more reasonable to consider Master Henry an Englishman who had worked at Reims than a Frenchman; cf. HHY, 3–4.

Montreuil—EMF, I. ii, 741.

note Langlois—E. Lefèvre-Pontalis in *Bulletin Monumental*, 1922, 480.

p. 68.   Jean des Champs—E. Mâle: *Art et Artistes du Moyen Age*, Paris, 1927, 122–37; *Congrès Archéologique*, C, 1937–8, 360 ff.

For Spain I depend mainly on Street and B. Bevan: *History of Spanish Architecture*, 1938.

p. 69.   Las Huelgas—J. Gonzalez in *Revista de Archivos*, LIII, Madrid, 1947, Num. 1. I owe my knowledge of this important item to the kindness of Dr. Xavier de Salas.

Italy—C. Enlart: *Origines françaises de l'Architecture Gothique en Italie*, Paris, 1894; G. V. Arata: *L'Architettura Arabo-Normanna e il Rinascimento in Sicilia*, Milan, 1914; G. Agnello: *L'Architettura Sveva in Sicilia*, Rome, 1935; G. di Stefano: *L'Architettura Gotico-Sveva in Sicilia*, Palermo, 1935.

See also L. Réau: *Histoire de l'expansion de l'art français*, Paris, 1928–33; Réau and G. Cohen: *L'Art du Moyen Age et la civilization française*, Paris, 1935.

p. 70.   Flanders—M. Laurent: *L'architecture et la sculpture en Belgique*, Paris and Brussels, 1928.

Holland—see Bibliography.

Prague—A. Podlaha: *Führer durch den Dom zu Prag*, 1906; K. M. Swoboda: *Peter Parler*, 4th ed., Vienna, 1943; M. S. Briggs: *City of Baroque and Gothic*, 1946; *Magic in Stone*, 1947.

CHAPTER VI

p. 73. Anglo-Norman school—e.g. M. Aubert: *Notre-Dame de Paris*, 177–8; FAO, 83, 141–2.
English glass-painters—see p. 50¦above—Read quoting Le Vieil: *L'Art de la peinture sur verre* ...., Paris, 1774, 24, from Chartulary of Abbey at Braine-le-Comte and *Index Coenobiorum Ordinis Praemonstratensis*.

p. 75. Alexander—see p. 28 above.
Lock—HMC, *Wells*, I, 35; II, 550–1.
Dereham—A. H. Thompson in AJ, XCVIII, 1941.

p. 76. Old Sarum—J. P. Bushe-Fox: *Old Sarum* (Official Guide), 1936.
Lincoln—J. W. F. Hill: *Medieval Lincoln*, Cambridge, 1948, 114.
Eleanor Crosses—The accounts printed in full in B. Botfield: *Manners and Household Expenses of England* (Roxburghe Club), 1841; cf. J. Hunter in *Archaeologia*, XXIX, 1842, 167.
Walter of Hereford—see p. 22 above.

p. 77 Persia—C. Desimoni in *Atti Liguri di Storia Patria*, XIII, 1877–84, Genoa, 537–698, prints from P.R.O., Exch. Tr. of Receipt, Misc. No. 49 the full accounts for Sir Geoffrey de Langley's embassy from Edward I to the Ilkhan Kaikhatu in 1292. Robert "Sculptor" was one of the party. For Persian buildings see A. U. Pope: *A Survey of Persian Art*, 1938, II, esp. 1103–1118.
Canterburys—W. R. Lethaby: *Westminster Abbey and the King's Craftsmen*, 1906, 180–92; Harvey in *Arch. Cantiana*, LVIII, 1946, 36; Lambeth MS. 242, ff. 27, 28, 33v., 43v., 52, shows Master Michael at work for the prior at Canterbury, and also going to London to work on the Prior's house at St. Mary-le-Bow in Cheapside, from 1275 to 1280. For information concerning the Prior's house in London I am indebted to Miss M. B. Honeybourne.
Chaumont—E. Lefèvre-Pontalis in *Congrès Archéologique*, 1902–3.
Kentish tracery—distribution map in HGE, fig. 69; cf. *ibid.*, pp. 42, 48–9.
Ramseys—Lethaby: *op. cit.*, 188–96; Harvey in BAA, 3 S., VI, 1941–3, 40–2; HHY, 7–9; HGE, 50–1, 57–8. A detailed study of the Ramsey family and their work is in preparation.

p. 78. Bridlington and Limoges—F. Bond: *Gothic Architecture in England*, 125; R. Fage: *La Cathédrale de Limoges*, 1926, 31, 52.

p. 79. Ireland—see Bibliography. I have also used extensively the Reports and Guides issued by the Commissioners of Public Works in Ireland.
Kilkenny—J. Graves and J. G. A. Prim: *St. Canice's Cathedral, Kilkenny*, 1857.

p. 80. Scotland—see Bibliography; also R. S. Mylne: *Master Masons to the Crown of Scotland*, 1893.

p. 81. Matthew Paris—T. Borenius and E. W. Tristram: *English Medieval Painting*, Florence and Paris, 1927, 13–14.
Avignon—contrary to the statement, often copied, of Lasteyrie (LAF, II, 571) there is no evidence that Jean Lavenier of Paris made the tomb of Pope John XXII, who died in 1334; see L. H. Labande: *Le Palais des Papes* ...., Marseille, 1925, II, 139. Lavenier's tomb for Benedict XII, made in 1342–45, was modelled on that for John XXII. Two English *master* masons are known to have worked at Avignon: (1) Hugues Wilfred, who built the Chapel of the Angels in Notre-Dame des Doms, c. 1315–22; (2) "Mag. Johannes Anglicus", who was one of seven masters concerned in building the walls of the Palace alongside N.-D. des Doms in 1340, and who was already working at Avignon in 1336. See F. Ehrle: *Historia Bilbiothecae Romanorum Pontificum*, Rome, 1890, I, 614; C. H. Schaefer: *Die Ausgaben der Apostolischen Kammer* (Vatikanische Quellen, Bd. 2, 3), 1316–35, Paderborn, 1911, 290; 1335–62, 1914, 51, 252, 681. A master painter Thomas the Englishman was also working in the Palace in 1333; Schaefer, 1316–35, 310–11.
Santes Creus—P. Lavedan: *L'Architecture Gothique en Catalogne*, Paris, 1935, 33, quoting Puig i Cadafalch in *Anuari de l'Institut d'Estudis Catalans*, VII (1921–6), 123–38; Puig i Cadafalch in *Ensayos Hispano-Ingleses—Homenaje a Walter Starkie*, Barcelona, 1948, 313–14, where it is emphasized that Fonoyll's work is by far the earliest Flamboyant (Curvilinear) in Spain. I owe these references to Dr. Xavier de Salas.
English influence on the Continent—F. Bond: *English Church Architecture*, Oxford, 1913, II, 619; CGB, 145–8; FAO, 278–80.

CHAPTER VII

p. 83. Angers—*Congrès Archéologique*, 1910; Ch. Urseau: *La Cathédrale d'Angers*; L. de Farcy: *Monographie de la Cathédrale d'Angers*, 1902–5.

p. 84. Bordeaux—*Congrès Archéologique*, 1939.
Toulouse—*ibid.*, 1929; R. Rey: *La Cathédrale de Toulouse*, 1929.
Valence—*Congrès Archéologique*, 1923.
Poitiers—*ibid.*, 1903.
Bourges—A. Boinet: *La Cathédrale de Bourges*, Paris, n.d.

p. 85. Hall-churches—see E. Lefèvre-Pontalis in *Bulletin Monumental*, LXXXI, 257–309.
Winchester—the building of the retrochoir and Lady Chapel is fixed between 1202 and 1239 by *Annales Monastici* (RS), II, 78, and CLR, 1226–40, 433, which refers to "the new work of St. Mary's Chapel".
Southwark—the new work was begun after a fire of 1207.
Temple Church—the new choir was consecrated in 1240, and on 7th January 1239/40 Henry III had presented a candlestick to "the new chapel of the New Temple"—CLR, 1226–40, 438.
Lambeth—CLR, 1240–45, 13; this agrees with the details and mouldings of the existing chapel.

p. 86. Ste.-Chapelle—I find that this view receives support from Dr. Joan Evans in her *English Art 1307–1461*, pp. 66–7.
Kenilworth—Harvey in AJ, CI, 1946, 96.
St. John's Clerkenwell—Sir Alfred Clapham in *Some Famous Buildings and their Story*, n.d.

p. 87. Catalonia—mainly from Lavedan, see p. 81 above, note. (Santes Creus)
p. 88. Gerona Conference—Street, appendix.
 St.-Denis—PSD, 46–50.
p. 89. Germany etc.—largely from CGB, 115 ff.
 Lichfield—the Lady Chapel was founded by Bishop Walter de Langton, but most of the work seems to have been done between his death in 1311 and 1337—Bodleian MS. Ashmole 794, ff. 2v., 5v., 42, 55, 56.
 Strassburg—J. Walter: *La Cathédrale de Strasbourg*, Paris, 1933; FAO, 189 and n.; O. Schmitt: *Gotische Skulpturen des Strassburger Münsters*, Frankfurt, 1924; Thieme-Becker, s.vv. Erwin, Rudolf.
p. 90. Naumburg—W. Pinder: *Die Bildwerke des Naumburger Doms*, Leipzig, n.d.
 Goethe—*Von Deutscher Baukunst*, 1771.

CHAPTER VIII

p. 93. England—the most satisfactory works for detailed reference are still F. Bond's two great books.
 Canterbury—see above, p. 77 note.
 Eleanor Crosses—see above, p. 76 note.
 St. Stephen's Chapel—see Harvey in *Burlington Magazine*, LXXXVIII, Aug. 1946, 192.
 Winchelsea—the existing portion of the church must have been built by 1307, for the great "Alard" tomb in the south aisle bears portrait heads of Edward I and his young second Queen, Margaret of France, whom he married in 1299. The old King's head appears to a larger scale outside the east window of this aisle.
 Joy—HMC, *Wells*, I, 220, 222; Somerset Record Society, VII, 137–8; Exeter Cathedral Fabric roll No. 2633 for 1346–7. I owe this last item to the kindness of Mrs. M. E. Clegg.
 Norwich—Chapter Muniments, Obedientiary rolls Nos. 1040, 1041; Roll 1042A shows that the south walk had been begun by 1327. The foundation of the cloister was in 1297, according to an anonymous interpolation in William Worcester's MS. "Itinerary" (Corpus Christi College, Cambridge, MS. 210, p. 226; ed. Nasmith, 1778, 302). But the rolls do not indicate work actually in progress until 1303–4 (roll No. 16).
 York—*Yorks. Archaeological Soc. Record Series*, XXI, 1897, 119; F. Collins ed.: *Freemen of the City of York* (Surtees Soc., XCVI) 1897, 16; RFY, 207n.
 Southwell—N. Pevsner: *The Leaves of Southwell*, 1945.
p. 94. Ramseys—see above, p. 77 note.
 Perpendicular—HHY; HGE; and in *Antiquaries Journal*, XXVII, 1947, 51 ff.
 Clyve—HWC, I, 186, 189, 193, 207–8; S. G. Hamilton ed.: *Compotus Rolls of the Priory of Worcester* (Worcs. Historical Soc., 1910), 20. Worcester Obedientiary Rolls, c. 69, 70, 71, 74.
 Eton etc.—WCC; cf. A. Oswald in *Proc. CAS*, XLII, 1949, 8 ff.
 Coventry—the details of the tower (1373–94, spire completed 1433) are very close to those of Skillington's great hall at Kenilworth Castle (1389–93); see Harvey in AJ, CI, 1946, 96.
 Merton—J. E. Thorold Rogers in *Oxford Documents* (OHS, XVIII, 1891), 314–37.
 Walberswick etc.—B.M. Add. Ch. 17634; and for Russell, Add. Ch. 40704, 40728, 40729; P.R.O., S.C.11/886, 887.
 Kessingland—wills in Ipswich Probate Registry: Robert Thurston, Reg. I, 104; Joan Mawsey, Reg. II, 29; Norwich Registry, John Bewcher, Reg. Neve, 40–1. I have to thank the Rev. Christopher Chitty, rector of Kessingland, for communicating the items from wills, and much other information; his account of the history of the tower appears in the *Kessingland and Carlton Colville Parish Magazine*, Sept.–Nov. 1949.
 Wastell—WCC; C. E. Woodruff and W. Danks: *Memorials of Canterbury Cathedral*, 1912, 208.
 Vertues—Lethaby: *Westminster Abbey and the King's Craftsmen*, 1906; *Westminster Abbey Re-examined*, 1925, 161–6; J. A. Robinson in *Proc. Somerset Archaeol. etc. Soc.*, LX, 1914–15, pt. ii, 1–10. Robert Vertue first appears as an apprentice at Westminster Abbey working with his father Adam Vertue for 19 weeks in 1474/5 (W.A.M. roll 23543), and thenceforward until 1479/80 (W.A.M. rolls 23545–552). He returned to the Abbey as a fully qualified mason in 1482/3, and worked there until 1490 (W.A.M. rolls 23558–563).
p. 95. Redman—see Harvey in BAA, 3 S., VIII, 1943, 50 ff.; and HTA, 29–31.
 Ireland—see above, p. 79 note.
p. 96 More—*Rotulorum Patentium et Clausarum Cancellarii Hiberniae Calendarium*, ed. E. Tresham, 1828, I, pt. i, 82, 128; British Museum Egerton MS. 1773, f. 22 ff.
 Ennis—C. O'Brien in *Architectural and Topographical Record*, I, pt. ii, 1908, 143–67.
p. 97. Scotland—see above, p. 80 note.
p. 98. Melrose—O. Delepierre in *Archaeologia*, XXI, 1846, 346 ff.
p. 99. Rothesay—W. D. Simpson in *Trans. Glasgow Archaeol. Soc.*, IX, X.
 Bridge of Tay—*Exchequer Rolls of Scotland*, 1529–36, 234.
 Ladykirk—*Accounts of the Lord High Treasurer*, 1500–04, lxxxiii, 347; 1507–13, 44, 446.
 Thom—*ibid.*, 1507–13, 46, 283.
 Dunfermline—see J. M. Webster: *Dunfermline Abbey*, 1948.
 France—see above, p. 59 note.
 Bayonne—*Congrès Archéologique*, 1939.
p. 100. Rouen St.-Ouen—A. Masson: *L'Église St.-Ouen de Rouen*, Paris, 1927.
 Raymond du Temple, Dampmartin—EMF, I, pt. ii, 748–9.
p. 101. Auch—*Congrès Archéologique*, 1929.
 Chambiges—EMF, I, pt. ii, 749–50.
 Paris St.-Jacques—J. Meurgey: *Histoire de la Paroisse St.-Jacques-de-la-Boucherie*, Paris, 1926, 178 ff.

Beauvais—V. Leblond: *La Cathédrale de Beauvais*, Paris, 1933. For the Midi, the standard work is R. Rey: *L'Art Gothique du Midi de la France*, Paris, 1934.

p. 102.　Albi—J. Laran: *La Cathédrale d'Albi*, Paris, n.d.

Uzeste—*Congrès Archéologique*, 1939; LAF, I, 270.

Tarascon—A. d'Agnel: *Les Comptes du roi René*, 1908-10.

Avignon—L. H. Labande: *Le Palais des Papes. . .* , Marseille, 1925. See above, p. 81 note.

p. 104.　Barcelona—J. Ainaud, J. Gudiol Ricart and F. P. Verrié: *Catálogo Monumental de la Ciudad de Barcelona*, Madrid, 1947; and see above, p. 68, 81, 87 notes.

Naples, Castel Nuovo—C. R. Cockerell in *Archaeological Institute, Proc. at Winchester 1845*, London, 1846, 33n., which however confuses Alfonso the Magnanimous with a 13th-century predecessor.

p. 105.　Martinez—J. M. de Azcarate: "Alvar Martinez, Maestro de la Catedral de Toledo" in *Archivo Español de Arte*, XXIII, no. 89, 1950, pp. 1-12. America—see Bibliography; and *Journal of the Society of Architectural Historians*, V, 1945-6 (Latin American Architecture Issue), Urbana, Illinois, 1947.

p. 106.　Portugal—W. Crumm-Watson: *Portuguese Architecture*, 1908; Visconde de Condeixa: *O Mosteiro da Batalha/Le Monastère de Batalha*, Lisbon and Paris, 1892.

p. 107.　Flanders—P. Fierens: *L'Art Flamand*, Paris, 1945; M. Laurent: *L'Architecture et la Sculpture en Belgique*, Paris and Brussels, 1928; P. Clemen: *Belgische Kunstdenkmäler*, 1923; and see Bibliography, Holland.

p. 109.　Hal—R. Hamann in P. Clemen: *op. cit.*, 203 ff.

Brussels—J. Duverger: *De Brusselsche Steenbickeleren der XIVe en XVe eeuw*, Ghent, 1933; *Brussel als Kunstcentrum in de XIVe en de XVe eeuw*, Ghent, 1935.

p. 110.　Brou—V. Nodet: *L'Église de Brou*, Paris, n.d.

Troyes—*Congrès Archéologique*, 1902.

Utrecht—see above, p. 42 note.

p. 111.　Germany—G. Dehio: *Handbuch der deutschen Kunstdenkmäler*, Berlin, 1914-28; rev. ed. E. Gall, I, II, 1935-8; G. Dehio: *Geschichte der deutschen Kunst*, 2nd ed., Berlin, 1921-31; CGB.

p. 112.　Parlers—see KPP; Thieme-Becker.

Vienna—see above, p. 22 note.

p. 114.　Zug—see E. P. Baker in *Archaeologia*, XCIII, 1949, 103 ff.

p. 115.　Bohemia—see Bibliography.

p. 116.　Parlers—Thieme-Becker; K. M. Swoboda: *Peter Parler*, Vienna, 4th ed., 1943.

p. 118.　Hungary—see Bibliography.

p. 119.　Kassa—A. Nyári: *Der Dom zu Kaschau*, 1896.

p. 120.　Kolozsvár—L. Makkai and E. Vásárhelyi: *Kolozsvar/Klausenburg*, Budapest, 1944.

Vajda-Hunyad—I. Möller in *Magyarország Müemlékei*, III, Budapest, 1913.

Baltic—see above, pp. 107, 111 notes; also K. H. Clasen: *Die mittelalterliche Kunst im Gebiete des Deutschordensstaates Preussen*, Königsberg, 1927; C. F. Doll: *The Architecture of the Teutonic Order in Prussia* (reprint from *The Builder's Journal*, 1896).

p. 123.　Poland—see Bibliography.

p. 124.　Estonia—see S. Karling in *Rig*, 1939, 65-114; and see Bibliography, Baltic.

St. George—J. Roosval: *Nya Sankt Görans Studier* (Kungl. Vitterhets H. och. Ant. Akad., Mono. 13), Stockholm 1924.

Marienwerder—W. D. Simpson in *Proc. Soc. Ant. Scotland*, LXIV, 1929-30, 326 ff. (*Scottish Archaeological Studies*, 2nd series, Aberdeen, 1936, 302 ff.)

p. 125.　Roskilde—C. M. Smidt: *Roskilde Domkirkes Middelalderlige Bygningshistorie* (resumé in French), Copenhagen, 1949.

Scandinavia—see Bibliography.

p. 126.　Finland—L. Wennervirta in *Suomen Muinasmuistoyhdistyksen Aikakauskirja*, XXXVIII, 1930 (German summary: *Die gotische Monumentalmalerei in den Kirchen von Westfinnland und Åland*).

Trondhjem—P. A. Munch: *The Cathedral of Throndheim*, Christiania, 1859.

p. 127.　Italy—Sir T. G. Jackson: *Gothic Architecture in France, England and Italy*, Cambridge, 1915.

p. 128.　Sicily—see above, p. 69 note.

p. 129.　Dalmatia—Sir T. G. Jackson: *Dalmatia, the Quarnero and Istria*, Oxford, 1887.

Crete—G. Gerola: *Monumenti Veneti nell' isola di Creta* (R. Istituto Veneto), 1905-32, esp. vol. II, p. 17 ff.

Greece—see Bibliography.

Rhodes—see Bibliography.

Cyprus—see Bibliography.

INDEX

Mediaeval architects and artists are listed separately after the main index. Numerals in heavy type refer to the figure numbers of the illustrations. The letter "n" as suffix indicates footnotes on the text-page itself; the letter "a" that the references will be found among the notes on pp. 138–45. The Bibliography and Abbreviations have not been indexed. Place-names are given in the form commonly used in English, or in the language of their mediaeval unit. The polyglot place-names of Central Europe have been cross-indexed as far as possible.

147

INDEX OF ARCHITECTS

This index includes the names of mediaeval artists believed to have acted as architects;
carpenters are indicated by the letter C, and sculptors and carvers (including masons
known to have acted as sculptors) by S; where not otherwise indicated, the persons
concerned were masons.

INDEX OF ARTISTS

In some cases these artists worked in several media, but glaziers are marked G, and miscellaneous craftsmen are specified. The rest were painters.

TRONDHJEM

ICELAND

STAVANGER

LINK

MEXICO

SAN JUAN

SANTO DOMINGO

TEPEACA

SAÑA
GUADALUPE
LIMA
CUZCO

Matthew Paris 1248

Étienne de Bonneuil 1287

John 1274

Berntem

PAISLEY
GLASGOW
ST ANDREWS
MELROSE

ROSTOCK
STRALSUND

DUBLIN

LÜBECK

Gerlach 1400

John Morow 1450

Cornelius de Aeltre

Adam von Düren 1499

Hamburg

Hermann 1440

Nikolaus Fellen

John of Corfe 1334

NORWICH

HAARLEM

MÜNSTER

LINCOLN

LONDON

MAESTICHT

CANTERBURY

John 1274

BRUGES
BRUSSELS

DÜREN

Arnold 1471

MEISSE

Claus Sluter

COLOGNE

Gasei

Raoul 1174

ST QUENTIN

1385

Heinrich
Parler 1300

Veit St

CAEN

LAON

NUREMBERG

Raynard Fonoyll 1331

Hanequin of Brussels 1448

Janin Lomme 1411

PARIS

REIMS

Peter Parler 1353

Jan van Eyck 1428

Michael Sittow 1490

Ricardo 1180

LIMOGES

Jean des Champs 1248

SENS

CLERMONT

Hugh Wilfred 1321

STRASSBURG

GMÜND

ST DIÉ

FREIBURG

ULM

1344

PASSAU

J
V

John son of Tyno

Matthieu d'Arras

Villard de Honnec

SANTIAGO

LAUSANNE

LEÓN

Juan de Colonia 1442

RODEZ

BURGOS

PAMPLONA

NARBONNE

AVIGNON

MILAN

VENICE
ROVIGO

Antonio 1430

?Ma

Simone Martini 1336

GENOA

Pedro Balaguer 1414

PERPIGNAN

Raimond 1175

Pierre d'Angicourt 1270

SIENA

SEBEN

LISBON

TOLEDO

URGEL
LÉRIDA
STES
CREUS
MONTBLANCH

GERONA

BARCELONA

ROME

VALENCIA

1426

SEVILLE

PALMA

Guillermo Sagrera

1448

NAPLES

Or

TANGIER
CEUTA

PALERMO

| 0 | 100 | 200 | 300 | 400 | 500 | 600 | 700 | 800 | 900 | MILES |

| 0 | 100 | 300 | 500 | 700 | 900 | 1100 | 1300 | 1500 | KILOMETRES |